CHARLES I AND OLIVER CROMWELL

CHARLES I
AND
OLIVER CROMWELL

A STUDY IN CONTRASTS AND COMPARISONS

Maurice Ashley

Methuen · London and New York

First published in Great Britain in 1987
by Methuen London Ltd, 11 New Fetter Lane, London EC4P 4EE
and in the United States of America
by Methuen Inc, 29 West 35th Street, New York, NY 10001
Copyright © 1987 Maurice Ashley

Printed in Great Britain
by Redwood Burn Ltd,
Trowbridge, Wiltshire

British Library and Library of Congress
Cataloguing in Publication Data

Ashley, Maurice
    Charles I and Oliver Cromwell.
    1. Charles I, King of England   2. Great
    Britain – Kings and rulers – Biography
    3. Cromwell, Oliver
    I. Title
    942.06'2'0924   DA396.A2

    ISBN 0–413–16270–2

This book is dedicated to
Austin Woolrych in gratitude
for his generous assistance

Contents

Prologue:
CONFRONTATION

On 7 June 1647 Charles I, King of England, Scotland and Ireland, and Oliver Cromwell, Lieutenant-General in the New Model Army that had defeated him in the civil war, confronted each other and spoke together for the first time in Sir John Cutts's house at Childerley, a few miles from Cambridge. They must have seen each other several times before then. It is even possible that they had done so as children (they were much the same age), for Charles's father, King James I, had enjoyed being entertained by Oliver's uncle at his Elizabethan mansion of Hinchingbrooke, where the hunting gave the monarch enormous pleasure, for, as a contemporary envoy remarked, 'to his kingly pursuit of stags he was quite foolishly devoted'.[1] Young Oliver, who had been named after his wealthy uncle, lived in nearby Huntingdon; he must surely have been invited to play in the gardens at Hinchingbrooke, while Charles may on occasion have accompanied his father to the estate he loved so much for tracking down and killing the unfortunate stags.[2] Years later Oliver, who was to become a member of parliament for Cambridge, would have been in his seat in the House of Commons when in January 1642 Charles as King vainly attempted to arrest five of its principal members for high treason, thus precipitating the great civil war: one of the members accused was John Hampden, a Buckinghamshire squire, who was Oliver's first cousin and close friend. Finally, a year before they met face to face for the first time near Cambridge, Charles must have seen Oliver charging into battle on the field of Naseby, where the King suffered his severest blow in the war.

By 1644 the Royalists had lost most of the north of England to the Parliamentarians after the battle of Marston Moor, in 1645 the King's main army was crushed at Naseby; and in the autumn of the same year the south-west of England, the most Royalist part of the kingdom, submitted to the New Model Army commanded by the Yorkshire gentleman Sir Thomas Fairfax, with Oliver as his second-in-command. Realizing that he could not continue the struggle, Charles escaped from Oxford disguised as a servant, crossing Magdalen bridge as the clock struck three in the morning at the end of April 1646. He was convinced that what he had lost by war he could regain by diplomacy. His first intention was to find his way to London in order to plead his case before Parliament, and indeed he had sent a message to Sir Henry Vane the Younger, one of the leaders of the House of Commons and at that time an intimate friend of Oliver, asking him if he and his friends would invite him to revisit his capital so that he could negotiate peace.[3] But Charles was resolved not to fall into the rebels' hands if he could 'by any industry or danger' prevent it.

With two companions he managed to arrive at a tavern in Hillingdon, fourteen miles from London. But then – nobody quite knows why – he changed his mind and decided to turn back to throw himself on the mercy of the Scottish army, the paid allies of the Parliamentarians. Hopefully but wrongly Charles believed that the Scottish commanders, who were then encamped near the strategic town of Newark in Nottinghamshire, had committed themselves through the intervention of the French ambassador in England to treating him honourably, asking him to do nothing contrary to his conscience and, provided he agreed to a few concessions to their religious views, ensuring that he was restored to his throne in Whitehall palace. Soon he was to be undeceived. The Scots obliged him to order the surrender of Newark to them before they carried him off to Newcastle upon Tyne where they tried to convert him to the Presbyterian faith and demanded of him that it should be accepted as the state religion in England, as it already was in Scotland.

For eight months Charles remained the prisoner of the Scots in Newcastle, under constant pressure by persuasions and threats to change his religion and that of his English subjects. He complained, 'I never knew what it was to be so barbarously baited before.'[4] Quickly he came to understand that his captors had no intention whatever of allowing him to be more of a king in England that they had already made him in Scotland, and that they certainly did not mean to break with the English rebels in order to restore him to the position he had once held of sovereign by divine right. Reluctantly he felt obliged to inform his wife that the Scots would not make him 'a great and glorious king' if he satisfied them about religion.[5] In fact during the summer of 1646 the Earl of Argyll, the most powerful man in Scotland, went up to London and agreed that commissioners from the Lords and Commons could carry an ultimatum to the King which, if accepted, would deprive him of all real authority.

Vainly Charles played for time, but eventually the English Parliament paid off their Scottish allies, who left Newcastle for home after handing over their royal prisoner to the Parliamentarian commissioners. Charles was removed by the commissioners, headed by the Earl of Pembroke, who had once been his Lord Chamberlain, to Holdenby House in Northamptonshire, which his mother had bought for him. He was delighted to get away from the Scots who, he thought, had deceived and humiliated him; on his journey south he was gratified by the acclamations of the crowds who had flocked to see him pass and wished him well. But at Holdenby, where he arrived in mid-February 1647, he was not allowed his own chaplains or grooms of the bedchamber or other personal servants. Otherwise he was treated courteously; he read and played chess, and he pursued his private devotions unhindered. So he became increasingly affable, chatting to Pembroke, and when the Earl was taken ill, inquiring anxiously after his health and graciously visiting him, which, according to Pembroke's doctor, much helped his recovery. Charles's own health was excellent because he was abstemious and exercised himself by walking and playing bowls.

Charles also occupied himself in preparing a detailed answer to the propositions he had received from Parliament when he was at Newcastle. He offered to permit Presbyterianism being the state religion in England for three years and also agreed to hand over the control of the militia, that was in effect the armed forces of the kingdom, for ten years. Of course he refused to consent to any of those who fought for him being excluded from a general act of pardon, but he hoped that

> the two Houses of Parliament, as they are Englishmen and lovers of peace, by the duty they owe to His Majesty the King, and by the bowels of compassion they have to their fellow subjects . . . will accept of this His Majesty's offer, whereby the joyful news of peace may be restored to this languishing nation.

In putting forward these considerable concessions Charles was going against the advice of his most intimate counsellors. His Queen, Henriette Marie, being a French Roman Catholic, was indifferent about the future of the Church of England; she told her husband that if he were willing to accept Presbyterian supremacy for three years he might just as well accept it permanently. But she was insistent that he should on no account yield up control over the armed forces.[6] The King, who remained convinced that he was a wily negotiator, was obsessed by his belief that if only he could get back to London he could exact reasonable terms from Parliament. His answer made a favourable impression, especially on the peers left in the House of Lords. Earlier he had informed Lord Digby that once he was allowed to return to London he hoped 'to draw either the Presbyterians or Independents to side with me, for extirpating the one or the other, [so] that I shall really be king again'. 'If I cannot live as a king,' he had then added, 'I shall die like a gentleman.'[7] About the same time he told the Queen that 'he hoped to suppress both the Presbyterians and the Independents'.[8] He realized, he assured her, that he 'must accept loppings but no rooting up and so will be able to return as entirely to the Crown in a prefixed time'.[9]

Such were the views Charles expressed in confidence while he was a captive of the Scots. Now that he was the honourable prisoner of the English Parliament he became much more optimistic about his future. For he found out that the Presbyterian members of the House of Commons, led by Denzil Holles, the high-spirited younger son of the Earl of Clare, were at loggerheads with the Army which had defeated him. Indeed during Easter week 1647 he is said to have received a proposal from an officer of the Army that if he surrendered himself to its charge, he would be restored to 'his Honour, Crown and Dignity'. His reply was, 'We will not engage our people in another war', and he added piously, 'The Lord be merciful to my poor people. Too much blood hath been shed already. The Lord be merciful to my distracted kingdom when He accounts with them for rebellion and blood.'[10] Unquestionably Charles was sincere at that time. Yet within a year he was to plunge his kingdoms into blood again.

Meanwhile, Oliver Cromwell as an assiduous member of parliament, though still on the army payroll, had been struggling to reconcile the Army with Parliament. The difficulty was that no effective executive was in existence. The body known as the Committee of Both Kingdoms had been a kind of executive as long as the first civil war was being fought, but lost its need for existence once the war had ended and the Scots army paid off. Its executive functions were taken over by what was called the Derby House committee, which was dominated by Denzil Holles, who was to describe Oliver in his memoirs as one of 'the Grand Designers of the Ruin of Two Kingdoms'. John Pym, the veteran anti-papist, who was the acknowledged leader of the House of Commons when the war began, had died of cancer, leaving no accepted or capable successor. No Lord Treasurer or Chancellor or Secretary of State was functioning, and decisions were taken by a fluctuating majority in the House of Commons which still sought the agreement of an attenuated House of Lords. The Presbyterian leaders in the Commons demanded that the New Model Army should be drastically reduced in size and the soldiers given a choice between disbanding or serving in an expeditionary force to be dispatched to quell the rebellion in Ireland, which had broken out in 1641. But the rank-and-file of the New Model Army was understandably restive because its pay was many months in arrears while no compensation was being offered to the widows and disabled created by the fighting. And before the soldiers consented to serve in Ireland they naturally wanted to know who their commanders would be and what were their future terms of service.

Oliver soon recognized how unpopular the existence and upkeep of large armies had become to the general public once the Royalists had been defeated. In most towns and counties the urge to be rid of the unpleasantnesses of wartime was profound. Cromwell told General Fairfax about a long petition that had been presented to Parliament by the City of London which 'struck at the Army' just before Christmas 1646.[11] Then Oliver was taken ill, but after his recovery, which he considered miraculous, he warned Fairfax that 'there want not in all places men who have so much malice against the Army as besots them'.[12] Nevertheless, he persuaded himself that if the Army were fairly treated by the House of Commons it would disband or volunteer for service in Ireland.

Towards the end of March 1647, however, a 'Declaration of the Army' was drawn up, in which Cromwell's son-in-law Henry Ireton played an important part, requiring Parliament to pay all arrears owing to the soldiers, to pass an act of indemnity for offences committed during the war, and to compensate the widows and orphans of fighting men who had been killed. A similar petition was addressed by private soldiers to General Fairfax. As a member of parliament of many years standing, Oliver disapproved of the soldiers' petition on the grounds that they were attempting to dictate to Parliament with their arms in their hands.[13] A majority in the Commons reacted furiously; it voted a resolution to the effect that 'all those who still continue in their distempered condition and go on advancing and promoting that petition shall be looked upon and proceeded against as enemies of the State and disturbers of the public peace'.

The men that had won the war for Parliament enemies of the state? No more provocative denunciation was conceivable. However, once the leaders of the Commons realized that the Army was united in its demands they compromised by appointing Cromwell, Ireton and two other members who had been officers to go to the Army headquarters (then at Saffron Walden) in May to pacify the soldiers by promising them that an act of indemnity would be passed and eight weeks of their arrears paid immediately. Oliver warned the officers there that if they disobeyed the orders of Parliament nothing could follow but confusion. But after he had been in Saffron Walden for a fortnight he was obliged to report that he and his fellow commissioners had found the Army (in which privates as well as officers were allowed to express their views) 'under a deep sense of some sufferings and the common soldiers most unsettled'.[14] He thought they would disband if they were paid off, but doubted if they would agree to go to Ireland. The leaders of the Commons reacted unfavourably to the report; they drew up a plan to scatter the regiments, disband them if they refused to serve in Ireland and, if necessary, recall the Scottish army to protect them against their own troops.

Under these circumstances it was hardly surprising that both Parliament and the Army turned to King Charles, for if a constitutional government under his auspices were to be established, the general state of public confusion could be ended. In April the propositions originally presented to Charles at Newcastle were again sent to him at Holdenby House, while in the same month he received a message from the Army that he should take refuge in its ranks. At the beginning of May a rumour arose that regiments in Cambridge and Ipswich were planning to fetch the King from Holdenby,[15] in the middle of the month the House of Lords voted to bring the King nearer to London, and later the Commons were considering the same idea. Parliament also contemplated dispatching him to Scotland out of the reach of the New Model Army. At the outset of June the French ambassador in London reported home that the Presbyterian members of parliament 'were trying to prevent the King of England from falling into the hands of the Army'. But they failed to do so.

On 3 June George Joyce, a cornet (the lowest-ranking officer in the Army), after seizing the magazine at Oxford went to Holdenby with 400 or 500 cavalrymen and demanded to speak to the King. The small garrison then fraternized with the troopers and the garrison commander, a Presbyterian, fled. Charles, who had returned from playing bowls at Althorp, was woken from his slumber. After a conversation with Cornet Joyce he promised, provided he was asked to do nothing contrary to his conscience, to leave Holdenby with Joyce on the following morning. On 4 June, after being reassured about his safety and that of his servants, Charles asked Joyce to show him his instructions. Joyce told the King that he had no orders, but turned in his saddle and pointed to his long line of troopers. 'It is as fair a commission and as well written as I have seen a commission written in my life,' replied

Charles, smiling.[16] He then agreed to accompany Joyce to the royal hunting lodge at Newmarket. The Parliamentary commissioners who had brought him to Holdenby from Newcastle reluctantly went with him but, as one of the King's grooms of the bedchamber noted, Charles was 'the merriest of the company'. For, knowing all about the differences between Parliament and the Army, he hoped to be freer to negotiate his return to power once he ceased to be the prisoner of Parliament.

How far was Cromwell responsible for the abduction of the King? Just over a month before Joyce's exploit eight of the cavalry regiments in the New Model Army had each chosen two representatives or agents from their ranks – they came to be known as 'Agitators' – who had addressed letters to their generals complaining of their shabby treatment by Parliament. According to a pamphleteer writing six months after the event, it was Cromwell who had in fact ordered Joyce to go to Holdenby to seize the King.[17] But why did he select a cornet for the task? Joyce told Charles that he had received no orders; that same evening he wrote a letter saying, 'Let the Agitators know once more that we have done nothing in our own name but what we have done hath been in the name of the whole Army',[18] – and that same day he wrote a letter to Cromwell to be given to Colonel Sir Arthur Haslerigg or Colonel Charles Fleetwood, both members of parliament, if Cromwell were not available, stating that he would 'obey no orders but the General's' – that is to say those of Thomas Fairfax.[19]

Haslerigg and Fleetwood denied any knowledge of Joyce's doings: so might Cromwell have done. But by the time the letter reached Westminster Oliver had left London to join the Army headquarters. As Sir John Berkeley wrote in his memoirs, 'Cromwell stayed very late in London, for one who had been the author of that design.'[20] Oliver himself said that the King had been removed from Holdenby without his knowledge or consent and that he had with Fairfax's approval sent his cousin, Colonel Whalley, with two cavalry regiments to take the King back there. But Charles firmly refused to return, for he was convinced that he was in a position to profit from the differences between the soldiers and their paymasters. Charles spent the night of 4 and 5

June at Hinchingbrooke, no longer the estate of Sir Oliver Cromwell, who had been obliged to sell it, ruined by his extravagant entertainment of Charles's father. Next day the King arrived at Childerley, where he was to stay for three days.

Such was the background to the occasion on which Oliver Cromwell first spoke to King Charles I. Various officers, headed by Fairfax, rode over from Cambridge, where the headquarters of the Army now were. Fairfax | knelt | to | kiss | the | King's hands; Cromwell and Ireton did not but, according to Thomas Herbert, who had been appointed by Parliament to be one of the King's grooms of the bedchamber, they 'behaved themselves with civility and respect to the royal person, which made the King sometimes very pleasant in his discourse with them'.[21] Naturally, Charles wanted to know if Fairfax and Cromwell had given their authority to Joyce to fetch him from Holdenby; when they denied this, Charles retorted, 'Unless you hang up Joyce, I shall not believe what you say.'[22] After the officers returned to Cambridge they were all said to have praised the King highly 'for his great improvement. He argued his own and his subjects' case with each of them (one by one) to their final astonishment.'[23]

At Childerley Charles was described as having found 'good entertainment', but when he was allowed to proceed to his own house at Newmarket, where many of his subjects came to see him when he dined or supped in the Presence Chamber, he grew very cheerful indeed. He kept in perfect health by riding on the heath.[24] The Parliamentary commissioners headed by the Earl of Pembroke, who had first joined him at Newcastle, still stayed with him and the chief Army officers frequently visited him. No wonder Charles optimistically hoped that an agreement would soon be reached between the Army commanders and the Houses of Parliament to restore him to complete liberty. Soon events were moving in the direction he wanted.

On the same day that Joyce brought the King from Holdenby to Hinchingbrooke a Solemn Engagement was drawn up by the Army and approved by Oliver, who was anxious to sustain unity and discipline. It was proposed that a General Council of the Army should be formed consisting of, besides the general officers, two commissioned officers and two private soldiers chosen by each regiment to discuss the terms it was being offered by Parliament. For after they learned of the abduction of the King the leaders in the Commons had decided to conciliate the Army by, on the one hand, repealing the declaration calling the soldiers 'enemies of the State' and, on the other hand, promising to pass an indemnity for acts done during the hostilities and to increase the amounts of arrears of pay available on disbandment. At the same time they took steps to raise a force from soldiers already demobilized and out of the London militia, and by invoking help from the Scots.

The Council of War, through which the general opinions of the New Model Army found expression, rejected Parliament's revised offers. On 10 June a letter was delivered to the Lord Mayor, Aldermen and Common Council of the City of London demanding 'a happy settlement ... not as soldiers but as Englishmen'.[25] Yet at the same time the letter affirmed that the Army had no wish to interfere with the government for 'once the State has made a settlement we have nothing to say but to submit and suffer'.[26] The sting in the letter came near its end. For it added that to obtain the desires of the Army 'we are drawing near your City'. The London authorities were warned that if they were seduced into taking up arms in opposition to their 'just understandings' ruin might 'befall your great and populous city'.[27]

It has been suggested that this highly significant letter was inspired and possibly drafted by Oliver Cromwell. The officers who signed it were mostly his friends and relations – his son-in-law Henry Ireton, his cousin John Desborough, and his future second-in-command John Lambert. Although Fairfax's signature was appended, he afterwards asserted that it was done without his consent. In fact, at the same time he wrote a letter to the Speaker of the House of Commons stressing that he and his officers could exert little influence over their men when they were so much in want of pay.[28] The letter to the London authorities was hastily written and muddled in thought. If Cromwell, Ireton and their colleagues believed that the Army must submit to the State and eschew politics, why did they say, as they did, 'we have as much right to demand a happy settlement as we have to our money'?[29] And after insisting in this curious letter that 'we desire not to intermeddle with or in the least to interrupt the settling of the Presbyterian government', a week later Cromwell and his friends drew up accusations against eleven of the Presbyterian leaders in the Commons, compelled them to withdraw from the House and started sketching out their own plans for the future constitutional government of the kingdom, culminating in a document known as the *Heads of the Proposals*, which was debated by the General Council of the Army and later submitted to the King.

The growing conflict between the Army and Parliament rejoiced the defeated Royalists. After the King's abduction Edward Hyde, one of the King's most loyal servants, wrote to Lord Hopton, who was equally loyal: 'It is now in the King's power to have a just and honest and honourable peace by consenting to nothing but what constitutes it just.'[30]

While Charles was spending an agreeable fortnight in Newmarket in the company of his young cousin the Duke of Richmond, who had married a daughter of the first Duke of Buckingham, he was frequently visited by the chief officers of the Army. He told a friend that the Army 'speaks to me very fair which makes me hope well'. When the Army began moving towards London he was required to conform with its movements. First he went to Royston, twelve miles south of Cambridge, and then on 27 June to the Earl of Salisbury's mansion at Hatfield where, it being a Sunday, he was allowed to attend divine service according to the ritual of the Church of England. Thence, after the Army withdrew from St Albans to Reading, Charles enjoyed two days in Windsor Castle, but was then moved to Lord Craven's house at Caversham. He was in the care of Colonel Whalley, who was instructed not to let him escape, but he was permitted to have his own chaplains – Dr Gilbert Sheldon, a future Archbishop of Canterbury, and Dr Henry Hammond, whose nephew Robert Hammond was a colonel in the Parliamentarian Army and destined to play a large part in the last months of the King's life. As Charles later told the Scots commissioners, whereas at Newcastle and Holdenby House 'he was kept with all strictness and rigour', since he came into the power of the Army he had 'been used with much civility and far greater freedom than he formerly was'.[31]

Not only was he permitted to have his own chaplains but also some of his own servants. His children were brought to see him and he was allowed to correspond with his wife in France.

At Caversham Cromwell visited the King on 4 July and so did Ireton. What Oliver said to Charles on this occasion is not known. But according to Sir John Berkeley, who returned from France with messages from the Queen to her husband, repeating what she had said in 1646 and advising him to come to terms with the Presbyterian leaders, Ireton had already warned the King not to try to profit from the breach between Parliament and the Army. 'Sir,' he said, 'you have an intention to be the arbitrator between Parliament and us, and we mean to be it between your Majesty and the Parliament.'[32] Cromwell evidently thought that he might make more progress towards a satisfactory agreement by using Berkeley, whom he had met when Berkeley was the Royalist governor of Exeter, as an intermediary rather than by negotiating with Charles himself, whom he found difficult to talk to. He told Berkeley that

> whatever the world might judge of them, they would be found no seekers of themselves further than to have leave to live as subjects have right to do and to preserve their consciences; and as they thought no men could enjoy their lives and estates quietly, without the King had his rights, which they had declared in general terms already to the world, and would more particularly very speedily, wherein they would comprise the several interests of the royal, Presbyterian and Independent parties, so far as they are consistent with each other.[33]

However, when Berkeley, on Cromwell's advice, received permission from General Fairfax to visit the King, Charles said he did not trust the leaders of the Army because they would not accept any promises of future favours from him for themselves. Cromwell, it was said, was to have been promised the earldom of Essex – the Earl, who was the first commander-in-chief of the Parliamentarian army which defeated the King, having recently died without heirs – and also be appointed Captain of the King's Guard.[34] From the other side Berkeley himself was offered a bribe of £1,200, which when he refused made the 'general officers' (he does not tell us who they were) think he was 'an engaged

Presbyterian'. When Oliver came to see him Berkeley assured him that he was 'as much Presbyterian as Independent', but he preferred the Independents because they favoured the King's restoration.

Though Oliver was disappointed that Charles was not franker with him and 'tied himself too strictly to narrow maxims', he told Berkeley at Caversham that 'he had lately seen the tenderest sight that ever his eyes beheld, which was the interview between the King and his children, and wept plentifully at the remembrance of it, saying that never man was so abused as he in his sinister opinions of the King, who, he thought, was the uprightest and most conscientious man in the three kingdoms' and added that he was grateful to Charles for rejecting the proposal of the Scots that he should impose an exclusive Presbyterian government of the Church on both his kingdoms as the price of his restoration.[35] Nothing illustrates more clearly how emotional Oliver was. When Berkeley repeated this story to the King he was not in the least pleased, for he thought he was merely being made the tool of the Army to achieve its particular ends. He was unshaken in his belief that Cromwell could be bought.

Oliver was in fact still hoping to attain a comprehensive settlement between the Army, the King and Parliament. But he was handicapped because at this stage what the rank-and-file of the Army wanted was the immediate satisfaction of their grievances over pay and security for their future in civilian life; therefore they were agitating for an advance on London in order to compel Parliament to do what they wished. So before he could negotiate further with Charles Oliver had first to satisfy the Army about his good intentions.

Here then, during the summer of 1647 in the prime of their lives, the two men who had fought each other in the civil war struggled to find a political solution that would restore the nation to peace. Charles had convinced himself that the divisions between the victorious Army and the Parliament that had started the war against him would enable him by offering a few concessions and by bribing Oliver to regain his lost power. Oliver, both as a successful soldier and an experienced member of parliament, hoped that he could work out a comprehensive settlement that would reconcile the Army, the House of Commons and the King. The characters of these two protagonists in this, one of the most dramatic years in British history, were very different, but the problems they were facing were much the same. The contrasts and comparisons between them is the subject of this book.

2

THE CHILD IS FATHER OF THE MAN

Wordsworth's line 'the Child is father of the Man' has become a commonplace. It was once believed that an adopted child, if lovingly cared for, could throw off the influence of poor heredity. But modern research has laid additional emphasis on heredity; certainly neither Charles nor Oliver owed much to their experiences in childhood which could not equally convincingly be attributed to heredity.

The Stuarts had been kings of Scotland ever since the fourteenth century. On the whole, they had been likeable and cultured monarchs. The first Stuart, Robert I, was praised for his 'innate sweetness of disposition' and the next Stuart, Robert II, was described as being 'sweet, pacific and indolent'. James I of Scotland was a musician who composed songs. James II founded a university. James III patronized the arts and encouraged native architecture. James IV was a fine linguist who was the patron of learning and literature. James V was a Renaissance prince who spent a great deal of money on the arts, including literature and architecture. But what all the Scottish Stuarts had in common was the need to sustain their positions by contending against ambitious noblemen: the Black Douglases, the Red Douglases, the Homes, the Hepburns, the Hamiltons, the Campbells and the Gordons. Except for Mary Queen of Scots, the Stuarts managed to survive by playing off these noblemen against one another; and since the Stuart monarchs rarely had the military resources to crush Highland chieftains and Border earls they relied on diplomatic ingenuity more than on warfare to maintain peace in their realm. Thus most of Charles I's characteristics – his ability to charm when he wished to do so, his aestheticism and his pride in his negotiating skill – can be derived from his ancestry.

Oliver Cromwell owed much to heredity. He was above all the child of the Reformation. His family derived its wealth and social position from the dissolution of the monasteries begun by King Henry VIII's Vicar General, Thomas Cromwell, who adopted and gave his name to Oliver's great-grandfather. The area in which Oliver was born had proved little resistant to the forces of the Protestant Reformation: there were relatively few recusants – Catholics who refused to attend Anglican services – as compared with those to be found in pockets in the north and in the western midlands.

King Charles I had been born a weakling; he was hastily baptized because he was scarcely expected to live. His mother, Anne of Denmark, presented her husband, King James VI of Scotland, with eight children, only three of whom grew to be adults. When two and a half years after Charles's birth his father set out on a leisurely drive to London, where he was to succeed Queen Elizabeth I as ruler of England and Ireland, and a few weeks later Queen Anne followed him there with her eldest son Prince Henry, it had been decided to leave their second son behind in Scotland because he was sick with fever. Charles was to remain in Dunfermline castle near Edinburgh, where he had been born, under the care of a guardian and a governess; although he was slow to walk and talk, he owed his survival to their devoted care.

A year after his arrival in England James despatched an English doctor to examine his second son in the summer of 1604. He was reported to be well enough to be brought to London, where he occupied what had previously been his brother Henry's quarters in Whitehall palace, but he was still frail and suffering from rickets, caused no doubt by a poorly balanced diet. Attendants had to carry and support him when at the age of four he was ceremoniously created Duke of York.

Charles was then placed in the charge of Sir Robert Carey and his wife. Carey was an ambitious man who made his mark with Charles's father by being the first to bring him news of the death of Queen Elizabeth I. Sir Robert fully realized that he was undertaking a dangerous job, for should the child die when in his responsibility he might lose his lucrative position at the Court of

Whitehall. 'The Duke was four years old when he was first delivered to my wife,' he wrote in his memoirs:

> He was not able to go, and scant stand alone, he was so weak in his joints, and especially his ankles, insomuch as many feared they were out of joint.... The King was desirous that the string under his tongue should be cut, for he was so long beginning to speak as he thought he would never have spoken.[1]

The doctor who had vouched for his improvement in health before he was allowed to come to England continued to examine him and an osteopath was employed, but it seems that it was chiefly Charles's own efforts in exercising himself, together with Lady Carey's motherly affection, that helped the Prince to overcome his youthful disabilities. Sir Philip Warwick was to record in his memoirs that the future King 'though born weakly, yet came through temperance and exercise to have as firm and strong a body as that of most persons I ever knew'.[2] It was this continuing good health that helps to explain his capability to sustain the vicissitudes that the future held in store for him.

Nevertheless, Charles was slow in learning to talk and was always to stammer. He was never to be more than five feet four inches tall, though most, but not all of the artists who painted him did their best to conceal this fact from posterity. Once his physical infirmities had been overcome Charles was far from unhappy. His mother loved him and he loved her: he was with her when she was dying and was to be the chief mourner at her funeral. He was fond too of his elder brother who was athletic, serious-minded, a patron of the arts, independent in character and had many admirers.[3] Henry was six years older than Charles. His sister Elizabeth was four years older. She had been named after Queen Elizabeth I, who accepted her as a godchild. Vivacious, enchanting and good-looking – she inherited her mother's golden hair – she worshipped her elder brother, but also cared for her 'dear brother Charles', as he always did for her, notably when she met with misfortune.

The winter of 1612-13 was crucial in Charles's life. In November 1612 his brother Henry died of typhoid fever; in February 1613 on St Valentine's day his sister Elizabeth married Frederick the Elector Palatine, with whom she had fallen in love, and was carried off to Heidelberg by her ambitious young husband. Charles was not yet twelve, but he had already assumed some of the ceremonial duties of his station. Now he had to welcome the Elector Frederick to Whitehall palace, act as chief mourner at his brother's funeral, and be the best man at his sister's wedding. Left devoid of the companionship he had so much appreciated, he was for a time, most unusually, taken ill himself.

James I was a conscientious father. He appointed a Scottish divine to be his son's tutor (subsequently he became Provost of Eton) and Charles mastered Latin and Greek without difficulty as well as learning French, Italian and some Spanish. At the age of eight he had been able to write to his brother in Latin and told him that he was 'reading the Colloquies of Erasmus from which I trust to learn both the purity of the Latin language and elegance of manners'.[4] 'There were few gentlemen in the world,' Sir Philip Warwick thought, 'that knew more of useful or necessary learning than this prince did.'[5] He was also taught to play tennis, to fence, to ride, hunt, and dance. But what was more significant for his future was his study of theology, which had impressed his elder brother sufficiently to tease him by saying he would one day become Archbishop of Canterbury.[6]

Both King James and Prince Henry were pronounced extroverts and in his early youth Charles dwelt in their shadow, from which he was to emerge very gradually. Writing about him when he was fourteen, soon after the death of his brother, one of his chaplains said: 'He had more understanding than the late Prince of his age and is in behaviour shy, grave, sweet, in speech very reserved without any evil inclinations and willing to take advice.'[7] Like Henry, he found the vulgarity of his father's Court distasteful and preferred the company of his mother. King James and Queen Anne had ceased to live together in 1607 after the birth of their youngest daughter. The King then relapsed into the homosexual habits which had been notorious before he left Scotland, but followed the curious principle of seeking the Queen's approval of his men favourites before he adopted and ennobled them.

His first notable favourite was Robert Ker or Carr, a handsome

Scotsman, whom he first created Viscount Rochester and then Earl of Somerset and to whom he vainly tried to teach Latin. Not surprisingly Prince Henry took an intense dislike to him, more especially as he could see his father fondling and kissing him in public. However, Somerset grew overconfident about his good fortune and took to railing at and upbraiding his master at all hours of day and night. After he wedded a noblewoman of great beauty but doubtful morals (a wedding approved by the King, who never objected to his men favourites being married) he tended to neglect James, which enabled a young Gentleman of the Bedchamber, sponsored by the Archbishop of Canterbury and described by the Bishop of Gloucester as 'the handsomest-bodied man of England', by name George Villiers, to take his place. Charles – he was crowned Prince of Wales on 4 November 1616 – at first naturally felt jealous of Villiers, who was created Earl of Buckingham two months later, for Villiers was only eight years older than he was but was accustomed to address the Prince, just as his father did, as 'Baby Charles'. However, Buckingham was a much cleverer and more charming man than Somerset, while King James was anxious that his son and his new favourite should become friends, and that was soon achieved.

It was significant of the relationship between Charles and his parents that at his father's request Charles had tried to persuade his mother to make a will when she was dying; after she did so and left her valuable jewellery to the Prince, this angered James so much that Charles was obliged to apologize and seek Buckingham's intervention to obtain his father's forgiveness. At a sumptuous banquet given by Buckingham at his country house in the summer of 1618 this peculiar trio – the widowed King, his homosexual favourite and his shy and diffident son – rejoiced together: 'the end whereunto it was designed [noted a contemporary] of reconciling His Highness gave it the name of the Prince's feast'.[8]

Nevertheless, Charles's character was shaped more by his mother and brother, both of whom died before he came of age, than by his father or Buckingham. His mother loved masques, most of which were designed for her by men of genius, Ben Jonson providing the libretto and Inigo Jones the setting. She acted in some of the masques herself and patronized the theatre.[9] The beautiful Queen's house at Greenwich, still standing today, was built for her. She collected jewellery, spent lavishly on her clothes, and had perfect manners – when James's cousin, Arabella Stuart, first visited his Court she found everyone discourteous except the Queen.[10] Prince Henry was a collector too, who bequeathed to his brother books, coins, paintings and Florentine statuettes. Like his mother, Prince Henry delighted in and performed in the Court masques and was fond of music as well as of acting. Otherwise neither he nor Charles cared for the goings-on at their father's Court.

After James had reached the promised land of England he became grossly extravagant and both the Scotsmen, who came with him, and the courtiers, whom he selected, hung about hoping to profit from his prodigality. The Jacobean Court was replete with sycophancy and corruption. The King was lax in discipline, swore frequently, and embraced his favourites in public. Inside the sprawling Palace of Whitehall the nobility were protected from arrest for debt. At times drunkenness was rife. After one banquet plates and dishes piled high on tables crashed to the floor, reminding a Venetian who was present of a severe hailstorm in midsummer. Anyone could find their way into the Court, slipping through the gates when the porters were not watchful, so that thieves and pickpockets could circulate and pilfer. But most of the stealing was done by dishonest officials and royal servants. Though parasitic courtiers profited from free food and wine, it was costly to keep up appearances. They were expected to gamble for high stakes – James himself gambled – and were liable to be poisoned by rich indigestible dishes. 'Allured by the glamour and excitement of the Court,' Professor Stone writes, 'many noblemen lived out their futile lives in a vain struggle for office and profit that left them cynical, servile and impoverished.'[11] There were to be found pimps and procuresses. Sexual permissiveness was accepted, at any rate among gentlemen, as readily as drunkenness. Venereal disease was common. Some of the behaviour at Court was obviously disgusting.

Such were the surroundings of Charles in his youth. The contrast between the way in which his father behaved and the ideals he tried to instil into his son was striking. Before King James left Scotland he had written a book called *Basilikon Doron* for the benefit of Prince Henry, in which he taught his son his duty towards God as a Christian, how to conduct himself in the kingly office, and how to behave 'in indifferent things', that is apart from politics and religion. Although originally only seven copies were printed, it was reprinted twice and was studied by Charles. It opened with a sonnet which began:

> God gives not Kings the stile of Gods in vaine,
> For on his throne his Scepter do they sway:
> And as their subjects ought them to obey
> So Kings should feare and serve their God againe;
> If then you would have a happier reigne
> Observe the Statutes of your heavenly King,
> And from his Law make all your Lawes to spring.[12]

God, James told his son, 'made you a little God to sit on his throne and rule over other men'. This patriarchal theory of government was, paradoxically, much more applicable to the Tudor monarchs of England than to the Stuart rulers of Scotland, who were invariably circumscribed in their authority by the power of border warriors and Highland chieftains and later of their Presbyterian ministers.

Yet it has to be emphasized that James was writing out of his experience as King of Scotland, not of England. Once he settled in England he wrote little and learned slowly about its politics, misunderstanding the growing strength and independence of the House of Commons. He adhered to the belief that he was 'the husband' and 'the whole isle his lawful wife' or, speaking in a more lofty vein to the English Parliament in 1610: 'Kings are not only God's lieutenants upon earth, and set upon God's throne, but even by God himself are called Gods.' In an earlier book, *The Trew Law of Free Monarchies*, he argued that some kings had ruled before there were any parliaments: 'The kings were the authors and makers of the laws and not the laws of the kings.'[13] So, to his mind, parliaments simply existed for the making of good laws dictated to them by kings. On more mundane matters James advised his son to 'serve his appetite with few dishes' and 'let all your food be simple without composition or sauces', to be moderate in clothing, to be careful in choosing a wife and never to forgive witchcraft, wilful murder, incest, sodomy, poisoning and false witness.[14] Charles could scarcely fail to see that his father did not always follow his own rules. Nevertheless he loved his father, but also feared him. The Venetian ambassador noted that when the Prince was sixteen 'he was very grave and polite' and that 'his chief endeavour is to have no other aim than to second his father, to follow him and do his pleasure and not to move except as his father does. Before his father he always aims at suppressing his own feelings.'[15]

So it is fair to say that while Charles often found the realities of his father's Court unpleasant, he was deeply impressed by his theories of kingship. Since God had created monarchs to govern their subjects as benevolent parents, who cared for their children as husbands cared for their wives, the Church was essential to the well-being of effective royal authority. The King might be the Supreme Governor of the Church of England, but he could not sustain the government of his dominions without its backing.

One may attribute to Charles's friendship with Buckingham the growth of a less dependent attitude towards his father. When at first Charles was jealous of Buckingham's influence on James, he was sixteen years old and Buckingham twenty-four, a notable gap in human experience. But after Buckingham had been successful in winning Charles's favour and later reconciling him to his father over the affair of the dead Queen's jewels, Charles found in Buckingham the friend of whom he was sorely in need. Having lost his mother, brother and sister, at eighteen he was going through the homosexual phase which most men undergo before they become polygamous. Buckingham well knew how to exert his charm, becoming the substitute for the brother Charles had lost six years earlier. Charles called him Steenie, as did James, and Buckingham still spoke of 'Baby Charles'.

By then Charles had overcome his physical weaknesses: he became a better horseman than his father (who frequently fell off) and a keen huntsman, while King James was particularly pleased with the way his son performed in the tiltyard. He also interested himself in politics; when a parliament was called in 1621 he often attended the House of Lords and also listened to speeches, notably those of Sir Edward Coke, the distinguished lawyer whom his father had dismissed from the court of King's Bench, in the House of Commons. Vainly he attempted to defend Francis Bacon Viscount of St Albans, who was impeached for accepting bribes in his capacity as Lord Chancellor. But the subject which most concerned him, as it did his father and both Houses of Parliament, was the fate of his only sister and her husband, the Elector Palatine, Frederick Henry.

Three years earlier Frederick had accepted an offer from the Protestant nobility of the Crown of Bohemia in place of Ferdinand, Archduke of Styria, a pious Roman Catholic Habsburg prince, who had in fact been elected King the year before. Before the Elector closed with this invitation he consulted his father-in-law, who felt considerable doubts about the wisdom of his doing so, especially as the Archduke Ferdinand was about to succeed (also by election) to the throne of the Holy Roman Empire with the immense influence that this position commanded. In any case James did not approve of rebels – he had had enough of them in Scotland. Charles, however, was delighted that his beloved sister was to be crowned a queen. But she was only to be 'a winter queen', for next autumn her husband was decisively defeated by the Emperor Ferdinand's army at the battle of the White Mountain outside Prague. Meanwhile, a Spanish army in alliance with the Emperor began the occupation of Frederick's Electorate of the Lower Palatinate. James I, who prided himself on being a prince of peace, determined to help his son-in-law by diplomacy and not by war. But when Charles's sister wrote from her enforced exile begging for her father's assistance to save herself and her husband from ruin, Charles and the Earl of Buckingham were eager to lead a crusade on her behalf.

The Parliament of 1621, in which Charles had been active, was deeply exercised over the destiny of the Elector Palatine, for it feared that a Counter-Reformation headed by the Emperor and the King of Spain, both members of the Habsburg family, might overthrow Protestantism throughout Europe. It voted money to sustain an English volunteer force that was trying to regain the Lower Palatinate for Charles's brother-in-law, and urged

King James to prepare to make war on Spain, as Queen Elizabeth I had done so successfully. But James would not allow foreign policy to be dictated to him by the House of Commons, and when the Commons protested he dissolved Parliament and tore the protestation from the journal of the House in January 1622.

Nine months later the news reached England that the Elector Palatine's capital of Heidelberg had fallen to the imperial forces and that an English garrison which was defending it had been overwhelmed. Charles and Buckingham now pressed the King to intervene. He agreed to send a firm note to the King of Spain because it was his conviction that only through an understanding with Spain could his son-in-law's restoration to his hereditary possessions be procured. Charles, it was said, was playing with the idea of leading an army of 20,000 men to the rescue of his sister and was planning campaigns. But he did not openly differ from his father's more cautious policy. Undoubtedly his attitude to his father was ambivalent. Yet it was not until the last years of King James's reign that he began to show he had a mind of his own.

Of Oliver Cromwell it has been said that 'the birth of a child in an obscure family in an obscure English town was not a matter of general interest'.[16] However, the fact is that the Cromwells were one of the most important and influential families in Huntingdon, which was the capital of a county not far from Cambridge. Thomas Cromwell Earl of Essex, when he was at his prime, had adopted his nephew Richard Williams, the son of a Welsh brewer, who assumed his uncle's name and called himself Williams alias Cromwell. Benefiting from the cheap purchase of confiscated monastic lands, including the nunnery of Hinchingbrooke, he founded a family eminent in Huntingdonshire. When Oliver married he also signed himself Williams alias Cromwell. Both his father and his grandfather had represented Huntingdon in Parliament. So he scarcely belonged to an obscure family.

Oliver's father was clearly influenced by the Puritan movement that had burgeoned in the later years of the reign of Queen Elizabeth I. He sent his son to the local grammar school, whose Master, Thomas Beard, was an enthusiastic Puritan who wrote a book demonstrating that the Pope was Anti-Christ and another entitled *The Theatre of God's Judgments Displayed* to prove that the system of rewards and punishments administered by the Almighty in the hereafter applied 'even in this life'. Beard became a close friend of the Cromwells and if, as has been assumed, he beat Oliver when he was a child, Oliver did not resent it.[17] Then Oliver's father sent him to Sidney Sussex College in Cambridge, a nursery of Puritans with a Master who was an eminent Calvinist divine; he left a diary in which he noted all his own shortcomings ranging from over-eating to 'wicked and adulterous thoughts'.[18] Oliver remained there for only a year because the early death of his father obliged him to return home to look after his mother, who was widowed for a second time, and no fewer than six sisters. His father had bequeathed a relatively small estate to support so large a family, but somehow they managed. When Oliver was twenty-one he left home for a time to study at one of the Inns of Court; while he was there he met the daughter of a reputable and wealthy merchant whom he married and brought back to live with his mother and brood of sisters in Huntingdon.

Oliver was an athletic young man more attracted to outdoor sports than book learning. An early biographer wrote that though he was 'of a nature not averse to study and contemplation, yet he seemed rather addicted to conversation and the reading of men and their several tempers than to a continual poring over authors'.[19] Indeed the only books it is certain he read were the Bible and Sir Walter Ralegh's *History of the World*, which argued that 'ill doing hath always been attended with ill success'. Oliver recommended it to one of his sons as 'a body of history' that would 'add much more to your understanding than fragments of story'. At Cambridge he learned enough Latin to be able to converse in it with foreign diplomatists after he became Lord Protector; he was also said to excel in mathematics.

His eldest son was born in 1621 and his eldest daughter in 1624. Some biographers have spoken of 'lost years' in Cromwell's life before he married and have speculated whether, like some of his contemporaries, he might have learnt the military art as a volunteer in a Protestant army overseas. But really there were no lost years and as to his 'boisterious years', another favourite topic of his biographers, they merely exhibit the habit of historians repeating one another. As John Buchan wrote, his early marriage to a girl who proved an excellent housewife and a devoted mother does not suggest the rake.[20] At Huntingdon he continued, as Thomas Carlyle suggested, 'unnoticeable but easily imaginable by History, for almost ten years: farming lands; most probably attending quarter-sessions; doing the civic, industrial and social duties, in the common way; – living as his father before him had done'.[21]

The next important date in Oliver's early life was 1628. First of all, he was elected member of parliament for the borough of Huntingdon; secondly, his youngest and ablest son was born; thirdly, he underwent the emotional experience known as conversion. According to Sir Philip Warwick, Cromwell's physician Dr John Symcotts, who had settled in Huntingdon some time before 1628, had assured him

> that for many years his patient was a most splenetic man, and had fancies about the cross in the town [Huntingdon] and that he had been called up to him at midnight, and such unseasonable hours, very many times upon a strong fancy, which made him believe he was dying; and there went a story of him, that in the daytime, lying melancholy in his bed, he believed that a spirit appeared to him and told him that he would be the greatest man (not mentioning the word king) in this kingdom, which his uncle, Sir Thomas Steward, who left him all the little estate Cromwell had, told him it was traitorous to relate.[22]

This seems a good story elaborated on. Warwick stated that he met Symcotts in 1646 after Cromwell had become famous for his victories in the battles of Marston Moor and Naseby. Sir Thomas Steward had died in 1636. It might be hard to credit any of this second-hand story but for the fact that Sir Theodore Mayerne, the most famous doctor in England, had noted down in his case-book on 18 September 1628 that he had been consulted by Cromwell as a patient and found him 'very melancholy'.[23] It is also worth noting that Symcotts's sympathies lay with Parliament and so he was presumably not motivated in his recollections by political bias.

Ten years later Oliver wrote that remarkable letter to his cousin, in the course of which he said: 'You know what my manner of life hath been. Oh I lived in and loved darkness and hated the light. I was a chief, the chief of sinners. This is true: I hated godliness, yet God had mercy on me.'[24] He was speaking of his spiritual conversion, of the dawn of his belief that he was one of God's chosen, just as Charles was to believe, with his father, that he was a divinely chosen King. A friend of Cromwell's was to describe later with much more plausibility than can be seen in the effusions of Royalist biographers, whose lucubrations have recently been resurrected, this spiritual crisis from which he emerged when he was in his twenties:

> This great man [he wrote] is risen from a very low and afflicted condition; one that hath suffered very great troubles of soul, lying a long time under sore terrors and temptations and at the same time in a very low condition for outward things; in this school of afflictions he was kept, till he had learned the lesson of the Cross, till his will was broken with submission to the will of God.[25]

During these early years Oliver was active in local politics. He was appointed a justice of the peace, he questioned the way in which the Mayor of Huntingdon and the Aldermen had made use of the rights bestowed on them in a new charter granted in 1630, and later when he moved to Ely he defended the rights of fishing and pasturage enjoyed by his neighbours there, which had been infringed when a company had been formed to drain the fens outside the town. In both these cases he resented what he regarded as attacks on customary property rights.[26] At the same time he regarded the sacramental usages in services which were promoted by William Laud (who became Archbishop of Canterbury in 1633) as dangerous innovations and thought preaching and expounding the Gospel of Jesus Christ were more valuable than the communion service. Thus essentially, in his younger days, Oliver was a conservative. It was not until he became a leading figure in the government of the country that he espoused genuinely progressive ideas. Nevertheless, he showed himself to be politically minded, for after all he belonged to the ruling gentry who at least at local level had been what may be called 'establishment figures' ever since the justices of the peace became maids-of-all-work in the thirteenth century.

One fact that can be plainly seen about Cromwell's character in his early manhood was how volatile he was, as instanced by his outbursts of hot temper when he thought that wrongs had been done, though, when satisfied, his temper rapidly cooled. It was exemplified first when he criticized the Mayor and Aldermen of Huntingdon, who were appointed for life, before the Privy Council for violating the ancient rights of his fellow townsmen. After a settlement had been recorded he apologized for the words he had spoken 'in heat and passion' and asked that they should be forgotten.[27] Later, constituting himself the spokesman for the commoners of Ely, who had rioted in protest because their livelihood was endangered by enclosures of the fens, he was equally vehement. When other fenmen, who had rioted in east Huntingdonshire, came to put their case before a committee of the House of Commons, of which Edward Hyde was the chairman and Oliver a member, he sided with the fenmen and 'enlarged upon what they said with great passion'. Because Hyde tried to bring these 'very rude kind of people' to order Oliver accused him of bias and (according to Hyde) 'already too much angry' replied to the case put by the enclosers with such 'indecency and rudeness and in language so contrary and offensive ... with his whole carriage so tempestuous and his behaviour so insolent' that Hyde threatened to report his behaviour to the House of Commons.[28]

One factor common to these particular incidents was that in each instance Cromwell was acting in opposition to the Montagu family which, like that of the Cromwells, was one of the most influential in Huntingdonshire. The case that Cromwell brought against the Mayor of Huntingdon was referred for arbitration to Henry Montagu first Earl of Manchester, who was then the Lord Privy Seal, while his vigorous defence of the fenmen in east Huntingdonshire was directed against the same Earl because he had purchased lands which formed part of the Queen's jointure with a view to draining and enclosing them. In this second affair the Earl was represented by his son, Edward Montagu Lord Mandeville, who was later to become the second Earl of Manchester. The first Earl had purchased Sir Oliver Cromwell's mansion of Hinchingbrooke two years after the death of King James I, who had regarded it almost as his autumn residence. Sir Oliver then moved to another palatial house in the county where he lived to the ripe age of ninety-six. His second wife was an extremely wealthy widow. A contrast that has sometimes been drawn between the Montagus and the Cromwells, suggesting that the former were rising gentry and the latter declining gentry, is hardly correct. Indeed, the fact that the future Lord Protector was elected as a member for Huntingdon after his uncle had left Hinchingbrooke, while the other member was a Montagu, the third son of the first Earl of Manchester, indicates that they were equally influential in the county. No doubt they were rivals, but reasonably friendly rivals, who were both to side with Parliament against Charles in the years ahead. Moreover, Oliver's animosity was short-lived – otherwise he could scarcely have become the second Earl's right-hand man in 1643. Although Oliver and his namesake had their temporary financial difficulties they were never grave. Both families were members of the governing classes who had derived their wealth and position from the Protestant Reformation, engineered and carried out by Henry VIII and Thomas Cromwell.

Charles Stuart and Oliver Cromwell grew to manhood during the same phase of European history. They were both born at the end of the reign of Queen Elizabeth I, who had reluctantly been driven into war against the most powerful monarch in the world, the Habsburg King Philip II of Spain, and in support of the Dutch who were fighting for their independence. When Charles's brother-in-law defied the Austrian Habsburgs by accepting the crown of Bohemia he precipitated the Thirty Years War which was to dominate European politics for a generation. Prince Charles was eighteen and Oliver Cromwell was nineteen when this war broke out. Neither of them was immediately or directly involved in it because Charles's father strove for peace and conciliation and Cromwell was not yet a member of the parliament which was to clamour for war against Spain. But Charles's sister pleaded with him for help and Oliver, passing through that spiritual agony which preceded his conversion, was in the process of becoming a fanatical Puritan to whom the Roman Catholic Church, on which the Habsburgs depended during their contest against rebels and heretics, was anathema. Religion was central to the characters of both these young men, but in very different ways. That is the subject of the next chapter.

3

MEN OF GOD

What is Puritanism? Up till recently it has usually been thought to consist of the doings of spoil-sports and kill-joys who deprive people of the right to enjoy themselves in their own way. As Cromwell once said, people must be made to do what is good for them, not what pleases them.[1] The range of prohibitions and penalties for disobeying the code of morality prescribed in the Old Testament was extended once the Puritans governed the country. Imprisonment could be imposed for fornication and death for adultery. Sabbatarianism was strictly enforced; no games or amusements were permitted on Sundays. Taverns and alehouses were closed down.

But basically the Puritans were, as a contemporary observed, 'the hotter kind of Protestants'. With a few exceptions all Puritans agreed that man was born sinful ever since Adam was tempted in the Garden of Eden. Oliver Cromwell's son-in-law, Henry Ireton, said: 'Men as men are corrupt and will be so.'[2] In the order of nature man was utterly depraved. Only in the order of grace could the truly converted Christian acquire a new and better character; he was still left open to temptation, though the subjective assurance of salvation that he obtained placed the believer somewhat apart from the sinner.

Oliver's conversion when he was a young married man was a fairly typical experience. As has justly been observed:

The Puritan's procedure was first to enlighten the unregenerate man about the nature of sin, then to lead him to the conviction of his own guilt before God. Only when thoroughly roused and humbled by the deadly pollution of sin ... was he encouraged to find comfort in the promises of the gospel.[3]

Those of Oliver's biographers who have maintained that his confession that he had been 'the chief of sinners' must have had some substance in it can hardly have studied the many parallel instances of conversion in the seventeenth century. As the Puritan Richard Sibbes explained in 1630, 'God knows that we are prone to despair for sin.'[4] After all, did not St Paul write, 'This is a faithful saying and worthy of all acceptation that Christ Jesus came into the world to save sinners, of whom I am the chief'?[5] The repentant sinner sued for grace and suffered mental and physical agonies before he was convinced that he was indeed one of God's chosen. Even then the certainty may never have been complete, for on his death-bed Cromwell enquired of his chaplain if it was possible to fall from grace and, when comforted, murmured, 'Then I am saved, for I know that once I was in grace.'[6]

What animated Oliver and his fellow Puritans was their dread that what they regarded as Popish superstitions might be revived after Charles came to the throne and married a Roman Catholic wife; thus the holy community which they envisaged as the ideal state of society could be undermined. When Henry VIII promoted the Protestant Reformation in his kingdom during the sixteenth century all he did was to replace the Pope by making himself Supreme Head of the Church of England and by setting about the destruction of the monasteries. The Roman Catholic rituals were left untouched, though they were to be modified during the reign of his son, Edward VI, who died young. But when Henry's daughter by a Spanish mother succeeded Edward she had comparatively little difficulty in restoring Catholic practices, even if reconciliation with the Pope proved more difficult. After Mary's death her half-sister Elizabeth I repudiated the Papacy, signed Acts of Supremacy and Uniformity and introduced a revised prayer book, which the Puritans condemned as 'picked out of the popish dunghill'; she then assured the Spanish ambassador that she was resolved to restore religion 'as her father left it'.[7]

The thirty-nine articles defining the doctrine of the Church, which were approved by the Queen in 1563, though somewhat ambiguous in their phraseology were barely acceptable to those

Protestant bishops who had returned from exile in Geneva and elsewhere because their minds had been schooled in the reformed theology as taught by John Calvin. The early Puritans demanded that popish practices should cease, objecting, among other things, to the wearing of surplices by the clergy, to the use of the ring in the marriage service, to signing with the cross, to the rite of confirmation and to bowing at the name of Jesus, all aspects of worship permitted in the Church of England today. It has been argued by some historians that the early Puritans were fully justified in their attacks on these practices because magic, superstition and ignorance were so widespread in the seventeenth century.[8] However, the Puritan leaders were themselves superstitious enough, as was instanced when Cromwell and the Council of Officers listened to Mrs Elizabeth Poole of Abingdon – whom the Royalists understandably described as a witch – after she had told them that she had been honoured with a series of visions from the Most High wherein had been manifested to her 'the disease and the cure of the kingdom'.[9]

For Oliver, as for most Puritans, the Bible was the sole authority on matters of religion, it was the fountain of truth, the body of rules which the Christian must follow, the lamp that must light his way. Since the Reformation the Bible had been translated into English: the Geneva version with its Calvinist commentary was that which Oliver first read, but most of his knowledge derived from the Authorized Version published on the instructions of Charles's father in 1611 when Oliver was twelve years old. The ordinary Puritan was not expected to interpret the teaching of Scripture himself, though in practice he often did so. Its meaning was expounded by preachers; at the outset of the Puritan movement 'prophesyings' took place in which learned clergy explained the meaning of some chapter of the Bible while their audience sat with the Geneva version on their laps following the appropriate texts. Thus preaching was accepted by Oliver as an essential part of religion and at times he is known to have preached himself. One of his earliest surviving letters refers to the support of a 'lecturer', that is to say a Puritan preacher without a cure, in Huntingdonshire.[10] Most Anglican clergy regarded the communion service as more important than a sermon and many of them preferred reading homilies to preaching. The appointment by laymen of 'lecturers' to expound the Scripture where the parish clergy were 'dumb dogs' was frowned upon by King Charles and banned by Archbishop Laud, especially as such lecturers were not subject to episcopal discipline. In his letter Oliver wrote that 'they that procure spiritual food ... are the more truly charitable, truly pious'. He regarded preaching as the highway to Christian enlightenment.

But in his early life Cromwell was most emphatic and outspoken in his detestation of bishops, for he was convinced that they were inclined to Popery. In his first recorded speech in the Commons (11 February 1629) he told the House how his old schoolmaster had informed him that when he wanted to refute a clergyman who 'preached flat Popery' he had been forbidden to do so by the Bishop of Winchester, Richard Neile, later to become Archbishop of York, a close friend of William Laud.[11] In the famous Long Parliament Oliver signed a protestation (3 May 1641) which aimed to frustrate 'the designs of priests and Jesuits and other adherents of the See of Rome' to undermine the 'True Reformed Protestant Religion, expressed in the Doctrine of the Church of England' and a fortnight later he was instrumental in introducing a bill to abolish all archbishops, bishops, deans and archdeacons because their government of the Church was 'prejudicial and very dangerous', spreading Popish tenets and rituals to the detriment of the Christian faith.[12] Earlier (on 9 February 1641) he had argued against those who defended episcopacy that he saw no necessity for 'the great revenues of bishops' and stated that 'he was more convinced touching the irregularities of bishops than ever before because, like the Roman hierarchy, they would not endure to have their condition come to a trial'.[13]

This animosity against bishops dated back at least to the time when Thomas Cartwright, Lady Margaret Professor of Divinity at Cambridge University, had insisted in the 1560s that episcopacy had no basis whatever in Scripture and might therefore, as Cromwell was advocating eighty years later, be abolished 'root-and-branch'. Yet none of the bishops appointed during the reigns of Queen Elizabeth I, King James I or King Charles I were in any sense bad men. What had changed since the Middle Ages was that the bishops were no longer wealthy magnates or great statesmen. Even Laud, whom Charles appointed Archbishop in 1633, was the son of a Reading clothier and Archbishop Neile of a tallow chandler. John Selden, an eminent lawyer and colleague of Cromwell, wrote in his *Table Talk* that bishops were formerly ambassadors or relatives of great noblemen 'so born to govern the State' while in the reigns of the early Stuarts they were men 'of low condition, their education nothing of that way – he gets his living and then a greater living, and then a greater than that, and so comes to govern'.[14] Queen Elizabeth and her favourites made money out of her bishops in a variety of ways. 'The fortunate few,' wrote Christopher Hill, 'grabbed at the lands of the bishops by means of long leases, of exchanges, of outright seizures or by the traditional method of inserting themselves into administrative positions in the Church.' The result was that bishops sometimes adopted dubious financial expedients to maintain their position and bring up their families. And although they were seldom absentees from their sees and were reasonably conscientious about their duties, few of them were outstanding preachers – even Bishop Lancelot Andrewes, Charles's favourite preacher, was more notable for his euphemisms than his comprehensibility.

That Charles because of his aesthetic outlook and Laud because of his passion for administrative tidiness provoked Oliver and his friends into the belief that they were introducing ritualistic innovations into the English Church has been agreed by most modern historians. But what cannot be contended is that theological innovations had anything to do with the matter. Since the time of St Paul it had been accepted by most Christian teachers, above all St Augustine, that it was the will of God alone that determined whether men were to enjoy everlasting life and that this could only be revealed to the individual believer by faith. Paul wrote: 'For by grace are ye saved through faith; and that not of yourselves: it is a gift of God. Not of works, lest any man should boast.'[15] For the conviction that man could earn salvation by living a good life was to question the omnipotence of the Almighty.

This theological dogma was emphasized by Protestants at the Reformation. Martin Luther had stated that people were made right with God only by the divine initiative of grace as received through God's gift of faith. John Calvin taught double predestination. God chose who were to be saved and who were to be damned: this was determined by the Almighty prior to and apart from any worth or merit on a person's part. The saving work of His son, Jesus Christ, was limited to the elect. His grace could not be turned aside.

This doctrine was accepted throughout the Church of England. Cranmer, the archbishop appointed by Henry VIII, wrote: 'He that doth good deeds yet without faith cannot have life.' Archbishop Whitgift, Queen Elizabeth's 'little black husband', laid it down in the Lambeth articles of 1595 that this doctrine of double predestination was an unquestionable truth. Bishop Lancelot Andrewes said: 'The moving or efficient cause of predestination to life is not prevenient faith or perseverance with good works . . . but only the will of a beneficent God.' Archbishop Laud declared: 'Man lost by sin the integrity of his nature and can not have light enough to see his way to heaven but by grace.'[16] It is of course true that Laud stated that his soul abominated the doctrine that 'God from all eternity reprobates far the greater part of mankind to eternal fire without any eye at all to their sin', but he recognized that individual Anglicans were at liberty to believe in the doctrine of predestination.[17] What he denied was that it was part of the official teaching of the English Church. He himself thought the question was beyond the reach of his faculties to resolve and he held all through his life that the Church was wise in avoiding too great an insistence upon difficult or controversial points of doctrine.

That no doubt was the reason why Charles in November 1628 declared it to be his will 'that all further curious research be laid aside, and these disputes shut up in God's promises as they are generally set forth to us in the holy scriptures and the general meaning of the Articles of the Church of England according to them'. But of course it is impossible to prevent people discussing religion. The argument that the doctrine of predestination made God the author of sin did not occur to Puritans like Cromwell. They accepted that man was utterly depraved since the Fall, but those who belonged to the Elect, who had been chosen as saints, must bear witness to their faith by living good lives.

It has been argued that the teachings of the Dutch theologian Jacobus Arminius, who maintained that the human will had to co-operate with God in salvation and that men were free to exercise their private judgement about the meaning of the Scriptures, penetrated into the Church of England after Charles became King. James I, a fairly typical Calvinist, had repudiated Arminius as a heretic; and though a belief in free will could be deduced from the first three Gospels and was accepted by the Jesuits, who would have found it difficult to explain to heathens the doctrine of predestination, it was not a major factor in the conflict between Charles and the bishops he favoured, on the one hand, and the Puritans on the other. It was because Laud and Neile stressed the value of the sacraments, through which God quickened grace in the Elect, and commended ceremonial in church services as lending beauty to holiness that they were dubbed 'Arminians', which was merely another way of claiming that they were poorly disguised Papists.[18] John Pym, who was the accepted leader of the opposition to the King in both the parliament of 1628 and those of 1640, has sometimes been called a moderate, but he was certain that he was one of the Elect, was fanatically anti-Catholic, and fancied that an Arminian conspiracy had followed the accession of Charles.[19] Some of his animosity against the bishops clearly rubbed itself off on Oliver Cromwell.

The Puritans thought that God's purposes were revealed through the Scriptures, through their own religious experiences, particularly after they were converted, when they listened to each others' depositions, and lastly through the testimony of events, 'God's providences'. Oliver always attributed his military successes solely to the will of the Almighty. When he captured Bletchington House, which was surrendered to him in 1645 by Colonel Francis Windebank (who was shot by the Royalists for cowardice), he told the Committee of Both Kingdoms, who ran the war, 'I hope you will pardon me if I say God is not enough owned: that hath much hindered our success.' Reporting the victory of Naseby to the Speaker of the House of Commons during the same year he wrote, 'Sir, this is none other but the hand of God and to Him alone belongs the glory wherein none are to share it with Him.' After the surrender of Bristol on 14 September in the same year he offered 'a full account of this great business wherein he that runs may read, that all this is none other than the work of God. He must be a very atheist that doth not acknowledge it.'[20] But where God did not bear clear witness through events, however faithfully sought, Cromwell was much less confident about the nature of His guidance.

When the Council of the Army was discussing the future of the kingdom in October 1647 he warned his fellow soldiers, 'I know a man may answer all difficulties with faith, and faith will answer all difficulties ... but we are very apt all of us to call that faith that perhaps may be but carnal imagination and carnal reasonings.'[21] In these debates he listened carefully to the testimony of others, but stressed that 'no man received anything in the name of the Lord further than [to] the light of his conscience appears' and confessed that while he thought it 'a high duty' to hearken to the voice of God speaking in any man the rule must be 'let the rest judge'. On this occasion he observed, 'I cannot say that I have received anything that I can speak in the name of the Lord.'[22] A month before Charles was executed Oliver told the House of Commons that God had not provided him with the means to give them counsel.

The final relatively easy defeat of the Royalists in the second civil war convinced Oliver that in his and Fairfax's victories they had 'beheld some remarkable providences and assurances of the Lord'. And although once again he warned about 'fleshly reasoning', he believed that 'the providences hung together, were so constant, so clear and unclouded that they must be meaningful'.[23] Nevertheless, at this crucial moment in his life when he was undecided whether Charles should be brought to trial for his war crimes, he and the army he then commanded in the north of England deliberately waited 'to see what the Lord will lead us to'. He was to hesitate once again, this time for many months, before he, like his modern counterparts in Africa and elsewhere, forcibly dissolved the parliament (or what remained of it) which had started the civil war. In addressing the assembly nominated by the Army, which replaced this parliament, he began his opening speech by reminding its members of 'the series of Providences wherein the Lord appeared, dispensing wonderful things to these nations from the beginning of our troubles to the present day'.[24] But not all Puritans were impressed by God's providences. For after he became Lord Protector and the argument was put forward that Providence had given him power, his republican critics retorted: 'That argument is like a two-edged sword, and a thief may lay as good a title to every purse he takes upon the highway.'[25]

Most people, fixed in their ways of thought, grow more intolerant as they grow older, yet a few become more tolerant. That was certainly the case with Oliver. It is true that towards the end of the first civil war he had written to the Speaker:

All that believe have the real unity, which is the most glorious, because inward and spiritual in the Body, and to the Head. As for being united in forms, commonly called Uniformity, every Christian will for peace sake study and do as far as the conscience will permit; and from brethren in things of the mind we look for no compulsion but that of light and reason.[26]

But here what he was mainly concerned about was preventing a rigid Presbyterian system of government being fastened on the Church, thus prohibiting decentralization with the principal authority allotted to local congregations. Indeed, he had regarded his own regiment as a gathered church. Only five members of the Assembly of Divines, set up by Parliament to constitute a Church of England bereft of the hierarchy of bishops and deans, fought for this principle of independence and at the end of the first civil war both Houses of Parliament acquiesced in the establishment of a Presbyterian system and the publication of a directory of worship superseding the Elizabethan prayer book.

It was not until after Charles and his Archbishop had been executed and Oliver as commander-in-chief of the victorious New Model Army approached full authority that he was faced with the practical difficulties of religious organization and the desirability of avoiding spiritual anarchy. He strongly advised the Nominated Parliament that 'if the poorest Christian, the most mistaken Christian shall desire to live peaceably and quietly under you – I say if any shall desire to lead a life of godliness and honesty – let him be protected'.[27] After he became Protector he strove to create a Church that would achieve unity in diversity while allowing toleration to all Christians who preferred to remain outside it. He introduced the Triers, who were chiefly clergy, to vet candidates for livings and Ejectors, who were laymen and had the duty of expelling ministers whom they found guilty of immorality, blasphemy or atheism. He did not interfere with the right of lay patronage and maintained the payment of tithes. It is clear that the Church of England Cromwell built up was pretty comprehensive and that in fact, as Sir Charles Firth noted, many orthodox Anglicans contrived to retain their livings, sometimes using portions of the Common Prayer Book from memory. Thus, by and large, the Cromwellian Church did not differ enormously from the old Church, the Triers and Ejectors replacing the bishops, deans and archdeacons.

Some modern historians have claimed that Cromwell had no use for the extreme sects of Fifth Monarchists and Quakers, but that is surely to misunderstand his religious position. As ruler of the country he could not assent to disturbances of the public peace, which were deliberately practised by both these sects. He assured the Fifth Monarchist leaders that he had no intention of persecuting godly ministers who preached the Gospel of Christ and the early coming of his personal reign, but he would not have them abusing their liberty or interfering with the rights of others. On more than one occasion he listened sympathetically to George Fox, the founder of the Society of Friends, and set him free from prison on the understanding that he would not take up 'a carnal sword' against the government. In both cases he was anxious to prevent religious freedom from degenerating into licence.

Oliver's toleration extended beyond the sects embraced in the official Church – Congregationalists, Presbyterians and Baptists. He saw that John Biddle, a Unitarian who was imprisoned for blasphemy, received an allowance. He attempted to mitigate the severe punishment imposed by the House of Commons on James Nayler, a Quaker who was accused of blasphemy, in his case for imitating Christ; he also questioned the right of the Commons to act as a judicature. As Lord Protector Oliver overruled his own Council of State by permitting Jews to return to England and set up a synagogue. Outside the Church he allowed rigid Anglicans to hold services privately in their own homes according to the Common Prayer Book. Only in Ireland during his campaign of 1649 did he eschew toleration. He then told the Governor of Ross: 'I meddle not with any man's conscience. But if by liberty of conscience you mean liberty to exercise the Mass, I judge it best to use plain dealing and let you know, where the Parliament of England have power, that will not be allowed of.'[28] But violent feelings about the behaviour of Irish Catholics were not new then and are not old now. Indiscriminate murder and terrorism were long Irish methods of political warfare, and public opinion in England had been incensed by the revolt of the Irish Catholics in 1641 and the death and destruction it entailed. In fact Cromwell was not speaking for himself but for Protestant England when he outlawed the Mass in Ireland.

His attitude to the Roman Catholics in England was very different. He assured Cardinal Mazarin, the effective ruler of France, in 1656 that under the Protectorate the English Roman Catholics had 'less reason for complaint as to rigour upon men's consciences than under the [Long] Parliament'.[29] That was vouched for both by the French ambassador in London and the English ambassador in Paris. In fact Roman Catholics were given scope to celebrate the Mass in private and in the chapels of foreign diplomatists. Oliver even had 'a Catholic favourite', the virtuoso Sir Kenelm Digby.[30] In sum, Cromwell was determined that men should not be punished for what they believed, but only for the way in which they behaved if it caused public disorder. 'Notions,' he insisted in 1654, 'will hurt none but them that have them' and earlier he said, 'I had rather a Mahometan were permitted amongst us than that one of God's children be persecuted.'[31]

Like Oliver, Charles was a convinced and devoted Christian who felt certain that he belonged to God's Elect and that he governed by divine right. (One modern historian puts it like this: 'Cromwell's notion of a calling was as brittle a theory of Divine Right as King Charles's had ever been.')[32] Clarendon wrote: Charles 'was very regular in his devotions .. the best Christian that age in which he lived produced.'[33] Sir Philip Warwick recorded:

His exercises in religion were most exemplary. In his own bed-chamber or closet he spent some time in private meditation ... never failed before he sat down to dinner to have part of the liturgy read to him and his menial servants. On Sundays and Tuesdays he came to chapel. No one better understood the foundations of his own Church and the grounds of Reformation than he did.[34]

The three theologians who most impressed Charles were Richard Hooker, whose monumental *Treatise on the Laws of Ecclesiastical Polity* was written in the last years of the sixteenth century; Lancelot Andrewes, whose elegant sermons were edited by William Laud; and Laud himself, whose conference or controversy with the Jesuit Father Fisher in 1622, in which he upheld the position of the Church of England, was subsequently published as a refutation of the Papacy. Those three books were recommended by the King for the edification of his eldest son, the future Charles II.

All these theologians believed in man's moral effectiveness in the world, even though he had been burdened with original sin. They thought that men possessed natural reason and therefore were capable of judging what was good and what was evil, whereas the Puritans distrusted reason (as Cromwell did, with his dread of 'fleshly reasonings') and considered that men were entirely corrupt and unable to choose rightly: they had to rely on and be guided simply by faith. Charles valued the sacraments as central to true religion – the taking of the communion was both a commemorative act and an efficacious means of grace. Because of this Charles disliked the treatment of the altar or communion table merely as a piece of furniture on which parishioners could leave their hats. He appreciated the meaning of ritual and ceremonial and favoured the wearing of surplices and other vestments. When he was crowned King of Scotland in Holyrood Palace he caused offence by having bishops wear their ceremonial robes and setting up an altar with chandeliers 'backed by a rich tapestry wherein a crucifix was curiously wrought to which the bishops were seen to bow and beck.'[35]

Such was Charles's theological outlook. To a fastidious aesthete the attitude of the Puritans to the beauty of holiness was incomprehensible. Although Cromwell is frequently blamed unfairly for vandalism and much of the destruction of statuettes and stained glass was done earlier, particularly during the reign of Edward VI, damage was unquestionably done by virulent anti-papists during the civil wars because they considered all relics of Roman Catholicism in English churches merited dismantling, while both armies used churches as stables and armouries – a practice that was regarded by the King as sacrilege.

But what was most important to Charles in regard both to the Church of England and the Kirk of Scotland was the function of bishops. He believed that the episcopacy maintained the Crown and the Crown maintained the episcopacy. Until his dying day he regretted that he had under pressure from Parliament signed an act in 1642 for the exclusion of bishops from the House of Lords. When he was a prisoner of the Scots army at Newcastle in 1646 he argued with Alexander Henderson, a distinguished Scottish divine who had been chosen to convert him to Presbyterianism, that episcopacy was approved in the Bible and that bishops were the successors of the twelve Apostles. He assured Henderson that bishops were a necessity in the Church, that episcopacy had always existed in England and that he was bound by his coronation oath to support it. He denied Henderson's argument that Henry VIII's Reformation was imperfect, he pointed out that his father as King of the Scots had instituted bishops in the Kirk and he insisted that Presbyterianism was not justified by anything in the Bible. Dr Gilbert Burnet, the historian, who studied the papers that passed between Charles and Henderson (Charles had no assistance of any kind in drawing them up), thought that the King had the better of the argument.[36]

Charles was pressed both by Scots and by the majority in the English Parliament to agree to the abolition of episcopacy if he were released from imprisonment and restored to his thrones. Queen Henriette Marie and several eminent Royalists urged him to accept Presbyterianism as a cheap way of regaining his regal authority, but the Queen at the same time begged him on no account to surrender control over the armed forces. Charles was adamant, however; he told his wife that the settling of Presbyterian government in the Church of England went utterly against his conscience. The bishops must stay, though he might allow 'a

toleration of conscience' to the Presbyterians. Then he made a
further gesture. He told the Parliamentarian leaders that he
would consent to Presbyterian government for three years provided that he and his household were allowed to continue to use
Anglican services and he was permitted to nominate twenty members of the Assembly of Divines still studying the future of the
Church of England at Westminster.[37] But privately he told the
Queen that she should invite the Pope to help restore episcopacy
– a fantastic idea.[38] And he explained to her that he regarded the
dependence of the Crown on the Church as equal in importance
to control of the militia, for 'people are governed by pulpits more
than the sword in times of peace'.[39] Indeed, he warned those who
urged him to accept an established Presbyterian Church in England that 'it would be in the power of the Pulpits (without trans-
gressing the law) to dethrone him at their pleasure or at least to
keep him in subjection'.[40]

But before he publicly made his three-year concession he
consulted three of the bishops whom he trusted most. He wrote to
the Bishop of London on 30 September 1646:

> I need not tell you the many persuasions and threatenings that have
> been used to me for making me change Episcopacy into Presbyterian
> government; which absolutely to do so is so directly against my
> conscience that (by the grace of God) no misery shall ever make me.
> Yet some kind of compliance to the iniquity of the times may be fit, as
> my case is, which at another were unlawful.[41]

At the same time he warned the Queen:

> The absolute establishing of Presbyterian government would make
> me but a titular King. A flower of the Crown once given away by Act of
> Parliament is not reduceable, and if the supremacy in church affairs
> be not one, I know not what is. The aim is to put the ecclesiastical
> power of the government from the Crown and give it to Parliament.
> They will also introduce the doctrine which teaches rebellion to be
> lawful.[42]

Reassured by the bishops whose advice he sought, Charles
offered the concessions which have been outlined, but later he
proposed that bishops should be retained, though assisted by
presbyters and their powers limited. He also suggested that full

liberty of worship should be allowed to all except Roman Catholics and atheists. Thus in theory at least he was willing to accept a Church of England not dissimilar from that which Oliver was to establish when he became Protector.

But it is plain from the King's private correspondence that in offering such concessions on the future of the Church he was playing for time and hardly being sincere. The Queen was clearly unable to grasp the casuistry when he expressed his willingness to accept a Presbyterian Church for three years but not permanently, and was unconvinced by his explanations. But it is not difficult to understand what Charles's real view was. Unlike many Puritans – but not Oliver Cromwell – Charles regarded the Church and State as inseparable. The Church upheld the monarchy and the monarchy sustained the Church. Soon after he had succeeded to the throne Laud, on the prompting of Charles's then favourite, the Duke of Buckingham, had written to all the clergy: 'We have observed that the Church and State are so nearly united and knit together that though they may seem two bodies, yet indeed in some relation they may be accounted as one... .'[43] When Charles was prisoner of the Scots in 1646 he told his Royalist advisers who wanted him to agree to a Presbyterian Church without quibbling that he had 'cast up what I was like to suffer, which would meet with that constancy that befits me', but was absolutely certain that such a change in the government of the Church was 'but a pretext to take away the dependency of the Church from the Crown' and he repeated to them what he told his wife: 'People are governed by pulpits more than the sword in times of peace.'[44]

In Charles's belief the Church of England followed an ideal middle way. Before he left Oxford in the spring of 1646 he had written to his eldest son, commanding him to be constant in his religion, 'neither hearkening to Roman superstition nor the seditious doctrines of Presbyterians and Independents', and not long before his execution Charles left a long letter for his son telling him that after much search he had reached the conclusion that the Church of England was 'the best in the world – not only in the Community as Christian, but also in the special notion, as reformed: keeping the middle way between the pomp of seditious tyranny and the meanness of fantastic anarchy.[45]

Charles was of course accused by many Puritans of being at heart a Roman Catholic (as two of his sons were to become), partly because his wife was a Roman Catholic and so were several of his ministers and courtiers and partly because of his penchant for ritual and ceremonial. Both he and his archbishop, Laud, accepted that the Roman Catholic Church was 'a true Church' and Charles once told a papal envoy that he was a Catholic and 'belonged to the Catholic Church', but he meant only that he was an Anglo-Catholic.[46] Never did he dream of bowing to the supremacy of an Italian Pope.

Apart from the question of the bishops, about whom Charles and Cromwell both felt so strongly, though in opposite ways, their main difference of outlook on religion was that the King laid much more significance on its political importance. Oliver was indifferent to forms of government; he pointed this out in the Putney debates. He then instanced the experience of the Jews, as recorded in the Bible: they were first governed by the heads of families, then by judges and lastly by kings, first elective and then by succession. 'If you make the best of it,' he argued, 'if you should change the government to the best of it, it is but a mortal thing. It is, as Paul says, "dross and dung in comparison with Christ".' It was enough for him that 'whoever ruleth over men must be just, ruling in the fear of God'.[47]

Charles's belief, however, was that he had been chosen by God to govern. In the book *Eikon Basilike*, published immediately after his death, Charles insisted that he could not live with the title of king, if it meant vasselage and a denial of the right to use his reason. 'I know no resolution more worthy of a Christian king than to prefer his conscience before his kingdom.'[48] In a speech which he intended to make at his trial but did not deliver he stated that he could not submit to the authority of the court 'without violating the trust which I have received from God for the welfare and liberty of my people'.[49]

Some modern historians have contended that Charles was insincere in his religion because in 1642 he chose 'Calvinist bishops', because he did not ask for the use of the Common Prayer Book when he was a prisoner of the Scots, and because he made little or no effort to save the life of Archbishop Laud. However, the majority of English bishops could be described as Calvinists, the Common Prayer Book was hardly essential for Charles's private devotions (even today regular churchgoers know the services, including the creeds, by heart) and the only way Charles might conceivably have saved Laud's life was by exchanging him for a high-ranking Parliamentarian prisoner and few such were available.

It has also been said that Charles introduced innovations into the Church which were provocative to the Puritans. But what were these innovations? The placing of the communion table at the east end of the churches? The wearing of surplices? Neither Charles nor Laud applied a mystical interpretation to the communion service: neither of them believed in transubstantiation or consubstantiation. A surplice had often been worn. And what was wrong with wearing a ring in marriage (people still do that today without any trust in its superstitious efficacy) or bowing at the name of Jesus? Charles certainly valued the sacraments, upheld the bishops, and sought to impose decency and order in church services. But he was not concerned about fine points of doctrine; he was reported to have said that 'so long as a man believed in Christ, he could save his soul in whatever religion he was born, baptised or bred'.[50] Therefore he actively discouraged theological controversy and stressed the value of good behaviour. Laud also worked to enforce silence on followers of Arminius and their opponents when they wrangled over the insoluble problems of free will and foreknowledge.[51] But neither Charles nor Laud repudiated the Protestant doctrine of justification by faith. It was the Puritans who wanted to transform the Church by rooting out of it every practice that savoured of 'popery'.

To Charles, as to Oliver, religion was paramount in life. No one who studies Oliver's letters and speeches or Charles's letters to his wife and eldest son can doubt that. But to Oliver as an extrovert (he was no mystic) God's guidance was to be found in events, while Charles took it for granted that the Almighty had chosen him to care for the welfare of his people: therefore in the last resort he could not be untrue to his conscience or violate his trust.

4

PRIVATE LIVES

Leaders of nations are rarely allowed to enjoy private lives, or if they do, have difficulty in concealing them from the general public. It is also true that they find few friends at the top. Some of Oliver Cromwell's closest friends and associates – John Lambert, Thomas Harrison, Henry Vane the Younger, Arthur Haslerigg – were alienated from him after he became Lord Protector. The case of Vane is particularly curious. Vane, according to Algernon Sidney, who knew him well, was a man of 'the mildest disposition imaginable' and 'an absolute master of naval affairs'.[1] He made himself wealthy as Treasurer of the Navy, a post in which he was highly competent, but towards the end of the Protectorate he became the victim of religious hysteria.

In 1648 Oliver called him his 'dear brother', sent him his love and had given him a nickname. Three years later in one of Oliver's few surviving letters to his wife he asked her to ensure that Vane looked after the business of his estate while he was away on active service in Scotland. But when Cromwell as commander-in-chief dissolved the 'rump' of the Long Parliament, of which Vane was a prominent member, he called him 'a juggler ... who had not so much as common honesty' and cried out loudly 'O Sir Henry Vane, Sir Henry Vane, the Lord deliver me from Sir Henry Vane!'[2] Yet after that Vane was invited by Cromwell to become a member of the assembly nominated by the Army which replaced the Rump. Not surprisingly Vane refused, opposed the Protectorate, and was imprisoned on the Isle of Wight for sedition. Lambert and Harrison, who were Oliver's closest colleagues and advisers before he became Protector, both quarrelled with him, Lambert because his own ambitions were not realized, Harrison because he was mixed up with sectarian plotters who claimed that the Protectorate was 'the reign of the beast', while Haslerigg was a dyed-in-the-wool republican who condemned Cromwell as a pseudo-monarch.

So Oliver lost most of his friends. Only within the confines of his own family was he at peace. He was indeed a devoted family man. His wife, born Elizabeth Bourchier, daughter of a London merchant, was a shadowy figure about whom little is known. To judge by her portrait she was a plump woman with dimpled cheeks and had the reputation of being a careful housewife. Lucy Hutchinson, the wife of a republican colonel, thought that while Oliver himself 'had much natural greatness, his wife and children were setting up for a principality, which suited no better with any of them than scarlet on an ape'.[3] Actually they adjusted themselves to their new positions with some facility. In a letter that Oliver wrote to his wife after his astonishing victory in the battle of Dunbar he said: 'I have no leisure to write much but I could chide thee that in many of thy letters thou writest to me, that I should not be unmindful of thee and thy little ones. Truly if I love thee not too well, I err not on the other hand much. Thou art dearer to me than any creature, let that suffice.' Another letter began: 'I love to write to my dear which is very close to my heart.'[4] Oliver's mother was a more distinctive character than his wife. She was described as a 'woman of ripe wisdom and great prudence' who reached her eighty-ninth birthday in Whitehall palace.

Of Oliver's eight children two sons died relatively young. The death of his eldest son Robert at the age of eighteen was 'a dagger to his heart', and his second son, Oliver, died during the civil war. His other children he tried hard to make good Christians. He was worried that his favourite daughter, Elizabeth, was 'being cozened with worldly vanities and worldly company' and he feared that his son Dick (Richard) was an idler with extravagant tastes who made pleasure the business of his life. When he married a girl he loved his father wrote to her 'As for the pleasures of life and outward business let that be upon the bye. Be above all things by faith in Christ.' Equally he warned his eldest daughter, Bridget, not to let her husband 'cool her affections after Christ'. Whatever his disappointments in his children, Oliver was a would-be dynast, for he named the idle Dick as his chosen successor and appointed his other son, Henry, Lord Deputy of Ireland.[5]

Oliver's two youngest daughters, Mary and Frances, who were still in their teens when he became Lord Protector, adjusted themselves to a more princely way of life. Both of them married sprigs of the aristocracy, one by her father's orders, the other for love, overcoming her father's objections. An entertaining anecdote relates that Oliver caught one of his chaplains on his knees before his daughter Frances in her apartment. When the chaplain was asked what he was doing there he asserted that he was not courting Frances, but asking her help because he was in love with one of her maids. Thereupon Oliver sent for the maid and saw that the chaplain married her.

On the whole, Cromwell's private life was happy. Nevertheless, he did not escape scandalous stories, mostly circulated after he was dead. One made out that a certain Elizabeth Murray by birth (how that name must have appealed to Oliver, his mother, his wife and his favourite daughter all bore that name, as did the Queen 'of famous memory' during whose reign he was born) was his mistress. The only evidence for this was that she told her future husband, John Maitland Duke of Lauderdale that she had saved his life by making a personal appeal to Cromwell after Lauderdale was taken prisoner following the Scots' defeat at the battle of Worcester. She was certainly a beautiful woman who might have appealed successfully to any man, but the likelihood is that she made up the story to impress him.[6]

Another candidate as Oliver's mistress was Frances, wife of Major-General John Lambert. Clearly Oliver was friendly with her, for he visited the Lamberts' house in Yorkshire and later their palatial residence at Wimbledon. Frances Lambert also followed her husband to Scotland when he was serving as Oliver's second-in-command there. She too was a beautiful woman and no Puritan; in a letter she wrote when she was in Scotland she asked that a scarf should be procured for her as, she explained, she had 'nothing to wear about my neck and I dare not go bare for fear of giving offence to tender saints'. Unquestionably Oliver admired her (she was about the same age as his second daughter). According to an Italian diplomatist, the favours and delicate attentions which his Highness has shown to this General's lady (though her beauty and distinction alone might merit this) may be assumed to have been solely directed to a quest for information regarding the designs of her husband, who for his part exposed his wife to much familiarity in order similarly to penetrate the designs of his Highness.[7]

That seems far-fetched. Oliver enjoyed the company of attractive women and invariably treated them with courtesy and consideration.

Instances of this are numerous. When engaged on his Irish campaign in 1650 Oliver showed himself to be 'a great servant' of the Marchioness of Ormonde, the wife of Charles I's Lord Lieutenant, much pitying her condition and allowing her to retain her estates. He also provided a ship to take Lady Inchiquin and her family out of Ireland, Inchiquin having been the King's President of Munster and Royalist commander there. Earlier, during the campaign of 1645 in England, Cromwell defended himself when reprimanded in the House of Commons for giving a pass to Thomas Chicheley, a Royalist, who had been a member of parliament for Cambridgeshire, to visit his wife there when she was seriously ill. During this same campaign he took another Royalist prisoner, Lord Percy, and found in his company 'a youth of so fair a countenance that he doubted his condition'. So he asked the young man to sing 'which he did with such a daintiness that Cromwell scrupled not to say to Lord Percy that being a warrior he did wisely to be accompanied by Amazons. On which that lord, in some confusion, did acknowledge that she was a damsel.'[8]

Life at Cromwell's Court in Whitehall palace differed markedly from that of King James I, where much gambling, overeating and overdrinking took place (thirty courses were served at one banquet), but was not so much a contrast with the Court of Charles I except that the King delighted in plays and masques, not permitted by Puritans. As one of Oliver's doctors remarked about the discipline that prevailed in his Court, 'no drunkard nor whoremonger nor any guilty of bribery was to be found'.[9] Oliver was fond of music. The chapel organ at Magdalen College, Oxford, where the President was a preacher much admired by the Lord Protector, was bought and played at Hampton Court. John Hingston, an organist, was appointed Master of Music and taught music to Cromwell's younger daughters. At Frances's wedding in Whitehall palace there was feasting and dancing and for Mary's wedding the poet and politician Andrew Marvell wrote two songs. Oliver was particularly fond of chamber music – Henry Lawes was a composer of outstanding ability whom he patronized – and music was played on occasions during dinner or as an entertainment for his guests afterwards. French ambassadors had no complaints about their treatment at the Protector's Court, where ample quantities of wine were provided for them. Oliver himself drank sack (sherry) and small beer and sometimes smoked a pipe. He was a temperate eater, who preferred roast beef to French cuisine or other foreign 'kickshaws'. Some of the curtains and paintings from Charles's vast collection were retained to decorate the Protectoral palaces.[10] Oliver had his portrait painted by Samuel Cooper and Peter Lely, but most of his portraits were the work of Robert Walker, copies being presented to rulers abroad, such as Queen Christina of Sweden, who was an admirer of his from a distance.

Although theatres were closed during the Protectorate Sir William Davenant, who believed himself to be an illegitimate son of William Shakespeare and managed to find favour with Charles I, Cromwell and Charles II alike, introduced the first operas to be performed in London. According to John Evelyn, they were 'after the Italian way in Recitative, Music and Scenes', though 'much inferior to the Italian composure and magnificence'.[11] One of them was called *The Siege of Rhodes* and another *The Cruelty of the Spaniards in Peru*. According to some accounts, the first actresses to perform on the English stage took part in them. Evelyn also noted in 1654 at the height of the Protectorate 'how the women began to paint themselves, formerly a most ignominious thing, and used only by prostitutes'.[12]

Most of his weekends Oliver spent at Hampton Court palace where he rode, hawked, hunted and played bowls. Charles also played bowls there when he was a prisoner and visited by

Cromwell's womenfolk. Like Charles, Oliver excelled in horsemanship and tried to establish the Arabian breed of horse in England, an achievement often associated with Evelyn's friend, Sidney Godolphin. Though Oliver reproved his elder children for being overfond of pleasure and reminded them to seek God through Christ, he enjoyed his recreations and was hardly a severe Puritan in the modern sense of the word.

In Charles's Court, as in Oliver's, decorum on the whole prevailed. Lucy Hutchinson observed: 'The fools and bawds, mimics and catamites, of the former Court [that of his father] grew out of fashion; and the nobility and courtiers who did not quite abandon their debaucheries, had yet that reverence to the King to retire into corners to practise them.'[13]

Charles earned the reputation of being abstemious himself. As Thomas Herbert recalled, he ate but few dishes – not more than three, according to Sir Philip Warwick. These were (as he used to say) 'agreeable to his exercise, drinking but twice every dinner and supper, once of beer and once of wine and water mixed, only after fish a glass the beverage he himself mixed at the cupboard, so he would have it; he very seldom ate and drank before dinner or between meals'.[14] He insisted that grace should be said before the start of a meal and sometimes said grace himself. Like Oliver, he did not care for fancy dishes made with elaborate sauces; his appetite, wrote Warwick, was 'to plain meats and though he took a good quantity thereof, it was suitable to easy digestion'.[15]

Even when he was a prisoner Charles took exercise regularly and since his childhood was never unwell. His reputation for abstemiousness stretched beyond the courtiers, and Lucy Hutchinson thought that he was 'temperate, chaste and serious'.[16] Again, like Oliver, he was lavish in giving advice to young people. When noblemen or gentlemen about to travel abroad came to kiss his hand 'he would give them good counsel, leading to moral virtues' and expressed the hope that they would keep 'good company'. He instructed the Prince of Wales how he should use 'the graces and gifts bestowed upon him so that he might weed out all vicious inclinations'[17] and advised his daughter Elizabeth on the right books to read. It is hardly too much to say that while he was in power Charles's conduct, in modern terms, was much like that of a Puritan.

Some thought that Charles did not treat people sufficiently graciously and that he tended to be indolent. Certainly in his youth he was shy and reserved and was said to blush at the use of an immodest word. His latest biographer thinks that he was 'an intensely private man, who, faced with something or someone he neither liked nor could control, retreated into the security of his own court'.[18] It is perhaps more correct to say that by the time he came to the throne Charles had evolved a fixed conception of the meaning of kingship and of how a king ought to behave, and was, therefore determined never to lose his dignity and rarely lost his temper. He schooled himself to treat triumphs and disasters in much the same way. When he was first told of the assassination of his friend Buckingham he showed no immediate sign of his deep distress. After he signed away the life of Strafford he concealed his tears. Alexander Henderson wrote of him when he was at Newcastle that 'never man saw him passionately angry nor extraordinarily moved either with prosperity or adversity nor did he complain or bemoan his condition'.

Few men change their character or behaviour after they reach the age of twenty-five, as Charles was when he came to the throne. Admittedly he was not a strong character who made up his mind about what he wanted and stuck to it – he preferred to manoeuvre. The members of the House of Commons blamed the mistakes made before the civil war on his evil counsellors, particularly the Earl of Strafford and Archbishop Laud, and modern historians have tended to accept the view that they were the guilty men. But the fact is that Charles did not care to have tough men around him. He preferred supple courtiers like Francis Cottington, George Digby and of course the Duke of Buckingham. When Laud wanted Charles to appoint Strafford as his Lord Treasurer after the death of the Earl of Portland the King rejected the idea out of hand and later chose the Bishop of London for the post. As has already been noticed, Charles made little effort to save the life of William Laud, badgered to death by an infuriated mob.

Charles won a justifiable reputation for being one of the most magnificent and knowledgeable patrons of the arts among the princes of the Renaissance. He was influenced in his taste by three of those who were closest to him in his youth, his mother, elder brother, and the first Duke of Buckingham. His mother, besides her delight in masques and flamboyant clothes, also cared for Italian paintings. Prince Henry had wide tastes and was a discriminating collector. Buckingham was an admirer of Caravaggio, Titian and Tintoretto; his London home, York House, was furnished with fine paintings, sculptures and velvet hangings. He also acquired a Michelangelo, two Raphaels and two Leonardos. Some of his pictures, as well as sculptures, were bought from Rubens, who painted him on horseback.

An older patron of the arts, who is known to have influenced Charles, was the fourteenth Earl of Arundel: he was particularly fond of Holbein. Arundel had been Earl Marshal to James I, but after Charles became King he threw him into the Tower of London after banning him from the Court, nominally because he disapproved of his son's clandestine marriage to a lady distantly related to Charles, whom he had intended for another bridegroom, but in fact because he had aroused the animosity of Buckingham. In 1628 they were reconciled and they shared the services of Rubens and Balthazar Gerbier, who had been the curator of Buckingham's collection at York House. The King sketched a little himself and was undoubtedly a connoisseur; he was even able to detect the difference between a genuine Rubens painting and a painting done by one of Rubens's many pupils. He knighted Rubens and Anthony Van Dyck, who settled in London as a Court painter. Rubens painted the famous ceiling in the Banqueting Hall at Whitehall celebrating the union of the kingdoms of England and Scotland in the person of James I. Van Dyck's portraits of Charles picture him as a hero and an emperor, but in them there have also been detected 'a delicate refinement, anaemic melancholy and a tired resignation as if the artist foresaw the King's future destiny'.[19]

One of Charles's best known purchases was the collection of the Duke of Mantua who, being hard up, was willing to dispose of his masterpieces by Titian, Raphael and Tintoretto among others for cash down.[20] Charles also bought a collection of statues from Mantua, the total cost of his acquisitions coming to some £25,000. At the time his agent carried out this *coup* the Duke of Buckingham was trying to relieve the French Protestants in La Rochelle who were being threatened by Cardinal Richelieu, the First Minister of France. Charles's financial agent, Sir Philip Burlamachi, protested that he could not find the money to pay for all these art treasures as well as the provisions needed for Buckingham's expedition. For strategic reasons it is extremely doubtful if this amphibious operation could possibly have succeeded, and in any case its cost amounted to hundreds of thousands of pounds. Taking a broader view of history, one can say that it was a pity that Oliver Cromwell and his friends decided to sell off a large part of the King's goods, including his superb paintings, at a very modest price to meet the heavy expenses involved in winning the civil wars. Today they would have been worth a fortune and made the royal collection the envy of the civilized world.

Besides his delight in painting and sculpture Charles, like Oliver, was fond of music and could himself play the violin. He patronized plays and masques, having a private theatre in his palace. Sir William Davenant succeeded Ben Jonson as poet laureate; Charles's favourite playwrights were Beaumont and Fletcher, not Shakespeare. Until he was forced to leave London his pleasure in the arts and out of doors his enjoyment in hunting and playing bowls, together with his personal religion, enabled him to retreat into an agreeable private life, cocooned away from the cares of state.

Before his marriage at the age of twenty-five much stress was laid upon Charles's shyness and sensitivity, his modesty and immaturity. He was also fastidious, tended to stutter and was reputed to be chaste. His surrogate elder brother, the Duke of Buckingham, introduced him to the pleasures and mysteries of sex. When the prince was eighteen he seems to have been engaged in an affair for which his father gave him 'a good sharp potion', but Buckingham 'took away the working of it by the well-relished comfits' he 'sent after it'.[21] Who the lady concerned was is not known. Three years later, however, he was attracted by a beautiful young girl who was a niece of Lord Bacon. Referring to a comet that had appeared in the sky during the previous year, Charles composed this verse in her honour:

Heaven's wonder late, but now earth's glorious ray
With wonder shines; that's gone, this new and gay
Still gazed on: in this is more than heaven's light
Day obscured that: this makes the day more bright.

'New and gay' was an anagram of the young lady's name – Anne Gawdy.[22] She was made much of by Charles and Buckingham, a blazing star that soon disappeared. Later, when Buckingham and his wife were at Court, Charles and the newly widowed Frances Duchess of Lennox often made up a foursome. Frances, by birth a member of the prominent Howard family, headed by the Duke of Norfolk, had first been married to the son of a London alderman by profession a wine merchant; she next married the ninth Earl of Hertford and finally the second Duke of Lennox, who was also created Duke of Richmond. Thus she climbed up the social ladder, greatly to her own satisfaction. Her third husband was related to Charles, and she was said to have been 'much courted and respected by the Prince'. One of his recent biographers even suggests that he had a daugher by her, but the evidence for this is flimsy, especially as she was into her late forties.[23] In any event, a year or so after he met her Charles was off to Spain, accompanied by Buckingham, with the intention of marrying the sister of King Philip IV of Spain.

Charles had been much attracted by a portrait of the Infanta Maria, which had been sent to him by the English ambassador in Madrid, and had therefore persuaded his father to allow him to woo her in person on the spot. After glimpsing the seventeen-year-old blonde princess in the flesh, as Buckingham reported to King James I, 'Baby Charles himself is so much touched in the heart that he confesses all he ever yet saw is nothing to her'. At the same time Sir Endymion Porter, who was one of Charles's attendants, wrote to his wife: 'The Prince hath taken such a liking to his mistress that now he loves her as much for her beauty as he can for being the sister of so great a King.'[24] Indeed he made a fool of himself by climbing over a wall to get near her. But she did not want to marry a heretic, while Charles refused to change his religion, so, as will be seen, the negotiations broke down.

On their way to Spain Charles had also caught sight of another teenage princess, Henriette Marie, sister of the King of France, but was not particularly impressed. However, he had to marry a princess and she was the next best available. This time the negotiations proved more fruitful. The marriage treaty provided that the future Queen should have full freedom of religion, have her own chapels and take charge of the religious education of her children until they were thirteen. By a secret clause, signed by both Charles and his father, the treatment of English Roman Catholics, subject to penal laws which imposed heavy fines for not attending the Church of England on Sundays since the reign of Queen Elizabeth I, would be alleviated.

Neither the Spanish nor the French princess were beauties – the Infanta had a large mouth and Henriette Marie, who was still fifteen when, after a proxy wedding, she arrived at Dover, was small with a largish nose and prominent teeth, but brilliant black eyes. After she first saw Charles she burst into tears. Her entourage included a young bishop, a confessor and twenty-four other priests.

Charles failed to meet his wife at Dover, but they spent her second night in England at Canterbury in a locked room from which Charles emerged fully satisfied, 'unusually jocund and loquacious'. Nevertheless, the first years of her married life proved stormy. How far Buckingham was responsible for this is not at all clear. He tried to foist his mother, sister and niece upon the young Queen as ladies of her bedchamber, which she resented, while Charles objected to the omnipresence of her French attendants and priests. For her part the Queen refused to take part in her husband's coronation and was understandably worried when Charles failed to honour the secret clause in the marriage treaty by improving the position of her fellow Roman Catholics. Quarrels followed, and on one occasion the King used violence against her when she tried to call out of a window to her French friends below. Charles then ordered Buckingham to send away all her French priests and servants, using fair means or foul. Later a compromise was reached, but it was not until after Buckingham was assassinated that the marriage settled on an even keel. Their first son died soon after birth, but in May 1630 the future Charles II was born amid rejoicing, and the Queen at last acquired sufficient influence over her husband to benefit English Roman Catholics. But that caused Charles's private life to impinge upon his public life. For when he was forced to call two parliaments in 1640 the Queen and the King's chief ministers were accused of fostering a Catholic conspiracy or 'popish plot'.[25]

As civil war became imminent Henriette Marie flung herself with enthusiasm into the support of her husband against his enemies. She bought arms for him in Holland and, chancing every danger, landed them in Yorkshire; after some adventures she rejoined him in Oxford. There her youngest daughter was conceived. But growing depressed and ill, she stayed with Charles in Oxford for less than a year. Leaving her youngest child in the care of a governess, she then fled to France, claiming that by doing so she was risking her life for her husband 'that I may not incommode his affairs'.[26] He never saw her again.

The military situation now turned against Charles, he was compelled to escape from Oxford before it was surrendered to the Parliamentarian army in April 1646. It was during the year following the Queen's departure that an intimate correspondence began between the King and Queen, which has survived and throws a flood of light on their relationship. Charles was at first upset because Henriette did not write to him more frequently from Paris. Before he left Oxford he complained of a melancholy letter from her and expressed the fear that she was displeased with him; he begged her to write 'for nothing but wilful silence can look like unkindness between us'.[27] Then when he was a prisoner with the Scots he braced himself by assuring her 'thy love preserves my life' and that her kindness upheld his courage.[28] But when she insisted that he abandon his steadfastness to the bishops and Church of England services in order to regain his freedom, and he refused to do so, she threatened to retire into a nunnery and 'never meddle in his business again'. That distressed him deeply.[29] In November 1646 she wrote to tell him that he was cutting his throat by not following her advice and warned him that 'as long as Parliament sits' he would not be King.[30] She added that she would not set foot in England again, but would only pray for him. Furthermore, she instructed him not to think of escaping to join her in France. In effect the marriage had broken down. In Paris Henriette Marie had the agreeable company of her Master of the Horse, the fascinating Henry Jermyn. One of Charles's latest biographers writes:

> Impudent and scandalous remarks concerning the Queen and Henry Jermyn had recently come to his ears. Jermyn he knew as a faithful friend and servant of the Queen, but he remembered how her first request on their meeting at Edgehill [after her return from Holland] had been for a peerage for Jermyn. He was distressed, but was quite unbelieving of any scandal.[31]

That may be so. But he needed a woman's comfort and sympathy and felt terribly alone.

When Charles was still in Oxford he met a lady named Mrs Jane Whorwood. In fact he may have met her much earlier, for she was the daughter of one of James I's Court officials and the stepdaughter of James Maxwell, who had been one of Charles's grooms of the bedchamber. She had married Brome Whorwood, a Royalist of sorts, whose mother, Lady Ursula, lived in the village of Holton near Oxford. Oddly enough, it was at Lady Whorwood's house in Holton that Oliver Cromwell's eldest daughter, Bridget, was married to Henry Ireton by one of Oliver's favourite chaplains, William Dell, just before Oxford surrendered. Jane Whorwood was a tall redhead, well dressed and well spoken, who was devoted to the King. The contemporary historian Anthony à Wood wrote that 'she was the most loyal person to King Charles in his miseries as any woman in England'.[32] She does not appear to have been notably faithful to her husband. Before Charles fled from Oxford he seems to have entrusted a casket of jewels to her care, and later when he was at Hampton Court he gave her £500.

She was certainly the 'handsome' and 'bold' lady who was caught visiting him at Holdenby House, for her step-father had been allowed to rejoin the King's service there. She may easily have seen him often at Hampton Court, for no restrictions were imposed on his visitors there. Finally, she saw him again in 1648 when he was a prisoner at Carisbrooke castle on the Isle of Wight.

Jane Whorwood arrived there in February when Charles greeted her as 'his best Platonic Lover or Servant'.[33] In May she succeeded in hiring a ship on which she hoped the King would escape to Holland. The plan failed, but she was back on the Isle of Wight later that summer, meanwhile corresponding with Charles, who expressed his eagerness to see her. A woman servant, who could neither read nor write but was loyal to the King, managed to smuggle his letters in and out of the castle. On 24 July 1648 he wrote to Jane:

> Sweet Jane Whorwood ... I must tell you that without any difficulty you may see the King and speak to him, but ye will not get leave to speak privately with him ... by means of the new woman you may be conveyed into the stool room [lavatory] which is within my bedchamber while I am at dinner, by which means I shall have three hours to embrace and nip you (for every day after dinner I shut myself up alone for so long).[34]

Evidently this scheme did not come off, for some days later he wrote again to 'Sweet Jane Whorwood' to thank her for a letter and said:

> If you like not or fear impossible the way that I have set you down for a passage to me, all I count on is that you invite yourself to dinner to Captain Mildmay's chamber [Mildmay was one of his attendants appointed by Parliament to spy on him] which is next door to mine, where I will surprise you and between jest and earnest smother Jane Whorwood with embraces, which to be doing is made long by your most loving Charles.[35]

That plan does not appear to have worked either and Charles had to satisfy himself by writing further letters to Jane begging her not to leave the island. And he asked his friend Sir William Hopkins, who lived nearby in Newport, to tell her that 'if she would have a [further] letter she must come to fetch it herself: and yet to say the truth her platonic way doth much spoil the taste in my mind; and if she would leave me to my free cookery I should think to make her confess so herself'.[36]

Eventually Jane managed to see him in the castle at the end of August and again in Newport when he was permitted to stay there with Hopkins during negotiations with a delegation from Parliament. Previously the King's warder, Colonel Robert Hammond, a young officer trusted by Cromwell, had frustrated all schemes for a rendezvous, for Charles told Hopkins he had heard her 'sad story' and 'could not have believed that so much barbarity could have been done in anybody that pretended to be a gentleman'.[37] As the negotiations at Newport faltered Charles considered escaping from the island, but told Hopkins he would not let Jane know of his plan, not because he mistrusted her but because he did not want her to be involved in what might prove to be a hopeless business.[38] Jane then got away to London where in November she learned of the Army's demand that the King should be put on trial for his life. She came back to the island and sent a message to the King begging him to escape at once 'out of some door and not from the top of the house by ladders' and assuring him that a ship would be waiting for him.[39] Charles was not allowed to escape. The Army fetched him from the Isle of Wight to be put on trial for his life. When he stayed in Windsor *en route* to Westminster he received two letters from Jane, but their contents are unknown.[40]

Two or three days before his execution Charles took a ring from his finger which had an emerald set between two diamonds and asked Thomas Herbert, one of his attendants appointed by Parliament, who was with him until the end, to take it to a lady living in Westminster, who returned him a packet of jewellery left in her care, which he gave to his two younger children, who were allowed to see him in St James's palace on the night before he died. The lady may have been Jane Whorwood. At any rate as he left the palace to be marched to the scaffold Jane ran forward to greet him, 'their affectionate embrace' (writes Pauline Gregg) 'reviving the rumour that she had been his mistress at Hampton Court and Carisbrooke'.[41]

After their early squabbles Charles and Queen Henriette

Marie had found a way of living happily enough together during the halcyon days that preceded the civil wars. She had given birth to two sons and two daughters and after the recall of Parliament their youngest son, Prince Henry of Oatlands, was born. After the birth of the future Charles II the King had declared 'the only dispute that now exists between us is that of conquering each other by affection'. In 1641 it was fear over his wife's safety as the crowds, organized by virulent anti-Catholic members of parliament for the city of London, milled around Westminster, that finally induced Charles to sign away the life of the Earl of Strafford. He was to liken the menaces of the London crowds to a storm at sea or an earthquake and was to write: 'I am content to be tossed, weather-beaten and shipwrecked that she might be in a safe harbour.[42] But twice the Queen had left him, first in February 1642 and again in April 1644. In the autumn of 1646 she condemned him for his obstinacy and told him not to join her in France. Charles could scarcely be blamed if he sought love and sympathy from another woman who was absolutely devoted to him.

Kings and other heads of state have never enjoyed much in the way of private lives; the glare of publicity beats down on them. We can picture Oliver Cromwell smoking his pipe, sipping his ale and listening to music in the company of his family and a very few intimates. Equally one thinks of Charles I, the honourable prisoner of Parliament, in Holdenby House, in Hampton Court palace, and in the Isle of Wight longing for a break from his loneliness to embrace 'sweet Jane Whorwood' during the months before he died.

5

SOLDIERING – I

Neither Charles I nor Oliver Cromwell had taken part in a battle or a siege before the civil wars began. But the King knew a great deal about fighting on land and sea because he had been directly concerned in wars against Spain, France and most of Scotland during the first fifteen years of his reign. He had inherited and largely inspired the war against the far-flung empire of King Philip IV of Spain. For when Charles and his friend, the Duke of Buckingham returned empty-handed from their long stay in Madrid during 1624 they were filled with resentment at the treatment they had received there – Charles thought that the Spaniards 'had used him ill' and Buckingham was 'utterly disgusted' – so that they pushed King James I reluctantly into war during the last years of his life.[1]

In the first year of his own reign Charles had organized a combined operation against Spain under the command of Sir Edward Cecil, a grandson of Queen Elizabeth I's famous minister, Lord Burghley, while sending Buckingham to negotiate a military alliance with the Dutch, who had been at war with Spain for many years. The object of the expedition headed by Cecil was to sack Cadiz (or some other Spanish port) and seize a Spanish treasure fleet, but neither aim was fulfilled. Two years later Charles also landed himself in a war against France and promised assistance to the Huguenots or French Protestants who were in revolt at the port of La Rochelle in Poitou against the French monarchy, then governed in effect by Cardinal Richelieu. This time Buckingham in his capacity as Generalissimo took command of the amphibious operation, which ended in disaster. Before the fleet sailed Charles conscientiously visited Portsmouth and dined aboard the flagship. After Buckingham's failure to relieve La Rochelle and his assassination by a fanatic not long after his return, Charles went to Portsmouth for a second time to inspect the fleet setting out in a vain attempt to avenge the defeat of the previous year.

What Charles had learnt about warfare then was that amphibious operations were extremely difficult to organize and co-ordinate (as later British governments have discovered, for example at Gallipoli and Dieppe) and also extremely expensive. So he was forced to conclude peace with both France and Spain and concentrated on rebuilding his navy, paying for it by levying ship money.

In 1639 and 1640 Charles acquired further knowledge of warfare by launching attacks on the Scottish Covenanters whom he regarded as rebels when they repudiated his ecclesiastical policy. On this occasion Charles went to York twice, as he had been to Portsmouth, to oversee the military preparations. The first campaign again took on the character of a combined operation. The strategic plan was for an army to cross from Berwick-on-Tweed into Scotland while the fleet occupied Aberdeen from the sea and a force despatched from Ireland landed on the west coast of Scotland. But before Charles reached York on 30 March 1639 the Covenanters captured Edinburgh castle and secured Aberdeen. The King appointed the Earl of Arundel, the connoisseur of painting and sculpture, to be his commander-in-chief: according to Edward Hyde he was 'a man who had nothing martial about him but his presence and his looks'.[2] At his wife's request Charles selected the Earl of Holland, who had arranged her proxy marriage at Notre-Dame, to command the cavalry, and the Marquis of Hamilton, who actually had a modicum of military experience, but whose mother was a Covenanter, to take charge of the navy. None of these generals scored any success. The Earl of Holland led his cavalry into Scotland and then led it out again. Under pressure from his demoralized officers and advisers Charles abandoned the campaign without any serious fighting having taken place, signed a truce, and postponed further operations until the following year.

In the summer of 1640 Charles chose different commanders with the intent of overcoming the Scottish rebels. The Earl of

Arundel was replaced by the Earl of Northumberland as commander-in-chief, but before the campaign opened he was taken conveniently ill (he was to oppose the King in the civil war) and had to be replaced by Thomas Wentworth Earl of Strafford, who was no soldier and crippled with gout and other illnesses. However, the decisive position was held by Viscount Conway, a qualified officer, who was chosen general of the cavalry and stationed at Newcastle upon Tyne. Before Charles reached York again the Scottish Covenanters had already crossed the Tweed and were marching south. This time Charles himself took an active part, for he led an army out of York with a view to supporting Conway in Newcastle. But Conway, who earlier assured the King that the Scots would not invade the north of England, abandoned Newcastle while Charles fell back to York, acquiescing in a second setback and signing a humiliating armistice. So even before the civil war began Charles had revealed himself as a highly incompetent strategist.[3]

If Charles sampled war at first hand after he became King, Oliver was forty-three before he engaged in any military action. In view of his later triumphs as a commander the speculation has been offered that during 'the lost years' of his early life he might have served as a volunteer abroad, as some of his contemporaries – such as the third Earl of Essex and the future General George Monck – had done. But the records of English volunteers in the Netherlands and elsewhere are reasonably complete and it would be surprising if his name had not been mentioned by diarists. It is, however, likely that as a prominent figure in Huntingdon and Cambridge he trained with the local militia, which exercised annually.

Once civil war threatened in the summer of 1642 he sent down arms to the townsmen of Cambridge, which he paid for out of his own pocket, and moved the House of Commons to permit the raising of two companies of volunteers to defend the city. When he learned that some of the colleges were responding to an appeal from King Charles to 'deposit their plate in our hands for the better securing and safety thereof' Cromwell obtained leave from the House to go to Cambridge himself to prevent the plate from being sent to the King. Although the President of Clare Hall managed to dispatch some of the plate from St John's College to the King, evading Cromwell and his militiamen, who were stationed on the main road between Huntingdon and Cambridge, by using by-roads, once Oliver entered Cambridge itself he was able to prevent any further plate from being sent and arrested an officer and party of soldiers ordered by Charles to convey the college plate to York.[4] On 15 August Parliament was notified that 'Mr Cromwell in Cambridgeshire had seized the magazine and the castle at Cambridge and hath hindered the carrying of plate from that university; which, as some report, was to the value of £20,000'.[5] Two days later Cromwell and the Mayor of Cambridge were commanded to ensure the safety of the town and exercise the trained bands and volunteers.

In his expedition to Cambridge Oliver worked in co-operation with his brother-in-law, Valentine Walton, one of the two members for Huntingdonshire, where Oliver was born, and it was here that he was to enlist a troop of horse (numbered 67) to fight for Parliament after Charles declared war by raising his standard at Nottingham. As Professor Abbott wrote, 'The contrast between a sovereign surrounded by his Court and an army rapidly growing in numbers and enthusiasm for his cause, and a relatively obscure member of parliament haranguing prospective volunteers in the market place of a small English town was as striking as that between the men who were, in time, to be the chief protagonists of the ensuing civil wars.'[6]

Throughout the first civil war Charles himself was Captain-General of his army, while it was not until he took part in the battle of Naseby that Oliver as Lieutenant-General of the cavalry in the New Model Army became the avowed second-in-command to Sir Thomas Fairfax, who was appointed Captain-General in February 1645. Before that Cromwell had served in one of the three armies raised by Parliament, but not in the main army under the first Captain-General, the Earl of Essex.

Charles made Robert Bertie first Earl of Lindsey, who was sixty years old, Lord General (or Lieutenant-General) of his army at the outset of the civil war. These ranks are somewhat misleading, for at the same time Charles appointed Prince Rupert of the Rhine, his nephew, who was twenty-two, to command the cavalry, and Sir Jacob Astley, who was sixty-three, as Sergeant-Major-General in charge of the infantry. When a disagreement over tactics arose before the first important battle of the war, which was fought at Edgehill in Warwickshire, Charles as Captain-General overruled Lindsey's advice, preferring that of Rupert. Thus, from the beginning, Charles was effective commander-in-chief. Annoyed at being overruled, Lindsey resigned, fought in the battle as colonel of his own infantry regiment, and was killed. Charles replaced him with Patrick Ruthven, a Scottish soldier of fortune, who had served under the famous King Gustavus Adolphus of Sweden, hero of the Thirty Years War in Germany. Gustavus Adolphus had dubbed Ruthven 'field marshal of the bottles and glasses as he could drink immeasurably and preserve his understanding to the last'. But Ruthven never commanded in a battle during the civil war. He was an 'adviser', who has been likened to a modern chief of staff. He was nearly seventy at the start of the war and in November 1644, being old and tired and over-fond of the bottle, was replaced by Prince Rupert, who thus became Lord General as well as Master of the Horse. Nevertheless, he had to obtain the agreement of Charles as Captain-General to all his military plans, and that was by no means always forthcoming. Unquestionably, therefore, Charles was the supreme commander of the Royalist army and its ultimate destruction was his own responsibility.

As a military organizer Charles learned from experience. To begin with, he had appointed Commissioners of Array to summon the local militia and persuade it to fight for him; he also commissioned prominent men in their own counties as colonels to raise regiments for him. In 1643 he gave precise orders to local gentry about how to regulate their garrisons. His reliance on members of the aristocracy without military knowledge or training as commanders proved a mistake except in the case of the Earl of Newcastle. By the end of that year, however, he realized that dependence on local populations working voluntarily under their leading gentry was not proving effective, and instead he began appointing men of military ability without local influence to take command in the regions that were loyal to him. This naturally provoked local people, who felt that warfare with all its demands for service and money was being thrust upon them from outside. This resentment proved to be a telling factor against him.[7]

It was as a strategist that Charles most notably failed. The original belief on both sides was that one battle would determine the result of the war. Before the opposing armies met at Edgehill on 23 October 1642 the Royalist army was marching from Shrewsbury towards London. Although Charles had the better of the fighting and was able to stay on the field of battle while the Parliamentarians under the Earl of Essex withdrew, instead of continuing the advance on his capital Charles moved to Oxford, thereby conceding that the battle had been drawn and not really won. By the time the advance was resumed a fortnight later it proved to be too late, since Essex's army had arrived to reinforce the trained bands in London.

In the following year, 1643, the Royalists were successful everywhere except in eastern England, where Oliver was winning his spurs. In the north the Earl of Newcastle defeated Lord Fairfax and his son, Sir Thomas, who had raised an army for Parliament; in the south-west, where the Marquis of Hertford (a bibliophile rather than a soldier) held the nominal command but was assisted by one of the finest cavalry officers of his time, Sir Ralph Hopton, they secured a base in Cornwall from which Devonshire was overrun. After Hopton defeated a Parliamentarian army under Sir William Waller at the battle of Roundway Down in Wiltshire, Charles sent Prince Rupert to join the victorious western army which was thus able to storm and capture Bristol, the second busiest port in the country.[8]

Over the past hundred years historians have consistently affirmed that the Royalist strategy in 1643 was aimed at a converging advance upon London from the north, west and centre. Oxford was within four days' march of London and from there the main assault would have been launched, while the Earl of Newcastle and Sir Ralph Hopton carried out simultaneous pincer movements on the capital. But although military historians have inferred that such a plan was logical and feasible, no document has been found to substantiate the idea.[9] What in fact happened was that after the capture of Bristol Charles and his Council of War, meeting in Oxford, determined to besiege Gloucester, where Sir William Waller, the Parliamentarian general in the west, had retreated following his defeat by Hopton, ably supported by Lord Wilmot, at the battle of Roundway Down. If the Royalists managed to hold both Bristol and Gloucester as well as most of Wales, which was predominantly loyal to the King, the whole of the west would be in Charles's hands and there would be no danger of a flank attack if an advance were made on London.

Rupert clearly had misgivings about his uncle's strategy. Furthermore, Charles settled down in the second week of August to conducting a leisurely siege of Gloucester, promising generous treatment to its inhabitants if the town surrendered. The King then returned to Oxford to hold a conference, leaving the siege to be directed by Lord Forth. Rupert would have preferred an immediate assault on Gloucester by storm, but Charles refused to allow this because he hoped that its military governor would surrender voluntarily. Meanwhile the Earl of Essex had marched from London, skirting Oxford, and, with a force as large as that of the King, relieved Gloucester a month after the siege had begun. As soon as Charles heard the news of the relieving force he withdrew his troops.

Charles's strategy in 1643 has been defended by modern military historians who have argued that by besieging Gloucester he had lured Essex from his base and obliged him to fight a pitched battle on unfavourable terms.[10] However, it was chiefly owing to the energetic activities of Prince Rupert that this situation had arisen. For Charles was quite wrong in thinking that Essex would return to London by the same route as that by which he had arrived and so could easily be intercepted. The King was sitting in a cottage playing piquet with his chief of staff looking on when Rupert burst in to inform Charles where Essex was and how he proposed to cut off his cavalry from his infantry through a flank attack launched by a flying column. He did so and thus succeeded in slowing down Essex's movements with the result that the whole Royalist army had time to reach Newbury on the road from Hungerford to Reading before the Parliamentarians. Essex now had to fight his way through. Charles, who had been disappointed by the relief of Gloucester, then became eager for battle. Rupert favoured delaying tactics, especially as his cavalry was likely (as proved to be the case) to be handicapped by the hillocks and hedges around Newbury, but also because he knew the Royalist army was short of ammunition, which could, given time, be augmented by supplies from Oxford. The King rejected Rupert's advice and the battle was fought and lost. This was perhaps the most decisive battle in the first civil war since, had Essex been beaten and the London-trained bands which were with him decimated, nothing could have stopped Charles from reaching his capital.

Nevertheless, the military situation in the autumn of 1643 remained rosy from Charles's point of view. The Royalists were in full command in Yorkshire, the west and the south-west, and even in East Anglia, where Cromwell was making a name for himself, no serious losses had been incurred. At a Council of War held in Oxford during September it was resolved to form two new 'armies' (the word army is of course misleading, for such armies were smaller than modern divisions): one army was to be formed in Cheshire under the command of Lord Byron and another under Lord Hopton (as he now was) in south-west England. Both were to be reinforced with troops brought over from Ireland, where Charles's Lord Lieutenant, the Earl of Ormonde, had concluded a truce with the rebels who had attacked the English two years earlier. However, Byron was defeated at the battle of Northwich in January 1644 and Hopton at the battle of Cheriton in March. Moreover, the whole military position changed for the worse from Charles's point of view because the Parliamentary leaders had concluded an alliance with the Scottish Covenanters, who had already humiliated him, and, led by a distinguished professional soldier, Lord Leven, crossed into England that January with a sizeable force. Charles had been warned of the possibility of this happening, but with his usual phlegm had ignored it.[11]

The King was thus compelled to adopt a defensive strategy and any idea, if it had ever been formulated, of a converging movement on London was given up. The Earl of Newcastle vainly tried to impede the advance of the Scottish army, but in April was obliged to shut himself up behind the walls of York. The decision was now taken by Charles to dispatch Prince Rupert to raise the siege of York, where Newcastle was confronted not merely by the Scots but by the Parliamentarian army which had been campaigning in Yorkshire under the two Fairfaxes and by the army in which Oliver Cromwell was serving, commanded by the second Earl of Manchester.

Before Rupert left Oxford for Yorkshire by way of Lancashire he had pressed the King to maintain a strong central position in and around Oxford, with reinforced infantry garrisons in Wallingford, Abingdon, Banbury and Reading plus a body of cavalry able to manoeuvre in support of these garrisons. This would contain the Earl of Essex's army while Rupert himself went north and his brother Maurice was completing the Royalist hold on the west of England. But not long after Rupert departed on the campaign which ended with his defeat at the battle of Marston Moor, Charles changed his mind, presumably on the advice of Lord Forth, who had returned to Oxford after being with Lord Hopton during his defeat at Cheriton, and ordered the evacuation first of Reading and then of Abingdon. Charles might then have been surrounded and defeated by the Parliamentarian armies commanded by Essex and Waller. Rather than surrender to them, however, Charles managed to slip out of Oxford and made for Worcester. Now he had a slice of luck, for Essex, who was jealous of Waller and the separate army under his orders, elected to march south-west in order to relieve the port of Lyme Regis, which was being besieged by Prince Maurice, leaving it to Waller to cope with the King. But Charles succeeded in defeating Waller at the battle of Cropredy Bridge, north of Banbury, at the end of June.

A fortnight before this creditable victory Queen Henriette Marie gave birth to her youngest child, a daughter, in Exeter. She had asked permission from the Earl of Essex to leave Exeter to go to Bath for recuperation. When that was refused, she managed to escape to Falmouth in Cornwall, where she found a vessel to take her to her native France. Before she embarked she wrote the letter to Charles telling him that she was hazarding her life for him.[12] In fact it was agitated letters she had written from Exeter that induced Charles to leave Oxford and follow the Earl of Essex into Devonshire instead of joining Prince Rupert in the north of England. Since Devonshire and Cornwall were, on the whole, Royalist in sympathy, Essex allowed himself to be cornered and defeated by superior numbers at the battle of Lostwithiel. Then Charles contemplated besieging Plymouth, which was in the hands of the Parliamentarians, but, as Sir Edward Walker, his Secretary at War noted, 'His Majesty, who is not vindictive, thought it unfit to be attempted by assault or by siege.'[3]

In spite of his two victories – over Waller at Cropredy Bridge and over Essex at Lostwithiel – there were three other armies opposing Charles which were still intact: the Yorkshire army under Fairfax, the East Anglian army under the Earl of Manchester and the large Scottish army under Leven. Moreover, Rupert's devastating defeat at the battle of Marston Moor in July had offset Charles's victories. On his way back to Oxford Charles's route was blocked at Newbury, where a second battle was fought on 27 October. The King managed to withstand the superior Parliamentarian forces, which were directed not by a commander-in-chief but by a committee or Council of War, and eventually the King got away relatively unscathed, though abandoning his wounded, baggage and cannon. On his way back he met Rupert, whom, despite his defeat in Yorkshire, he had just appointed general of all his forces in England. With Rupert and an army of 15,000 men Charles returned to Newbury, where he retrieved the artillery he had left behind in Donnington castle, but a third battle was not fought there, though Rupert favoured it and so, on the other side, did Oliver Cromwell.

Thus ended the campaign of 1644. But any hope that Charles may have nursed of beating his enemies piecemeal or of marching on London were frustrated. Indeed, his strategy in that year of sending Rupert north with what proved to be misleading orders,[14] and himself marching to rescue his Queen, meant in the end that he had weakened his armies and thrown away the advantage of having an area for manoeuvre round Oxford. And the strategy he followed in 1645 of leaving Oxford without any precise idea of where he was going – north, west or east – was fatal. Although in the previous November he had appointed Rupert to be his commander-in-chief in place of Lord Forth, whom he had raised to an earldom by way of compensation, Charles remained Captain-General and ultimately took all the decisions about the future course of the war. On the whole, he seems to have accepted the advice of the last commander or courtier who spoke convincingly to him.

As for Rupert, he had no illusions about the King's prospects and disliked the dispersal of the Royalist resources. Charles had sent the Prince of Wales, who was not yet fifteen years old, to Bristol to act as nominal commander-in-chief in the west with an independent Court, a military adviser (Lord Hopton) and a Council of State. Yet George Goring, who had distinguished himself at Marston Moor, was given a separate command as Lieutenant-General of the Horse, while Rupert was sent into the west to restore order there. When Rupert returned to Oxford that May he advised Charles to fight the Scottish army in Yorkshire, which had been weakened because the Marquis of Montrose had been winning victories for the King in the Scottish Highlands, but although Charles agreed to this plan in principle, he also sent Goring with much of the Royalist cavalry to besiege Taunton in Somerset, which was still held by the Parliamentarians. Furthermore, after capturing Leicester Charles turned his army back to Oxford under pressure from courtiers who were alarmed lest General Fairfax and the New Model Army, which Parliament had created as a unified force to win the war, should successfully besiege the city, thus threatening the safety of the womenfolk they had left behind. But Fairfax broke up the siege and advanced to confront Charles's army.

Once again Rupert counselled withdrawal northwards and once again he was overruled. After Charles's destructive defeat at the battle of Naseby, which followed, Rupert advised the King to make a treaty with the Parliamentarians as the only way left open to him 'to preserve his posterity, kingdom and nobility'. Charles's answer was that, speaking as a mere soldier or statesman, 'I must say there is no probability but my ruin', yet 'because he believed God will not suffer rebels and traitors to prosper' he must fight on.[15] But when a month later Prince Rupert, who earlier in the war had captured Bristol, was obliged for what he thought were sound military reasons to surrender it to Fairfax, Charles dismissed him from all his offices.

If little can be said in favour of Charles as a stategist, he showed himself to be a capable tactician and a brave officer. At the battle of Edgehill he had accepted Rupert's advice to abandon his original intention of marching to Banbury and instead deployed all his forces on that Warwickshire hill. Before the battle he inspected all the brigades of horse and foot and 'spoke to them with great courage and cheerfulness which caused huzzas through the whole army', and 'in the crisis of the battle the King's presence had done much to steady the infantry'.[16] When it was suggested to him after the infantry had been repulsed that he should leave the field with as much of the cavalry as he could collect, he rejected the proposal as dishonourable and spent the night quartered on the hill, where it was bitterly cold.[17]

In the next year at the first battle of Newbury Charles adopted sensible tactics in trying to drive back the Parliamentarian infantry, supported by artillery, who occupied a hill in the centre of their line, but was thwarted by the desperate courage of the London-trained bands who fought there under the Earl of Essex. 1644 was Charles's *annus mirabilis*. At the beginning of June in that year Oxford was menaced by two armies, that of Essex, which was concentrated at Islip and aimed to cross the Cherwell river to the north of the city, and that of Waller, which was based on Abingdon and advanced on Oxford from the south. Charles then decided to break out of Oxford by night in the expectation that he would draw his enemy after him. With a force of 3,000 foot, 4,000 horse and some light guns Charles went by way of Burford and Evesham to Worcester where he was 'joyfully received by that loyal people with significant expressions of love and duty'. After much manoeuvring the King fought and defeated Waller near Banbury. The battle was fought across the Cherwell by equal forces, Waller trying to cut off Charles's rear troops from his main body. But the Parliamentarian cavalry were repulsed and Charles, realizing what was happening, recalled his vanguard and sent his own Life Guard to the assistance of the Earl of Cleveland, who commanded the leading brigade in the rear guard. So effective was Cleveland's second repulse of the Parliamentarian cavalry under Lieutenant-General John Middleton that the enemy, thinking 'the devil had come upon them in a cloud of dust', were completely routed and abandoned their guns.[18]

After this battle Charles withdrew to Evesham.[19] While he was there, as has already been noted, he resolved to march south-west to protect the Queen. By the time Charles reached Exeter Henriette Marie had fled to France but the King, co-ordinating four Royalist forces, boldly closed in on Essex's army along a fifteen-mile front. Essex himself got away by sea and his cavalry managed to escape the cordon, but his infantry surrendered and marched away dispiritedly to Portsmouth. The King, it has been justly said, 'never showed more vigour and ability' than in this battle 'where he proved himself a commanding officer in fact as well as in name'.[20]

On returning from Cornwall to Oxford Charles again distinguished himself in another battle, the second battle of Newbury, because his defensive positions were such that the Parliamentarians divided their forces and failed to prevent him from retiring in good order. However, had Charles not detached troops to relieve Banbury before the battle began he might again have been victorious. Thus in 1644, whatever his errors as a strategist, Charles proved himself an extremely able tactician.

But in the vital battle of Naseby in the following year Charles played a negligible part. Although Rupert was now his commander-in-chief, the King allowed him to take charge of the right wing of the cavalry instead of leaving it to his brother Maurice. Had Rupert stayed with Charles and the reserve in the centre on Dust Hill, where an excellent view of the whole battle-field could have been maintained, some sort of control over events might have been exercised. As it was, Charles remained there with quite a large reserve, consisting of his own horse Life Guard, under the command of Lord Bernard Stuart, who had done well at Cropredy Bridge, plus cavalry from Newark, Prince Rupert's infantry regiment and the infantry Life Guard under the second Earl of Lindsey. After Rupert had impetuously charged off the field, leaving behind him some of the Parliamentarian cavalry on their left wing and Cromwell, who was victorious on the Parliamentarian right wing, the Royalist infantry in the centre were then attacked by cavalry and dragoons as well as by the Roundhead infantry under the experienced Major-General Skippon. Charles evidently threw in his infantry reserve, but when he tried to counter-charge Cromwell's cavalry with his reserve of horse the Scottish Earl of Carnwath seized the King's bridle and, crying with an oath 'Will you go upon your death?', pulled the royal charger away from the enemy. The defeat here was largely Charles's own fault because he had sent Goring with his cavalry back to the south-west when they were needed in the north. He still remained sanguine and had one last tactical victory to his credit when in August of that same year he succeeded in raising the siege of Hereford, which was being conducted by the Scots under the Earl of Leven.

Looking back on Charles's military career as a whole, it is clear that he made decisions that proved wrong frequently through ignoring the advice of his nephew Rupert, who proved himself a capable strategist and a daring cavalry commander. Charles had refused him permission to form a flying column after the battle of Edgehill to thrust on to Westminster where he might have occupied the Houses of Parliament. In 1643 he would not allow Rupert to storm Gloucester before the town was relieved; then he failed to follow the Earl of Essex after the town's relief with sufficient speed to fight him in open country where the Royalist cavalry might have been victorious instead of in the enclosed country around Newbury. In 1644 he sent Rupert 'peremptory commands' lacking in sufficient lucidity, which induced the Prince to fight the battle of Marston Moor on unfavourable terms.[21] In 1645 he rejected Rupert's advice not to return to Oxford after the siege of Leicester. Afterwards he failed to move north sufficiently swiftly to avoid having to fight the New Model Army with an inferior force.

Finally, having appointed Rupert as his effective commander-in-chief, he brusquely dismissed the Prince when he felt obliged to surrender Bristol, maintaining that Rupert could have held out in the ancient fort and medieval castle until he was relieved. In fact, such relief would certainly not have been forthcoming, for the Parliamentarians possessed strength enough to surround the port completely by land and sea. Finally, Charles's decision to throw himself on the mercy of the Scots after escaping in disguise from Oxford was less sensible and less heroic than submitting to a siege which might well have ended honourably.

One facet of Charles's military approach derived from his character. Because he believed he had been chosen by God to rule over his people as a loving father he was genuinely appalled by the horrors of war between himself and any of his subjects. That was one of the reasons why he failed to employ his military following to seize Hull and its valuable magazine in April 1642 after he had been defied by its governor, Sir John Hotham, who, incidentally, went over to the King at a later stage in his career. It is likely that if Charles had acted more forcefully the garrison would have surrendered; instead he was content with protests on paper.[22] The Queen was astonished – she told him, 'I would have flung the rascal over the walls.'[23] But Charles reflected later: 'I was resolved to bear this and much more with patience,' for it was 'a hard choice for a king that loves his people and desires their love either to kill his own subjects or be killed by them'.[24] When Prince Rupert advocated a forced march on London after the battle of Edgehill Charles was dissuaded by the fear that the Prince, 'being a young man and naturally passionate', might set fire to the capital.[25] It took time for Charles to recover from the shock of civil war. He confessed that he was 'exceedingly and deeply grieved by the carnage' and was left stunned and lethargic. So, as Sir Richard Bulstrode, who fought in the battle, wrote, 'Our King trifled away his time in taking Banbury and Broughton House ... places of very little consideration and so marched very slowly towards London where the Earl of Essex with his army arrived before him.'[26] At Gloucester in the following year Charles rejected Rupert's advice to make a frontal assault on the city because he was so upset over the heavy loss of lives by officers and men during the storming of Bristol.

Following his victory at Cropredy Bridge, wrote Sir Edward Walker, 'His Majesty, according to his wonted clemency, desirous to avoid the destruction of his subjects, and willing by all fair means to reduce them to their due obedience, sent a message of grace and pardon to all officers and soldiers of Waller's army, which was refused.'[27] Four months later at Lostwithiel Charles allowed the Parliamentarian infantry to march away with their colours flying and actually gave them an escort to prevent them from being abused, plundered and pillaged by the local inhabitants. Charles recorded in his *Eikon Basilike*: 'I never had any victory which was without sorrow because it was on my own subjects.'[28]

Doubtless Charles was sincere when he asserted in 1647 that he would not engage his poor people in another war. So far as he was concerned he had fought his last battle; yet by signing a secret engagement with the Scottish Royalists, headed by John Campbell Earl of Loudoun (the Scottish Chancellor), the Earl of Lauderdale and the Earl of Lanark (brother of the first Duke of Hamilton), at Carisbrooke castle on 26 December, in which he agreed to large concessions over religion in return for the promise that an army would be sent from Scotland into England to restore him to his government and 'the just rights of the Crown', he had provoked a second civil war. Indeed, as Jack Ashburnham wrote, he had 'far greater hopes of being restored than ever he had whilst (in person) in arms'.[29]

No one denies that Charles was a brave soldier, even if he did not charge at the head of his cavalry as Rupert and Oliver did. Clarendon rightly observed that he was 'very fearless in his person', though, he added, 'but in his riper years not enterprising'. He showed himself an astute commander in the campaign of 1643, but at the big battles of the first civil war – Edgehill, the two battles of Newbury and Naseby – he remained on horseback at the rear with the reserve, but proved unable to intervene decisively at any stage.

In theory Charles had one immense advantage over his enemies: he exercised an undivided command as Captain-General and in a rough sense was his own Minister of Defence. The Parliamentarians, on the other hand, lacked a unified command. Though the Earl of Essex was by name Captain-General he was not entirely trusted by his own side (after all, he had first been appointed general by the King) and he was jealous when Sir William Waller and the Earl of Manchester were given separate armies. In 1644 the Committee of Both Kingdoms was constituted to co-ordinate military strategy but as its military members, such as Oliver Cromwell, were usually on active service its orders were either wrongly conceived or ignored. It was not until a united army – the New Model – was created in 1645 and after a while General Sir Thomas Fairfax, who superseded Essex, was granted a free hand that the superior resources of Parliament were utilized and prevailed.

Charles's strength was that he was courageous and never despaired. But he did not appreciate how to choose and handle men. In the war against the Scottish Covenanters he appointed amateurs as generals, thus antagonizing Essex, a man of military and naval experience. During the civil wars he treated the first Earl of Lindsey badly and dismissed Lord Wilmot, a capable cavalry officer, on an unjustified charge of treason. Admittedly Prince Rupert was a difficult character to handle, quick-tempered, touchy, easily aroused to jealousy, and little accustomed to English ways, regarding the Parliamentarians as mere rebels who should be dealt with harshly, but he was a commander of genius. Though Charles assured him that 'I mean not to trust you by halfs'[30] he constantly ignored his advice. By detaching part of his army to fight in the west of England during 1645 under the nominal command of his fourteen-year-old son he angered the Prince while, by simultaneously conferring an independent command on General George Goring, a notoriously unstable character, as Lieutenant-General of Horse, he created chaos.

Goring, who 'strangely loved the bottle, was much given to his pleasures and a great debauchee', refused to take orders from either the Prince of Wales's Council or from Prince Rupert. Furthermore, had Charles kept Goring with him in May of that year (as Goring wanted him to do) instead of despatching him to Taunton the King might not have been defeated at Naseby. Instead of following Rupert's counsel in that crucial year to march north and join the Marquis of Montrose, the finest general on the Royalist side after Rupert himself, he sent George Digby, his sycophantic Secretary of State, as Lieutenant-General with three cavalry regiments on a hopeless mission. Digby reached Scotland, but then fled with most of his officers to the Isle of Man, leaving their troops to shift for themselves. Digby was sent north by Charles after he had dismissed Rupert from all his offices for surrendering Bristol. The truth was that Charles's behaviour to

his commanders reflected one of the outstanding traits in his
character – he liked to divide and rule. As the Earl of Clarendon
observed, 'he did not love ... very confident men'.[31] Just as he
never gave his full support to the Earl of Strafford or Archbishop
Laud and preferred more obsequious ministers, so he failed to
put his entire trust in either Rupert or Montrose; and because he
lacked faith in himself as well as repudiating the ruthlessness
needed to be a successful general, most of his military decisions
derived from lesser men who sat in his Council of War and tended
to be pusillanimous.

6

SOLDIERING – II

Though Oliver Cromwell was undoubtedly Charles I's superior as a military strategist and more resourceful as a tactician, it has to be recognized that the science of generalship, as distinct from the art, has always consisted chiefly of the ability to organize. The training of troops, their commissariat, their regular pay have been essential to the success of warfare and without smooth lines of communication campaigns are rarely won. Attempts made in the war of 1939–45 to campaign without normal lines of communication – for example, in Burma – did not succeed, and both Napoleon and Hitler were defeated in Russia because their lines of communication were too far stretched.

Relatively little is known about the training of soldiers during the civil wars, though Oliver's remarks to his cousin, John Hampden, about the quality of the troopers that were needed to face 'gentlemen's sons and persons of quality' are familiar. And it seems plain that he believed not only that religious men would be 'valiant', but that only by relying on such men could 'those disorders, mutinies, plundering and grievances of the country which deboist [debauched] men are guilty of' be avoided.[1] Recent research has shown how in every county anger against the depredations of soldiers on both sides mounted and aroused a desire for neutrality at almost any price.[2]

Still, religious men, however ardent and courageous, needed training. Oliver set an example of this, for he spent much of 1643 recruiting and drilling troopers for his double cavalry regiment. Most of his men were freeholders who, according to a contemporary, were 'well armed within, by the satisfaction of their consciences, and without by good iron arms; they would as one man stand firmly and charge desperately'.[3] Oliver saw to it that his men were punctually paid and praised an officer 'who much improved his men in their exercise'.[4]

Though Cromwell invariably wrapped up what he had to say in religious terms, it is clear that he insisted on firm discipline. When he became commander-in-chief in 1650 he told Major-General Thomas Harrison, himself a fanatical Christian martinet, that even if the militiamen who were called to the colours were of poor calibre and he (Oliver) had 'much such stuff to deal with in those sent to him in Scotland', yet with good officers put over them they were 'reforming daily'.[5]

All the military writers of the time paid lip service to the importance of training and discipline. Prince Maurice of Orange, a highly successful general, thought that in drill and weapon training lay the secrets of victory. But so far as his troopers were concerned, Prince Rupert of the Rhine – Charles's commander-in-chief after 1644, who, like Cromwell, was primarily a cavalry officer – does not appear to have done much training. His latest biographer states baldly that 'details of the training imposed by Rupert are lacking'.[6] Plainly, most of the cavalry officers and troopers brought their own horses with them, knew how to ride, and could quickly be taught how to charge the enemy brandishing their swords (and not firing their pistols and carbines until they had engaged) but, as Rupert was to find to his cost, they could not easily be rallied after their first successful charge. On the other hand Oliver, notably at the battles of Gainsborough, Marston Moor and Naseby, was able to halt and steady his cavalry and obviously this was owing to careful training.

To begin with, Oliver insisted that 'honest godly men', 'honest men that fear God' made the best officers and soldiers. In this he concurred with one of the greatest generals of his age, King Gustavus Adolphus of Sweden, who maintained that good Christians made the best soldiers. But it is to be noticed that initially Oliver excluded Anabaptists from this category. He wrote to his friend Oliver St John in September 1643: 'My troops increase, I have a lovely company, you would respect them if you knew them. They are no Anabaptists, they are honest sober Christians'.[7] In the following month he told his cousin, Sir Thomas Barrington, from whom he asked prayers and money:

'Truly mine (though some have stigmatized them with the name of Anabaptists) are honest men, such as fear God, I am confident the freest from unjust practices as any in England, seek the soldiers where you can.'[8]

Why were the Anabaptists excluded from the lovely company of honest Christians? It was a term that was very loosely used, but Anabaptists were accused of holding extreme beliefs – for example, denying the resurrection of the body – and they were even confused by some Puritan gentry with the Arminians, who rejected predestination. More to the point, they or some of them, like the later Quakers, objected to wars and military service. Yet when later in 1644 Oliver became Lieutenant-General in the army of the Eastern Association, commanded by the Earl of Manchester, he remonstrated with Major-General Lawrence Crawford, a keen Scottish Presbyterian reluctant to allow authority to extreme sectarians, for putting an Anabaptist (Lieutenant William Packer) under arrest when he was 'a godly man'. He also defended another officer (Lieutenant-Colonel Henry Warner) whom Crawford had 'turned off' on the ground that he was an Anabaptist. 'Admit he be an Anabaptist, shall that render him incapable to serve the public?' demanded Oliver. 'The State in choosing men takes no notice of their opinions, if they be willing faithfully to serve that satisfies.'[9] Evidently he changed his mind about Anabaptists; as so often in his career, Oliver learned from experience. When the Reverend Richard Baxter, a Presbyterian, went to visit Cromwell's soldiers after the battle of Naseby he asserted that 'Independency and Anabaptistry' were most prevalent and that 'Separatists, Anabaptists and Antinomians' were most honoured under Cromwell.

Oliver's energetic actions in Cambridge, his formation of his double cavalry regiment and his evident ability in training and disciplining his troopers meant that when Parliament decided to form a new army in the group of counties known as the Eastern Association, he was the obvious choice to be second-in-command to Edward Montagu second Earl of Manchester, who was appointed Sergeant-Major-General of the Associated counties on 10 August 1643. Cromwell was at first one of four cavalry colonels under Manchester, but on 22 January 1644, presumably with Manchester's approval, he became Lieutenant-General of Horse and Foot.[10] Thus within eighteen months he rose from being a captain to the rank of lieutenant-general.

In so far as he held any religious opinions, Manchester was a Presbyterian, but in building up his army he aimed at its being commanded by 'godly officers without respect to sectarian differences' and initially he always placed Cromwell 'in chiefest esteem and credit' with him. But early in 1644 Oliver's attitude underwent a radical change. According to Manchester, he expressed contempt for the Assembly of Divines, which was planning a new Church of England aligned to that of the Scottish Kirk. Oliver then, again according to Manchester, showed his animosity against the Scottish nation, whose army had entered England as the paid allies of the Roundheads, and desired in the army of the Eastern Association only 'such men as are of Independent judgment'. Though it is an exaggeration to say that he aimed to pack Manchester's army with his own adherents, he was certainly antagonized by Crawford's behaviour. The Scots, for their part, contended that Manchester was too lenient with Cromwell. It was admitted that Oliver was 'a very wise and active head, universally loved as religious and stout', but 'being a known Independent most of the soldiers who loved new ways put themselves under his command'.[11] So while Charles was always ready to seek help from Scots or Irish to win the civil war, Oliver, because he found Scottish Presbyterianism distasteful, wanted the Army to be manned by Englishmen who possessed his own frame of mind, even if they were Anabaptists.

Of course, like Charles, Oliver was to begin with an amateur soldier. He was enthusiastic, eager to be actively engaged, but was not exactly clear where he was going. The members of the Eastern Association (which consisted of Cambridgeshire, Hertfordshire, Essex, Norfolk and Suffolk and later Huntingdonshire) had a diversity of aims. Many within the Association were simply anxious to keep the war out of their counties, to protect them against 'all sorts of plunderers', and to undertake limited defensive measures. The war party at Westminster, on the other hand, wanted to secure these counties against Royalist infiltration, while recruiting a fresh force to assist the main Parliamentarian army under the Earl of Essex in the principal theatre of action. Earl Grey of Wark, who preceded Manchester as Major-General of the Association, was ordered to lead the army raised there to Reading, where Essex was planning to attack Charles's Oxford headquarters, while Cromwell was left with a detachment to protect the northern flank of the Association.

After drilling his men for three weeks in April 1643 Cromwell was determined to take the offensive. During the first half of May he and two other colonels met on the road from Peterborough to Lincoln and after winning a skirmish at Grantham, which Oliver designated 'a glorious victory', prepared to advance on Newark, a key town on the route from Yorkshire to the Midlands, roughly half-way between York and Oxford, which had already been successfully defended by the Royalists from other Parliamentarian forces. At the end of May Oliver and four other officers were reported to have 6,000 men at Nottingham, but they were too late to intercept a convoy of ammunition, sent by the Queen, who after collecting arms for her husband in Holland reached Yorkshire that February. In fact the Lincolnshire committee blamed Oliver, among others, for the failure to obstruct the arrival of this valuable convoy at Oxford. What was worse, apart from one attack in which they were repulsed, Cromwell and his fellow officers remained inactive near Nottingham after Queen Henriette Marie herself arrived safely at Newark with 6,000 foot soldiers and some 3,500 cavalry. After spending a fortnight in Newark she left to meet Prince Rupert at Stratford on Avon and then rejoined her husband. Apart from the fact that one of the officers with Cromwell proved to be a traitor and, as Oliver rightly maintained, they had too few men directly to confront the force which accompanied the Queen, the events of May and June 1643 spelt military ineptitude.[12]

Having failed to prevent the Queen from rejoining Charles, the Roundhead forces in the Eastern Association concentrated on advancing northward in order to give help to their colleagues in Yorkshire, who were outnumbered by the Royalists under the Earl of Newcastle. Cromwell took Burleigh House near Stafford before going to the assistance of Lord Willoughby of Parham, who had occupied Gainsborough, which lies some thirty miles south-west of Hull. Newcastle had sent his younger brother, Sir Charles Cavendish, to relieve Gainsborough. When battle loomed Cromwell was in command of the cavalry on the right wing, but he kept three troops from his regiment in reserve. It proved to be essentially a cavalry contest and, at the end of it, Oliver sent his reserve to fall on Cavendish's rear; Cavendish himself was killed and the victory over him appeared complete. But soon Newcastle sent a large reinforcement, and Cromwell was compelled to retire southward.

Once he had relieved Lincoln as well as Gainsborough, the Earl turned his attention to the siege of Hull, which had been held by the Parliamentarians since the beginning of the war and was defended by Lord Fairfax and his son Thomas. Thus the pressure on the Eastern Association was relieved, enabling Oliver to return to Huntingdon and Cambridge where he concerned himself with recruiting the Parliamentarian strength and training his men. His reaction after the retreat from Gainsborough and his determination to put matters right was reflected in his correspondence. To the Commissioners of the Association, who functioned from Cambridge, he wrote: 'You see how sadly your affairs stand. It's no longer disputing, but out instantly all you can.' He was certain that God was still on his side and that God's blessings were coming in due season, as if He should say: 'Up and be doing, and I will help you and stand by you.' Oliver badgered the authorities in the Association for more cavalry and infantry, more weapons and more money.[13]

By the middle of September he had collected his 'lovely company' and on the 20th he was able to cross the Humber and confer with the Fairfaxes in Hull. It was decided to reinforce Hull with some of the Eastern Association infantry, while Thomas Fairfax with a detachment of cavalry, which were of little use in the defence of Hull, joined Cromwell and his new commanding officer, the Earl of Manchester, in the counties south of Yorkshire, where the Royalists still occupied Newark, Lincoln and Gainsborough. The Marquis of Newcastle (he had been promoted by Charles after his victories in Yorkshire) ordered these Royalists to combine and relieve Bolingbroke castle near Boston, which was being besieged by Manchester. The two armies confronted each other near the village of Winceby. The Roundheads had superior numbers, and the Cavaliers were routed chiefly by means of a flank attack carried out by the Yorkshire cavalry under Thomas Fairfax. Oliver was in the van, but his horse was killed under him at the first charge and the part he played later in the battle is not known. As late in the season as 2 November he and Fairfax captured the Royalist stronghold of Newark.

Thus 1643 was the year of Oliver's military apprenticeship. As has been pointed out, 'he had been engaged in three consecutive victories at a time when the Parliamentarian fortunes on the whole were on the wane'.[14] He had learned the value of charging the enemy with his cavalry at 'a good round trot', he had appreciated the importance of having some kind of reserve which could be thrown in when the battle reached its crisis, and he could see that the cavalry had become the queen of the battle. Above all, he had come to realize how essential and how difficult it was to collect and train men, pay them adequately and provide them with good weapons, for only then would they fight for their lives.

Another facet of Oliver's character that emerged as he climbed up the military rankings was his aggressiveness, which extended not only towards his Royalist enemies but also his own colleagues. This clearly owed much to the fact that he was, above all, a politician accustomed during his years of service in the House of Commons to the rough-and-tumble of debate. He did not conceal his opinions. He blamed Lord Grey of Groby, the head of the Midlands Association, for failing to meet him at Stamford with a view to marching on Newark and intercepting the convoy of munitions despatched by the Queen. He also criticized Grey for worrying about the defence of Leicester (which was in Roundhead hands) instead of attacking the enemy. He castigated the committee of the Eastern Association at Cambridge for not giving firm orders and seeing that they were obeyed. 'Raise your bands,' he urged, 'Get up what volunteers you can; hasten your horses . . . you must act lively: do it without distraction.' And he attacked Lord Willoughby of Parham, the major-general in command of the Parliamentarian forces in Lincolnshire, for surrendering Gainsborough and Lincoln to the Royalists, blaming him for having 'very loose and profane commanders'.[15]

Not unnaturally he was accused of casting dirt on deserving fellow officers, but unquestionably he was single-minded in seeking the means of victory, even though he was not averse to adopting that self-humiliating stance that was so characteristic of the Puritan gentry. As late as October 1651, when he was in supreme command of the triumphant army of the Commonwealth, he wrote to a friend in Boston in America: 'I am a poor weak creature and not worthy of the name of a worm ... you know my weakness, my inordinate passions, my unskilfulness and in every way unfitness for my work.'[16]

It was in 1644 that Oliver won his military reputation. At the start of the year he had received his appointment as lieutenant-general under Manchester and was made a member of the Committee of Both Kingdoms, the equivalent of joint chiefs of staff of the English and Scottish armies. This committee was in a strong position because the entry into the north of England of the Scottish Covenanting army of 20,000 men under a highly experienced general swung the balance in its favour against the King. The Marquis of Newcastle, who had hitherto dominated Yorkshire, was unable to stem the advance of the Scottish army and shut himself up in York with its splendid stone walls, where he was surrounded by the Scots and the army of the Fairfaxes and later by the Earl of Manchester's army, which had managed to lose Newark (it had been retaken by Prince Rupert) but had recaptured Lincoln.

At the end of June Prince Rupert, with an army which had occupied most of Lancashire (except the town of Manchester), arrived at York under peremptory orders from Charles to relieve the northern capital. The besieging armies then withdrew because the commanders feared they might be crushed between Rupert's relieving army and Newcastle's large garrison in York. Expecting Rupert would be advancing directly from the west, they stationed their main force, which included Cromwell in charge of Manchester's cavalry, around the village of Long Marston four miles west of York. But Rupert did not come the way they had anticipated and the allied commanders, greatly overestimating the size of the Royalist army, began to retreat south-west in the direction of Leeds and Bradford, where support for

Parliament was strongest, in order to gain time, secure a more advantageous position, and await reinforcements. The Round-head infantry went ahead while the cavalry of the three armies guarded the rear. But when it was realized early on 1 July that Rupert had already thrust out a cavalry screen to cover Marston Moor, which lay to the north of Long Marston, and when next day further cavalry arrived on the moor it became evident that Rupert was intent on fighting a battle. The Parliamentarian foot under the commander-in-chief Lord Leven were called back; a defensive line was then drawn up with Cromwell and Manchester's cavalry on the left, the infantry in the centre and the Yorkshire cavalry under Sir Thomas Fairfax on the right.

The battle of Marston Moor has often been described in detail, but there has been much argument about the part taken in it by Oliver Cromwell. The story that before the battle began Prince Rupert asked a prisoner 'Is Cromwell there?' suggests that he was already known widely as an enterprising commander. When Lord Leven ordered the allies to attack as late as seven o'clock that summer evening Cromwell led forward the front cavalry line on the left wing. Rupert, although he was the Royalist commander-in-chief, appears to have concentrated his attention on his right wing opposite Cromwell. He was taken by surprise because he had not expected to be attacked so late in the day, but the defensive lay-out with his squadrons interspersed with mus-keteers, to some extent protected by infantry lining a ditch, was intended to induce Cromwell to charge and only then, when his formation was broken, to be counter-charged.

In this first charge Oliver was wounded and the story has been told – and accepted by some modern historians anxious to dispa-rage his military genius – that he had to retire to the neighbouring village of Tockwith to have his wound dressed, while either Colonel David Leslie, who was in command of the third cavalry line on the left wing, dealt with the counter-charge headed by Rupert in person or even that Cromwell's *bête noire*, the Scottish Major-General Crawford, whose infantrymen were fighting to the right of the cavalry, took over the command. That Oliver received a slight wound in the neck is vouched for by the scout-master in Manchester's army, but no reliable evidence about his leaving the battlefield exists. One military historian, who is no admirer of Cromwell, has written that, 'though bleeding from his wound, Cromwell was not out of action and retained sufficient presence of mind to rally his men for a second bout'.[17]

After his victory on the left wing, Oliver kept his regiments of horse close and firm together in one body. Sir Thomas Fairfax's cavalry had been defeated by the Royalists on the right wing of the allied line. But Cromwell wheeled his cavalry eastwards and routed the victorious Royalists there. Finally he joined with the infantry in a devastating attack on the Royalist foot, who had fought bravely enough in the centre. According to the Marquis of Newcastle's second wife, who no doubt heard the story of the battle from her husband, 'they showed such extraordinary valour that they were killed as they stood in rank and file'. One military historian has written that 'Sir Thomas Fairfax, as senior officer, probably took command of Cromwell's and Leslie's horse', that 'the masterly manoeuvre by Sir Thomas Fairfax assured final victory' and that 'Sir Thomas Fairfax must have directed the final and decisive attack'.[18] Thus 'the might-have-beens of history' become 'the must-have-beens of history.'

Neither Fairfax himself nor any of his biographers make any such claims. It is not even certain that when Fairfax rode across the battlefield to join the horse on the left wing – as Fairfax himself said he did – he met Cromwell or brought the first news of his own defeat on the right. Indeed it is not even true that Fairfax was at that time Cromwell's senior officer: they were of equal rank. Two of the men on the Parliamentarian side made different comparisons. One said Cromwell was 'the great agent of this victory' and that Sir Thomas Fairfax 'carried himself as bravely as a man can do'; the other wrote that in the service Lieutenant-General Cromwell 'merited most' and Sir Thomas Fairfax 'very much'. In the most recent assessment of the battle the author writes: 'It is certain that Cromwell need share the honour of the Allied victory with no one'.[19]

The defeat of Sir William Waller at Cropredy Bridge and of the Earl of Essex at Lostwithiel by King Charles counterbalanced the Parliamentarian victory at Marston Moor. Taking advantage of his membership of the House of Commons, Oliver criticized his superior officer, the Earl of Manchester, for lack of enterprise; and in order to get rid of both Essex and Manchester he lent his powerful support to a self-denying ordinance whereby no member of either House of Parliament was to be allowed to hold any office or military command during the remainder of the war and offered to lay down his own command. Sir Thomas Fairfax, who was not a member of parliament and had distinguished himself in the fighting in Yorkshire, was appointed to take charge of a New Model Army. Cromwell and Fairfax had been on pretty intimate terms, having fought together at the battle of Winceby, siege of York and the contest on Marston Moor. Fairfax was a man who made friends easily and such correspondence between him and Oliver as survives shows admiration and trust between them. Fairfax was given the right to appoint his own officers, subject to the approval of Parliament. He chose Phillip Skippon as his Major-General of Foot, but left the office of Lieutenant-General of the Horse open. Cromwell's commission was twice renewed for forty days, and two months after the New Model Army took the field in 1645 Fairfax asked and received permission from the House of Commons to appoint Oliver to the vacant post. It can scarcely be doubted that this had always been Fairfax's intention and that Oliver knew it.

In June 1645 Cromwell with 600 picked cavalrymen from East Anglia joined Fairfax in good time to take part in the crucial battle of Naseby. He advised Fairfax to take up a position which would encourage the Royalists to attack uphill. On the left of the line he stationed his future son-in-law, Henry Ireton, whom Fairfax promoted to be Commissary-General, on Oliver's recommendation, to take command of the cavalry there. Oliver himself drew up the cavalry in three lines on the right-hand side of the battlefield with his double regiment to the fore. Here he repeated his success at Marston Moor, first charging the opposing enemy cavalry, then driving it back past King Charles's reserve (it was at this point in the battle that the King vainly tried to organize a counter-charge) and finally, steadying his troopers, Oliver was able to lead them against the Royalist infantry, who had been heroically resisting superior numbers of Parliamentarian foot-soldiers in the centre. By the time Prince Rupert, unwisely allowed by Charles to take command of the cavalry on the Royalist right, had swept past Ireton as far as the village of Naseby to the south and returned to the fray, the battle had been lost.

It is true that the soldiers in the New Model Army outnumbered the Royalists in the infantry by about two to one and in the cavalry by three to two, but it has to be remembered that the New Model infantry consisted largely of untrained or sparsely trained men (that was why the infantry in the centre at Naseby were nearly defeated by the Royalist foot) and that Ireton was not a skilful commander. If doubt was cast by some contemporaries and later military historians on the part played by Oliver at Marston Moor, clearly the decisive victory at Naseby owed most to him because of his dexterous handling of his troopers, contrasting strikingly with Charles's inability to rally his cavalrymen. As the Earl of Clarendon wrote in his incomparable *History of the Rebellion,*

> the difference ... in the discipline of the King's troops and of those which marched under the command of Cromwell [was] that though the King's troops prevailed in the charge, and routed those they charged, they never rallied themselves again in order, nor could be brought to make a second charge again the same day.

As usual Oliver bestowed on God full credit for the Naseby victory 'wherein none are to share with Him', but he also gave Fairfax a pat on the back. He told the Speaker of the House of Commons, 'The General served you with all faithfulness and honour.'[20] Nothing is more remarkable about Cromwell's behaviour as a soldier than his willingness openly to praise or blame his superior officers. In later times generals only do this in their memoirs.

Some historians have observed that God was on the side of the big battalions in the two victories that made Oliver Cromwell famous, Marston Moor and Naseby. But what proves him to have been a general of outstanding ability was two later victories when he was in supreme command, Preston (1648) and Dunbar (1650). In these two battles Oliver had fewer soldiers than his opponents – at Preston 8,600 against 17,600 and at Dunbar 11,000 against at least double that number.

Of course it is not the case that Oliver was always victorious. Curiously enough, one of the Royalist officers by whom he was twice defeated was of completely opposite character to his own, Colonel George Goring. He had, as has already been noticed, a reputation for debauchery, comprising excessive drinking, lying and wenching; he had to put up with a whining wife, a semi-invalid unable to bear him children. He was an audacious soldier. When in the spring of 1645 Cromwell was ordered by the Committee of Both Kingdoms to isolate Charles in Oxford he besieged Farringdon, seventeen miles south-west of Oxford, telling the military governor: 'If God give you into my hands, I will not spare a man of you, if you put me to a storm.'[21] But Goring surrounded his headquarters and beat him off. Earlier, in the second battle of Newbury, when Cromwell was engaged in an outflanking movement, Goring successfully counter-charged Cromwell's cavalry force and defeated him with inferior numbers. In Ireland and Scotland Oliver also suffered setbacks. In spite of the fears engendered by his drastic actions at Drogheda and Wexford, in southern Ireland he was defied first at Kilkenny and then at Clonmel.

At Clonmel four of his attempts to storm the town were frustrated; in the last attempt his men were caught in a death trap prepared for them by the governor, and the result was a massacre first of the infantry and then of the cavalry. The Irish garrison was safely evacuated. The siege of Clonmel has been called 'the most disastrous episode in Cromwell's whole military career'.[22] In Scotland too he sustained losses in trying to capture Edinburgh in 1650 and Stirling in 1651. One distinguished historian wrote that before the battle of Dunbar Cromwell had been 'thoroughly outgeneralled and showed himself halting and irresolute'. But here his military genius extended to valuing the importance of sea power, which enabled him to overcome all obstacles.

Just as it has been claimed that David Leslie or Thomas Fairfax were the real heroes of the battle of Marston Moor, so it has also been argued that it was the young Yorkshire officer John Lambert, by his successful harrying of the Scottish Engagers army, who was the true victor in the Preston campaign; and it has been contended too that it was either John Lambert or George Monck who achieved the extraordinary victory obtained under Oliver's command at the battle of Dunbar. Lambert's biographer attributes both the plan of the battle and the result to his hero, and one of Monck's biographers says that Cromwell failed to give his hero the praise that was his due. But no serious evidence has been found to rebut Oliver's statement that the plan for the battle was his own, and in any case his was the responsibility. In fact the victory at Dunbar was the epitome of Oliver's military genius.

In all his battles Oliver showed boldness and vigour. Unlike most of the campaigns in the Thirty Years War in Germany, when siege after siege took place and battles were regarded by generals as hazardous and dangerous, Cromwell always believed that 'to fight the enemy was his business'. In contrast with King Charles, ever painfully aware that he was fighting his own subjects and therefore unwilling to inflict unnecessary suffering, a commendable view, Oliver was a ruthless commander. Though in general he was popular with the rank-and-file of his men, underneath his geniality (as Sir Charles Firth wrote) 'lay a fiery temper which sometimes flared up into vehement utterances or sudden bursts of passion'. And he was, as Hilaire Belloc observed, 'as he believed, the instrument of an implacable God'. At most battles he was carried away momentarily and even in retrospect by passionate exuberance. Both at the battles of Marston Moor and Dunbar he rejoiced that the Lord of Hosts made the enemy 'as stubble to our swords'. When confronted with resistance by Roman Catholic soldiers in Ireland, he was enraged by what he regarded as their idolatry. At the siege of Basing House, the fortified manor of the Roman Catholic Marquis of Winchester, he allowed his men to kill a quarter of the garrison and indulge in unlimited plundering. At the siege of Drogheda he ordered St Peter's church, where a hundred Roman Catholic soldiers refused to surrender, to be set on fire and afterwards reported sadistically how they cried out, 'God damn me, I burn, I burn!' Even at the battle of Dunbar where the enemy were fellow Puritans he exclaimed, 'Now let God arise and his enemies be scattered!'

Oliver was invariably on the attack, carried forward, as he was convinced, by the wrath of God. Charles, except during his campaigns of 1639 and 1640 against the Scottish Covenanters, was always at heart on the defensive. For example, in his famous letter to Prince Rupert of 14 June 1644 he warned him 'If York be lost, I shall esteem my Crown little less.' Again as has been noted before, following his defeat at Naseby and the loss of the battle of Langport immediately afterwards, when Rupert advised him to make peace on the best terms he could get, he admitted that 'as a soldier ... there is no probability but my ruin'.[23] So basically he was a defeatist, though, like Oliver, he expected God to work miracles because his cause was just. By contrast Oliver was always on the offensive: he felt certain, even in the darkest hour before the battle of Dunbar, that ultimate victory was assured. Essentially that was the difference between the two men.

7

RULERS AT HOME

One is accustomed to think that statesmen governing a country are chiefly concerned with domestic affairs, promoting prosperity and public welfare, organizing the national finances, and introducing necessary legislative reforms. But in fact governments are usually largely occupied with foreign affairs and the defence of the realm. This was particularly the case in seventeenth-century England. Much of the time spent both by Charles I during the sixteen years before the civil war broke out and by Oliver Cromwell when he was Lord Protector was absorbed in questions of foreign policy rather than problems at home, except for security.

Neither Charles nor Oliver regularly attended meetings of their Privy Council or Council of State. Charles's Privy Council met on Wednesdays and Fridays in the afternoon, when it discussed routine matters but had limited policy-making functions. Moreover, the membership of the Privy Council was too big for effective decisions. It was in committees of the Council that the real work was done. So understandably Charles often attended meetings of committees, particularly those that dealt with the navy and trade.[1] Oliver's Council of State, on the other hand, had, according to the terms of the Instrument of Government, which established the Protectorate, far-reaching powers. Initially it contained only thirteen members and met five or six times a week.

Before Parliament assembled in September 1654 the Council acted as a legislature, reading ordinances two or three times before submitting them to the Protector for his approval. As a rule, Oliver did not preside over the Council himself except when questions of importance were being discussed. For example, he was there when a scheme for establishing a bank was being considered and again when the reform of the Court of Chancery was the main subject. Whereas in March 1654 Oliver was present at only one meeting of the Council, in the first week of May he was present at three out of four meetings and in October 1655, although he was far from well at the time, he managed to be at five Council meetings in the week.[2] That was unusual. But it seems that he was often there when foreign policy was the principal topic. Thus in the period between July 1656 and May 1657, when the Commonwealth was at war with Spain, Oliver attended nearly half the meetings of his Council of State.

So far at any rate as domestic affairs were involved, Charles has been accused of being indolent and lethargic. As evidence for this, it has been pointed out that Lord Falkland, who was Lord Deputy in Ireland in 1631, complained that the King seldom read papers and left all decisions to his secretaries of state.[3] However, few men in positions of supreme authority waste their time over matters of routine. One of Charles's latest biographers concludes that he was 'eager, assiduous and hard-working' and notes that he insisted on being consulted by his ministers on all significant questions.[4]

Clearly men who govern great nations need to look after their health, find time for exercise and relaxation, and avoid being burdened with details. King Louis XIV of France, the contemporary of Charles and Oliver, was a conscientious ruler who planned his days methodically but allowed himself specific time for recreation. Charles, like his father, enjoyed hunting, riding and playing bowls and his habits also were as regular as clockwork. That left him in excellent health. But as Protector Oliver spent every weekend at Hampton Court where he went out riding or listened to music, sometimes going there on Friday and not returning until Tuesday (it has been claimed that he invented the English weekend), but he did not leave the cares of State behind and was rarely in good health during his Protectorate. He was extremely conscientious; it has been said, no doubt with justice, that he 'had at his finger-ends at all times that intimate knowledge of the details of administration ... which enabled him to direct affairs as few administrators have done at any time'.[5] Charles has been accused of 'pettifogging concern for trivia',[6] but this is far truer of Oliver. No one who studies his surviving correspondence can avoid feeling that he spent too much time on minutiae, so that in the end overwork helped to kill him.

The eleven years between 1629 and 1640 have often been dismissed as the eleven-year 'tyranny'. But Charles I's government during this era must be seen in perspective. Both Queen Elizabeth I and King James I had managed without calling a parliament for lengthy periods. Parliament had to be summoned when the kingdom was at war or threatened with war so that the necessary sinews could be provided. After the death of the Duke of Buckingham Charles was quick to end the wars with Spain and France; and although he did what he could to obtain the restoration of the Palatinate to his nephew Charles Lewis, whose father, after vainly defying the Emperor in Vienna, had died in exile in 1632, the King's efforts were confined to diplomacy. So he did not need the help of Parliament.

The early years of Charles's personal rule were ones of economic depression. Owing to bad harvests between 1629 and 1631 the price of bread doubled.[7] Soldiers and sailors, disbanded after the end of the wars initiated by the Duke of Buckingham, produced unemployment and swelled the number of vagrants who roamed the country seeking work or charity. Bishop Laud insisted that the dearth was 'made by man and not by God', so Charles's government bestirred itself to grapple with the problem of poverty.

The opening years of the King's personal rule were therefore marked by a number of orders sent from the central government to the justices of the peace throughout the kingdom, instructing them how to cope with scarcity of food, the spread of infection owing to plague and the threats to the maintenance of public order from desperate men out of work. In January 1631 a commission under the Great Seal nominated a majority of members of the Privy Council to supervise the enforcement of the existing poor laws. Magistrates and overseers of the poor were told exactly what they were expected to do and were required to deliver regular reports. The government aimed to keep down the price of food by stopping the export of grain, demanding its equitable distribution, and punishing hoarders. To prevent disorders arising through resentment at the price of bread, the number of alehouses, where outcries focused, was to be sharply reduced and houses of correction were to be built to set at work able-bodied poor or, as it was put perjoratively, 'sturdy vagabonds'.[8]

None of these measures to cope with an economic and social crisis were in any way new. A bad harvest, a plague in London and depression in the woollen textile industry had previously invoked the publication and distribution of books of orders; they had been issued to justices of the peace ever since the middle of the reign of Queen Elizabeth I. Although the attempts by the central government to solve these problems in 1630–1631 were not particularly effective, it is clear that Charles and his ministers fully recognized and accepted their responsibilities; they were extremely energetic in stimulating the local authorities both directly through orders and proclamations and through arranging periodical visitations by justices of the assizes to inspect the work of the magistrates. The Book of Orders, one modern historian has claimed, 'was the start of a programme for the reformation of society and the reinvigoration of local government'. It also aimed to tackle 'the symptoms of dearth and poverty'.[9] But of course, as may be learnt from the history of later times, there is a limit to what governments can do to reduce unemployment and poverty.

The economic problem with which Charles concerned himself most was the draining of the fens in eastern England. The Great Fens covered an area of some 400,000 acres; it was a wilderness of bogs, pools and 'red-shoals' scattered over six counties, where the rivers overflowed the land in winter and at times in summer too. The inhabitants subsisted by keeping geese, cutting willows and catching wild fowl; a contemporary dismissed them as 'a rude and almost barbarous set of lazy and beggarly people'. The objective of the draining was to prevent floods and provide proper irrigation so that the reclaimed land could be cultivated. Charles, who was lord of a number of manors in the area known as the Hatfield Level, which lay to the south of the mouth of the river Humber, began by employing an outstanding Dutch engineer, Cornelius Vermuyden, and stipulated that before he started work he should obtain the consent of the commoners, to whom 6,000 acres of the drained land were to be allotted. Five years later a much more ambitious scheme was launched to drain the Great Level, which lay around the Isle of Ely and covered some 100,000 acres, a project in which the Earl of Bedford was the chief undertaker. This draining scheme took over five years to complete and provoked widespread rioting by the displaced commoners.[10] In 1638 the King superseded Bedford as undertaker and made short-term concessions to the commoners.

Both Cromwell's father and his rich uncle Oliver had been Commissioners of Sewers and favoured local drainage enterprises. That Oliver himself thought well of these undertakings was shown when in 1649 Parliament authorized the first Earl of Bedford's son, a leading Roundhead, to complete the ambitious plan started by his father; for both Oliver and his eldest son were named among the Commissioners. But in 1637–8 Cromwell's sympathies evidently lay with the rioters, for it was 'commonly reported' that he offered 'to hold the drainers in suit of law for five years and that in the meantime they should enjoy every foot of their common'.[11] According to Sir William Dugdale's authoritative *History of Embanking and Drayning of Fens*, Cromwell was in May 1638 chosen 'to be the orator of the fenmen before the King's Commissioners of Sewers there in opposition to His Majesty's most commendable design'.[12] Later in the spring of 1641 Oliver was still acting as adviser to, and spokesman for, displaced commoners who lived near his home in Ely.

Historians tend to ascribe base motives to characters whom they do not admire. Thus Charles I has been condemned for the active part he took in the draining of the fens because, it is emphasized, he himself stood to gain substantially from the various schemes initiated during his reign. 'The Crown's chief interest in draining was undoubtedly financial,' it has been stated.[13] But other monarchs from Henry VIII to James I had recognized that to prevent this large area of their kingdoms from constant flooding was a necessary duty. There is no reason to suppose that Charles thought differently or was solely motivated by the profit he might make out of it.

As to Oliver, his motives in supporting the opposition of the commoners have been variously interpreted. Sir William Dugdale claimed that Cromwell was chosen as their spokesman 'by those who endeavoured the undermining of royal authority': thus his opposition 'to His Majesty's most commendable design' was politically motivated. That is clearly improbable. It was also suggested by Dugdale that Oliver's boldness in championing the poor fenmen was to make a name for himself and thus help secure his election as a member of parliament for Cambridge in 1640. But in 1638, when Oliver first took up the cause of the fen-dwellers, he can have had no reason to suppose that the King was going to call another parliament, and in any case the fenmen had no votes. The local landowners, who did have votes, were likely to benefit from the drainage schemes. Oliver was easily excited by what he considered to be injustices: the fact that Charles's part in promoting the drainage of the fens was included in the crimes attributed to him in the Grand Remonstrance of November 1641, by which Oliver set so much store, indicates that he and his fellow Parliamentarians were genuinely convinced that the commoners had been badly treated by the King.

During his period of personal rule Charles was deeply occupied in stimulating trade and industry. He was attracted by novel ideas such as, besides Vermuyden's methods of draining the fens, a plan to make soap out of local materials, a scheme to improve water supplies, and the use of human urine in the manufacture of saltpetre. No doubt he was over-sanguine about the likely success of such enterprises, but his optimism even during the darkest days of his life was one of his most striking characteristics. As one of his biographers has observed, 'Charles liked to see himself as an "advanced monarch", patronizing inventors and giving scope to innovation and improvement.'[14] He was also anxious to promote commerce, frequently attending the meetings of the Committee for Trade and Plantations, and tried to succour industry by protectionist means. He did, however, forbid the planting of tobacco in England (as Cromwell was to do later). Recent evidence seems to show that the British carrying trade made considerable progress in the 1630s.[15] On the whole, as long as the kingdom remained at peace under the government of Charles I, it enjoyed considerable prosperity.

After the death of Buckingham Sir Richard Weston, who had recently been appointed Lord Treasurer (having previously been

Chancellor of the Exchequer), initiated a policy of retrenchment in order to put the royal finances on a securer footing.[16] He succeeded in this by raising special revenues – which ranged from the sale of Crown lands to fines for the retailing of tobacco – and paying off most of the costs of the unsuccessful wars against Spain and France. He also invented or revived a number of expedients, such as fining well-to-do gentlemen who failed to apply for the order of knighthood; conferring monopoly privileges (called patents), such as those given to manufacturers of playing cards and dice; fining Roman Catholics who did not attend Anglican services; and increasing the rents obtained from farmers of the Customs. By the time Weston died in 1635 Charles's revenues, yielding about £618,000 a year, almost met his expenditure, while his debts amounted to about £1,163,000, much of which were obligations that would never be repaid and 'worried no one but the unfortunate creditors'.[17] At the same time Weston managed to reduce expenditure, notably by cutting down the royal pension list.

It has often been taken for granted that the two ministers who exercised most influence on Charles and contributed to his unpopularity before 1640 were Thomas Wentworth, his Lord Deputy in Ireland, and William Laud, his Archbishop of Canterbury. But in fact Charles was rather nervous in his dealings with these two strong-minded men. Weston, on the other hand, whom he created Earl of Portland in February 1633, earned the King's confidence more than any other man except the Duke of Buckingham. When Laud, who disliked Portland intensely, accused him of being corrupt, Charles showed complete trust in him and it was not until Portland died that Wentworth was able to speculate with cash due to the Treasury from Ireland, to his own profit. Ben Jonson called Portland 'that Mine of Wisdom' and

> That waking man! that Eye of State!
> Who seldom sleeps! Whom bad men only hate!

When Portland, who suffered throughout his Treasurership from bad health, died, Charles refused Archbishop Laud's pressure to appoint Wentworth in his place and consoled Laud by making him head of a Treasury Commission, a post for which he was unsuited. Later Charles chose William Juxon, the Bishop of London, to be his Lord Treasurer, the last ecclesiastic to occupy a high ministerial post in England. Charles's preferences were at least of honest men, who did not accept office simply as a means of feathering their own nests.

Neither Portland nor his successors at the Treasury had much to do with the revival of the tax – or, more exactly, rate – known as ship money (it had been imposed by royal prerogative in the reign of Queen Elizabeth I), which is attributed to Charles's Attorney General, William Noy. Charles was an enthusiast for the navy. Its strengthening was called for by the many seizures of English merchant ships by pirates and privateers and by the need for the protection of fishermen. The rate was first levied on port towns and maritime counties, which had the option of either providing ships or money to pay for them. In 1635 ship money was extended to the whole country on the ground that everyone was concerned with the defence of the realm. Charles, however, insisted that the poor should not be assessed for the tax and it was largely a land tax. The money collected was paid directly to the Treasurer of the Navy and, to begin with, met most of the cost of the equipment and maintenance of the fleet. Thus until Charles embarked on the war against the Scottish Covenanters he was financially secure. Commerce and industry were flourishing and the Customs revenue increased. Sir Philip Warwick thought that 'no nation in the world enjoyed more peace and prosperity'. The Earl of Clarendon wrote that 'the like peace and plenty and universal tranquillity for ten years was never enjoyed by any nation'. An American historian has written: 'Few kings who sat on England's throne and few ministers who have counselled them appear to have been more genuinely desirous of the subjects' good than were Charles I and his principal counsellors.'[18]

Oliver Cromwell's period of personal rule, so far as domestic questions were concerned, was chiefly confined to the nine months that preceded the calling of his first Protectorate parliament. After that the Lord Protector was immersed in foreign affairs and constitutional disputes. By the terms of the Instrument of Government (1653) the Protector 'with the consent of the major part of the Council of State' was entitled 'to make laws and ordinances for the peace and welfare of England, Scotland and Ireland where it shall be necessary, which shall be binding in force until order shall be taken in parliament for the same'. This clause seems to have been slipped in as an afterthought, yet in fact eighty-two ordinances were promulgated during these months. The opinions of historians and biographers about them are extremely mixed. Lord Morley described them as 'a meagre show of legislative fertility'. John Buchan dismissed them as mostly 'police measures and minor matters of administrative reform', revealing 'a slow mind struggling towards that clarity which a legislative act demands'. Later historians, on the other hand, have spoken of 'the great series of reforming ordinances passed from January to December 1654' and have averred that Oliver 'aimed to rally men of experience behind a programme of measured reform'.[19]

It is generally agreed that Oliver was not a committed revolutionary. He hesitated to assume the chief executive power, and after dismissing the Rump Parliament he preferred to summon an Assembly of Saints, virtuous men nominated by the Army, both to govern and frame legislation. These Saints had, in his opinion, driven forward too fast and furiously, abolishing the Court of Chancery and voting in favour of a Bill abolishing lay patronage in the Church without providing necessary alternatives. The Protectorate government did in fact retain some of the measures passed by this assembly – notably the introduction of civil marriages and an act for the relief of creditors and poor prisoners (though substantially amended) – but at the same time it sought, as Oliver declared in his opening speech to his first parliament, to 'heal' and 'settle' the nation after the disruption of the civil wars. His aim, he stressed, was that 'the Ship of the Commonwealth' should be 'brought into a safe harbour'. But he insisted that it was his government's desire to reform the laws and reduce taxation, which may or may not be interpreted as a conservative policy.[20]

The ordinances passed before Parliament met, all of which were considered and approved by Oliver, dealt with financial matters, security, religion and poverty. The rather chaotic financial system that had functioned during the civil wars, which involved a number of committees, was brought to an end and the Exchequer course re-established, though the assessments, which paid for Cromwell's army, did not go through it. Only one measure concerned law reform: that was an ordinance passed by the Council of State in August 1654 'for the better regulation and limiting the jurisdiction of the High Court of Chancery and to the end that all proceedings touching relief in equity may be with less trouble, expense and delay than heretofore'. This ordinance comprised many valuable reforms, but it was not to the taste of lawyers, who had been obstructive and unhelpful while it was being prepared and discussed. In fact the Master of the Rolls and two out of three of the Commissioners of the Great Seal, who would have been responsible for putting the ordinance into effect, resigned in protest. Oliver accepted their resignations and compensated them liberally with other offices.[21] But it was frustrating for him; the new commissioners failed to make the ordinance work and he allowed it to lapse in 1657. Equally, when Oliver asked his second parliament to reform the criminal law by limiting capital offences to murder, treason and rebellion he obtained no response.

The judges, who were appointed by the Protector, were all first-rate men – 'just men', as he called them, 'men of the most integrity and ability'. His Secretary of State noted in the spring of 1654 that 'His Highness is very much resolved upon a good and solid reformation of the law ... and was also resolved to give the learned of the robe the honour of reforming their own profession'.[22] Yet Oliver's urgent pleas for law reform were never answered. This revealed the limitations of dictatorship, if a dictator was what he was.

It has, however, to be admitted that the 'just men' whom Oliver appointed or approved came to question the validity of the ordinances promulgated by him and his Council of State. When George Cony, a London merchant, refused to pay Customs duties or a fine levied on him by the Council for his default, he applied for a writ of *habeas corpus* and his barristers argued that the Instrument of Government was not part of the law of the land. The Lord Chief Justice, Henry Rolle, listened to their reasoning with favour. When the barristers were summoned before the

Protector and the Council of State, who ordered them to be put in prison for seditious and subversive behaviour, Rolle resigned his office. Two other judges, who questioned the validity of an ordinance of treason passed by the Council in 1654, were dismissed, according to Bulstrode Whitelocke, for 'not observing the Protector's pleasure in all his commands'.

Charles I had less difficulty with his judges. It was recognized that they only held office during the royal pleasure. Sir Edward Coke, who had stood up for the independence of the judiciary, had been dismissed as Lord Chief Justice (first of Common Pleas and secondly of King's Bench) by Charles's father. His successor was warned to take notice of Coke's fate. Nevertheless the Lord Chief Justice of the King's Bench at the outset of Charles's reign was dismissed for questioning the legality of forced loans collected by the Crown. One of the judges during the case brought against John Hampden for refusing to pay his ship money declared that the King was the law, 'a living, speaking and acting law'. Charles's proclamations, like Oliver's ordinances, were claimed to have full legal authority, though that was questioned. So it can be maintained that both for Charles and Oliver judges were still regarded as lions under the throne.

To return to the character of Charles's ministers during his period of personal power, admirers of the Stuart monarch have often blamed his downfall on Laud and Wentworth. In fact, far from being responsible for Charles's domestic (or foreign) policy, Laud and Wentworth, who became close friends, were highly critical of it. They described Portland as Lady Mora (delay) and the Chancellor of the Exchequer, Francis Cottington, as 'Lady Mora's chief waiting woman'.[23] Laud resented the fact that his friend was not called back from Ireland to become Lord Treasurer, which was, after all, the most important ministerial post. He blamed Cottington and Charles's Secretary of State, Sir John Coke, for intriguing against Wentworth. Laud wrote to Wentworth at the end of 1637 of 'the cancerous malady which possesseth the vulgar at this present, but certainly not the vulgar only' and thought it would be to the mutual advantage of them both were they ' "thorough" in the carriage of any business'.[24]

Undoubtedly the amount of intrigue that prevailed at Charles's

Court vitiated his domestic policy. Cottington was an able and experienced man, who looked the obvious choice as Treasurer. The Queen gave him her backing, but Laud was determined to prevent his appointment if he could and succeeded in his aim. At the critical time when the Treasury Commission was being dissolved Cottington was obliged to absent himself from Court because of an attack of gout. Laud then secured the King's ear; and as Charles tended to take the advice of the last person who spoke to him, Cottington lost the appointment.

It has often been said that there are no friends at the top. Oliver Cromwell, it has been claimed, had no friends, only agents. This is even truer of Charles, for his only confidants were the Duke of Buckingham and Queen Henriette Marie. Certainly he was on close terms with neither Laud nor Wentworth. One man with whom Charles might have been expected to be friendly was Thomas Howard second Earl of Arundel.[25] Arundel had been appointed Earl Marshal by Charles's father, and as a connoisseur and collector of paintings and sculptures was as knowledgeable as Charles himself. But, as has been seen, because of a minor delinquency Arundel was banned from the Court and Privy Council and thrust into the Tower of London. Two years later a reconciliation was arranged; when the first war against the Scottish Covenanters began Charles made him his commander-in-chief, a post for which he had no qualifications whatever. Charles's treatment of the first Earl of Bristol and the third Earl of Essex proved equally disadvantageous to him. In fact the King's lack of warmth and generosity and general aloofness meant that he had practically no friends during his period of personal rule.

As to Cromwell, his principal minister during his Protectorate was John Thurloe, who became his Secretary of State. It is absurd to describe him, as some have done, as Oliver's 'intimate friend', but he trusted him absolutely, much as Charles had trusted Richard Weston. Thurloe was certainly more honest than Weston, who made at least £14,000 a year out of his office. Thurloe's salary was a mere £800 a year and he had few perquisites, nor has any serious evidence been found to prove that he accepted bribes – not even a pearl for his wife.[26] When, because he was responsible for the Protector's intelligence service, Thurloe was put in charge of the Post Office, paying a quarterly rent for it, he felt able to boast that he had 'improved that office £4,000 per annum to the State voluntarily', which 'he might have put into his own purse'.[27] Unquestionably Thurloe was devoted to Oliver and admired him as 'a great man'.

One reason why men in positions of authority have difficulty in making and keeping friends is that they are obliged at times to rebuke them publicly. One of Oliver's closest friends and counsellors was Henry Ireton, who married his eldest daughter. So influential was Ireton with his father-in-law that it was said that 'Cromwell only shot the bolts that were hammered in Ireton's forge'. Yet when during the siege of Oxford Charles sent a message to Ireton proposing a general settlement and Ireton passed on the message to Oliver as his superior officer Cromwell publicly rebuked him in the House of Commons for writing to him about the matter instead of reporting it directly to Parliament. Similarly, when Prince Rupert surrendered Bristol in 1645 Charles condemned him 'who was so near to me as you are, both in blood and friendship' for 'so mean an action' and dismissed and publicly disgraced him. Just as Charles dismissed Rupert, Cromwell as Protector dismissed John Lambert, who was not only in effect the second-in-command of his army, but had replaced Ireton (who died in 1651) as his political mentor. No wonder Charles and Oliver had few friends.

The character and activities of the civil servants – to use an anachronism – or state servants under Charles and Oliver have been exhaustively analysed.[28] A major question that has been discussed is how far they were honest. During Charles's reign it is difficult to draw a line between what were legitimate payments earned by officials and what were forms of corruption. Fees paid by the Crown were generally small – clerks of the Privy Seal, for example, were paid £5 a year – and were supplemented by pensions or annuities or diet money (one thinks of modern luncheon vouchers) or free board, and officials were permitted to accept gratuities or presents for services rendered. The system of payment was so complicated that few people, including the King, could have understood it. Indeed one courtier said to another that the King was far too busy to look after their needs and therefore they themselves must look after them. Offices were bought and sold in the hope of finding profitable by-lines. Though some high-ranking officials were honest enough and hard-working, most were not: for example, the Cofferers of the Royal Household swindled the Crown of £10,000 a year by a simple and blatant accounting device.[29]

During the Cromwellian Protectorate reforms in the administrative system and higher salaries granted to state servants plainly increased probity and stimulated economies. To give two examples: the Wardrobe – the department of the Court responsible for buying furniture and fittings for the state departments in Whitehall, Hampton Court, Windsor castle and elsewhere – had its staff reduced in size from eighty to forty, while the accounts of the Keeper were closely scrutinized. The other example relates to the office of Master of the Ceremonies. Charles's Master of the Ceremonies, Sir Charles Cotterell, had an Assistant Master and a Marshal to serve under him and obtained an income of £1,000 a year from the office, largely derived from gratuities given him by foreign ambassadors resident in London. Oliver's Master of the Ceremonies, Sir Oliver Fleming, who happened to be one of the Protector's many cousins, was paid a salary of £200 a year, allowed no assistants and was forbidden to accept gratuities. Any expenses in which he was involved when entertaining diplomatists had to be specified before he received payment.[30]

In general it has been argued that 'a new kind of public service was coming into existence in republican England'.[31] Cromwellian officials were no longer drawn from an upper or ruling class but from what has been called a middling class of county and parochial gentry. It might be assumed that such men, being more modestly off, would be anxious to screw the maximum amount out of their offices. As a rule they were paid higher salaries than Charles's officials, but restricted from taking fees and gratuities. On the whole, it is clear that there was little venality or corruption during the Cromwellian Protectorate. Curiously enough, the men who appear to have done best out of their offices were republican stalwarts who were vehemently opposed to Oliver as Lord Protector: Sir Henry Vane the Younger, Sir Arthur Haslerigg and Major-General Thomas Harrison. Vane made a fortune out of his position as Treasurer of the Navy; Haslerigg took advantage of his post as Governor of Newcastle upon Tyne to buy up Royalists' land cheaply; Thomas Harrison, who had an odd taste for wearing fine clothes, obtained the lucrative office of Lieutenant of the Ordnance for two years and received compensation when the office was abolished. He could then afford to dress himself in a scarlet coat trimmed with gold and silver lace, though, apart from that, it is fair to say that his heart was not in earthly things.[32]

As to Oliver himself, the sum of £100,000 a year was specifically allotted for the upkeep of his household on the advice of a committee of the Council of State; this sum was again decided upon in August 1657 by Cromwell's Privy Council (appointed under the constitution known as the Petition and Advice) just over a year before the Lord Protector died. It amounted to about 3 per cent of the annual state expenditure. The cost of Charles's household was about 40 per cent.

These specific allocations of funds to pay for the cost of Oliver Cromwell's Court anticipated the Civil List introduced during the reign of King William III. Oliver had no extravagant tastes, as Charles had, except for the provision of dowries for his daughters and jointures for the wives of his sons. These he was able to provide out of the lands settled on him when he was a victorious general during the civil wars, which made him a rich man in his own right.

Charles I had nothing equivalent to a Civil List. Monarchs had always been expected to 'live of their own' except in times of war, when parliaments would vote taxes to meet the cost of raising an army and navy. So out of his income Charles could pay for paintings and sculptures, gifts for his wife and the upkeep of his palaces, as well as the sums needed for day-to-day government.

Nevertheless, it would be an exaggeration to say that in the upkeep of his household Charles was prodigal and Oliver parsimonious. Charles, it is true, seems to have spent annually about £78,000 on his household, chamber and wardrobe. Although Oliver was allowed £100,000 a year for domestic expenditure at the outset of the Protectorate he appears to have managed on £64,000. But when his Court became more monarchical in character in the autumn of 1657 the expenses of his semi-royal household rose to about £76,000 a year.[33] The truth no doubt was that the upkeep of the palaces and the payment of their staffs and other Court officials, together with the entertainment of foreign diplomatists and visitors, cost much the same whoever stood at the head of government. Charles had to rely on all sorts of expedients to pay his way. Oliver had the advantage of new taxes introduced by Parliament during the civil war – the monthly assessments and the excise – as well as Customs revenue, which Charles's parliaments had refused to grant him, and which increased in value during the Protectorate.

To sum up, the differences between Charles I's and Oliver Cromwell's periods of personal rule, so far as domestic affairs were concerned, were marginal. Both were conscientious men who had their subjects' welfare at heart and were sympathetic about the problems of the poor, although neither was able to do much to relieve them. Oliver allowed himself to be too much absorbed in minutiae, but neither of them could spare the time regularly to attend meetings of their Privy Councils. Each of them had able officials at their disposal, although Charles's state servants were more on the make than Oliver's were. Neither of them had more than a few personal friends and counsellors. Charles trusted the first Duke of Buckingham and the Earl of Portland; Oliver relied on Henry Ireton and John Thurloe. The idea of social reform meant little to either of them. Both believed that God had created men unequal. Charles was anxious to stimulate agriculture by the draining of the fens and commerce by strengthening the navy. Oliver hankered after the reform of the law, both civil and criminal; in particular he wanted the relief of poor debtors. But virtually nothing was achieved because of the obstruction of interested parties. Though both men lived in revolutionary times the only revolution that they saw was the birth of religious nonconformity, which was to colour British history for another three centuries.

8

DIPLOMACY AND WAR – I

At the outset of the seventeenth century the Spanish empire was one of the largest the world has ever known. In Europe it included Spain and Portugal, the Netherlands (modern Belgium and Holland), much of Italy – Sicily, Sardinia, Naples, Tuscany and Milan – and Artois and Franche-Comté, lying on the route from Spanish Italy to the Spanish Netherlands. In South America it comprised Mexico, Peru and Brazil; in Central America Cuba and most of the West Indies; in North America California; in Africa Oran, Ceuta, Tangier, Mozambique, Guinea and the Canary Islands; and in Asia, Ceylon and the Philippines. To pay for a big army and navy treasure ships brought gold and silver to Spain from the mines in Central and South America, which amounted during the last ten years of the sixteenth century to nearly 3 billion grams of silver and 19 million of gold.[1]

A great deal has been written both then and now about the decline of Spain.[2] The reasons assigned for it are numerous: financially, it was caused by the falling off of the silver supplies from America, the profligate minting of copper coins and the reduced yield of taxation in Castile. The population of Castile and Andalusia was reduced by a series of plagues: these meant a scarcity of labour, a rise in the price of food and a decrease in the output of wool, the basis of the Castilian economy. Politically, the destruction of the Spanish Armada in 1588, the revolt of the Dutch Netherlands (which had forced the Spanish government to agree to a truce in 1609), and unrest provoked by taxation demands in Catalonia and Portugal all weakened the global monarchy. Furthermore, with the opening of commerce across the Atlantic the trade of the Mediterranean was severely damaged. Thus the decline of the Spanish empire can be attributed to falling revenues, diminishing population, and defeats on land and sea.

All this has been recognized by experts on the history of Spain and no doubt contemporary Spanish ministers realized what was happening. Indeed one Spanish diplomatist argued that while the kingdom was at peace after the truce with the Dutch it had sunk into poverty and torpor and that it might be wiser to renew the war with the Dutch – and with England also – to ensure the preservation of the monarchy's power and authority.[3] But it is by no means certain that foreign statesmen were conscious of the frailty of Spain. King James I of England was convinced that the whole of Catholic Europe danced to the Spanish tune. And he was persuaded that a marriage alliance between the future Charles I and a Spanish princess would assist his finances by bringing a huge dowry (the sum of 2 million ducats was expected) – after all, the treasure ships loaded with silver were still arriving unmolested from America – and would also ensure the continuance of peace. Oliver Cromwell was to remind the House of Commons that Spain was 'a great and powerful State'.[4]

The advocate of Charles's marriage alliance with Spain was Diego Sarmiento Acunā Count of Gondomar, a wealthy Castilian nobleman who arrived in London as ambassador at the end of 1613. Charles was only thirteen at the time and negotiations proceeded slowly. In fact, while King James was converted by Gondomar to the idea neither King Philip III of Spain nor King Philip IV, who succeeded him in 1621, was enthusiastic about it. To begin with, Prince Charles was, as has been seen, infatuated with the notion of marrying a young and hopefully delightful blonde. It was he, and not the royal favourite, Buckingham, who persuaded James to allow him to go to Madrid in March 1623 to pursue his suit in person.[5] But the difficulties standing in the way of reaching an agreement were formidable. Apart from the fact that Philip IV's sister, the bride-to-be, was agonized at the thought of marrying a heretic, her brother fancied that if he kept Charles hanging around his Court long enough and stimulating his ardour for the marriage, the future King of England would become a Roman Catholic. He was made to listen at length to arguments put forward by the King of Spain's Confessor with the aim of converting him to the faith. Charles was in fact firm in his opposition to Popery. But both in Spain and in England people assumed that the reason why Charles had travelled incognito to Madrid wearing a false beard was because he was about to change his religion and be married at a Mass. What a triumph that would have been for the Counter-Reformation.

If Charles refused to change his religion, as he did, the marriage of a Catholic princess to a Protestant prince required a papal dispensation. So lukewarm was the young Spanish King's desire for such a marriage that he asked the Pope (Gregory XV) not to grant it. But the Pope believed that the marriage would be a valuable step towards converting England back to Roman Catholicism. The conditions that he approved were that the penal laws imposed on English Roman Catholics should be repealed and they should be allowed freedom of worship, that a large Catholic church should be opened in London where anyone might attend the services, and that when the Spanish Queen of England became a mother she should have her children baptized according to Roman rites and be responsible for bringing them up until they reached the age of twelve. The Spanish priests, who were to accompany her to England, were to wear their proper habits in public.

Against the advice of Buckingham Charles decided to accept these terms, which were reluctantly agreed to by Charles's father. The marriage treaty was signed on 25 July. But Charles was now informed that though the marriage might take place, it could not be consummated nor could the Infanta Maria return with her husband to England until sufficient time had elapsed to make sure that the King of England fulfilled his obligations under the treaty. Meanwhile Pope Gregory XV had died so it was necessary to await a dispensation from the new Pope. Charles, who had now been in Spain for nearly six months, was summoned home by his father. So he gave his authority to the Earl of Bristol, the English ambassador in Madrid, for the conclusion of the marriage by proxy when the dispensation arrived from Rome and he consented to wait until March for his future wife to come to England. But before he sailed Charles changed his mind and sent a message to Bristol cancelling the proxy. The reason why he did so is by no means certain. It may well have been because he was conscious of having failed in another duty he had taken upon himself when he first went to Spain.[6] That duty was to secure help for his only sister, Elizabeth, Queen of Bohemia, as she called herself, whose husband Frederick had managed to lose two thrones.

Frederick had been the Elector or ruler both of the Lower Palatinate on the Rhine, where Heidelberg was his capital, and of the Upper Palatinate west of Bohemia and was also head of the Evangelical Union, which included not only all the Protestant princes in Germany but also the kings of England and Denmark. When the Bohemians, the majority of whom were Protestants, invited Frederick in 1618 to become their king in place of Ferdinand Archduke of Styria, who was about to become Holy Roman Emperor and therefore the acknowledged overlord of Austria and Germany, Frederick had hesitated to accept the invitation, but eventually decided that it was the will of God that he should do so. It does not appear to be true that Elizabeth had told her husband that she 'would sooner eat sauerkraut at a king's table than feast on delicacies with an Elector', but she certainly agreed with her husband's decision to accept the throne of Bohemia and had tried to persuade her loving father to lend them active support.[7] But James I was always pacific; nor would the other German Protestant rulers give the Elector Palatine any assistance. So Frederick's determination to go to Prague, where he and his wife were crowned, proved disastrous.

The Emperor Ferdinand II, who had no army of his own, invited the aid of his kinsman in Spain and of the Duke of Bavaria, the most powerful and ambitious of the German Roman Catholic princes, in order to reassert his claim to rule over Bohemia. While a Spanish army marched from the Netherlands to occupy most of the Lower Palatinate Maximilian of Bavaria's forces moved into Bohemia. Charles's brother-in-law had few allies. France, the erstwhile enemy of Spain, would do no more than arrange for an amnesty between the Protestant Union and the Catholic League and James I would only allow a force of 2,000 volunteers to move into Heidelberg and two other fortresses. The Bohemian army consisted chiefly of untrained volunteers, and a contingent coming from Hungary to help it was useless and unpopular. Military defeat came quickly. The result was that Frederick and his English wife not only lost the crown of Bohemia but both the Lower and Upper Palatinates as well.

Their plight aroused consternation in Protestant England. Therefore, both Charles and his father came to hope that once an alliance with Spain was concluded Philip IV would insist that the Emperor Ferdinand II should restore the Elector Palatine to his hereditary title and possessions. While he was in Spain Charles had promised his sister that he would not consent to the marriage until he had first obtained satisfaction for her. However, Philip IV, who was only interested in the marriage if it contributed to the welfare of English Roman Catholics by gaining for them complete liberty of conscience, made it clear to Charles that he would not even discuss the restoration of his brother-in-law to his hereditary lands until after the marriage arrangements were completed.

It is not at all plain why Charles should have imagined that the Catholic King of Spain would interfere in the affairs of Germany in order to help a Protestant prince contrary to the wishes of his Habsburg kinsman in Vienna. When Charles raised the question with Count Olivares, Philip IV's chief minister, after James I had agreed to the conditions stipulated for the marriage, Olivares told him that the Spaniards would never ask the Emperor to reverse his policies and would never take up arms against another member of the Habsburg dynasty. In the end Charles had in fact committed himself to the marriage treaty without receiving any undertaking about the reinstatement of his brother-in-law to the Palatinate Electorate. Thus it seems likely that the reason why Charles instructed Bristol not to use his proxy was that it would gain time for him to consider what could be done to cheer his sister and her husband before the marriage negotiations were completed. Indeed, Parliament was assured that the King of England 'liked not to marry his only son with a portion of his only daughter's tears'.[8]

So Charles's misadventures during his six months in Spain shaped his future foreign policy. It had drawn him closer to Buckingham (whom James I had created a duke while he was

there), and Buckingham, who had quarrelled with Count Olivares while he was in Madrid, became violently anti-Spanish.

After he returned home Charles insisted even more firmly that
he would not honour the marriage treaty by allowing Bristol to
make use of his proxy until he received satisfactory guarantees
that the King of Spain would either by mediation or by force of
arms obtain the restoration of his brother-in-law to his thrones in
the Palatinate. The French ambassador in England noted his
extreme bitterness towards Spain.[9] For his part the Duke of
Buckingham had long given up any hope of goodwill from Spain;
he therefore devoted his energies to trying to construct an anti-
Habsburg coalition in alliance with the Dutch (who had been at
war with the Spaniards again since 1621) and if possible with the
French, who had been fighting against Spanish troops in Italy,
and he carried Charles along with him. Charles's father, who had
always prided himself on being a peace-maker, did not want to be
pushed into war in his old age, but was frequently ill and seldom
in London. He was persuaded into calling a parliament which
petitioned him to end the existing treaties with Spain and promised him assistance if war broke out in consequence. So he
reluctantly allowed Charles and Buckingham to carry on a militant diplomacy.

While Charles was engaged in pursuing an anti-Spanish foreign policy King James was induced to agree to a direct military
effort to regain the Palatinate for his daughter and son-in-law.
The arrangements he accepted were extraordinary. A mercenary
general named Count Ernst von Mansfeld, whose sole aim in life
was to employ any unscrupulous means of providing himself with
comforts in his old age, arrived in London during April 1624,
was put up in St James's palace, and made much of by Prince
Charles. He was promised money and allowed to recruit an army
of 12,000 men with whom it was intended that he should march
across Europe and overthrow the Spaniards who were in occupation of the Lower Palatinate. He was prohibited from enlisting
men who had some slight experience of soldiering in the trained
bands or county militia. The result was that the troops he
gathered together in Dover were the dregs of society; they terri-
fied the inhabitants of Kent, and before the embarkation took

place there many of them deserted. The French King, having promised to provide Mansfeld with some cavalry and to contribute to the cost of the expedition, refused to let this rabble land in France so instead they were shipped to Holland, sailing at – of all times – the end of January, and then went into winter quarters where many of them were half-starved or killed by plague. By the time the campaigning season opened in 1625 Mansfeld's army had largely melted away.

Thus the grandiose scheme for an anti-Habsburg alliance into which Charles had been pitchforked by Buckingham got off to a bad start. However, the Dutch, having long been fighting for their independence against Spain, were obvious allies and if Charles could effect a marriage treaty with France, the French monarchy, which resented being hemmed in by Spanish possessions in the Netherlands, Italy and Germany as well as by the Pyrenees, might also become valuable confederates.

The marriage treaty was concluded fairly easily. Charles was assured that Henriette Marie, the youngest legitimate daughter of King Henri IV, was 'the sweetest creature in France' and the princess, who was only fifteen, liked the look of Charles in a miniature she saw.[10] Cardinal Richelieu, the chief minister of Henriette Marie's brother, King Louis XIII, demanded that Charles and his father should guarantee in a separate and secret agreement (*écrit particulier*) that the lot of English Roman Catholics would be improved: this they eventually accepted. In May 1625 a proxy marriage was held outside Notre-Dame cathedral in Paris. But Charles's father had already been warned that the marriage could not be made dependent upon an agreement for the recovery of the Palatinate. When Buckingham arrived in Paris to bring over Henriette Marie and had conversations with Richelieu the Cardinal made it absolutely plain that he would not consent to any kind of political treaty, let alone the offensive and defensive alliance to which Buckingham aspired.[11]

Meanwhile, James I had died (on 27 March) and Charles was proclaimed King. Buckingham, who had in effect been James's leading minister, but had built up a close friendship with Charles while they were in Spain, was confirmed in all his offices and was appointed to a committee of the Privy Council established to advise the new King on foreign policy. Thus foreign policy remained unchanged except that James's extreme caution in diplomacy vanished. Charles hastened to assure his sister, as she herself observed, 'that he will be both father and brother to the King of Bohemia and me'. 'Now,' she thought, 'all will go well in England.'[12]

The preparation of a grand alliance against the two Habsburg powers centred on Madrid and Vienna and was an enormously expensive process. Charles assumed that a parliament which he summoned to meet soon after his accession to the throne would vote him generous subsidies. But when he opened Parliament in June 1625 he announced that it did not 'stand with his nature to spend too much time on words' and told the members nothing about the commitments involved in Buckingham's grand strategy. The House of Commons was more concerned about religious questions than military matters. One member observed: 'We know yet of no war nor of any enemy.' Because the plague was raging in London the King ordered the members to assemble for a second session at Oxford during August, harvest-time, which annoyed them considerably. When they were informed that £600,000 was needed for wars and an army another member asked who the enemy was against whom these preparations were being undertaken. He received no answer.[13]

By a variety of means, which included drawing on his French wife's dowry and pawning the Crown jewels in Holland, Charles raised the money needed for sending a fleet of nearly a hundred ships carrying 10,000 soldiers to begin an undeclared war on Spain. A treaty concluded at Southampton provided that twenty Dutch warships would join this fleet and another treaty, which Buckingham arranged at The Hague with the Dutch and the King of Denmark, was aimed at an offensive alliance against the Habsburgs by land and sea. Under the command of Sir Edward Cecil the Anglo-Dutch fleet set sail at the ridiculously late date of the first week in October. The expedition was almost as big a fiasco as Mansfeld's campaign in Germany. The naval force failed to intercept a Spanish treasure fleet, it abandoned an assault on Cadiz, and it lost hundreds of men through sickness and starvation, rightly blamed on corrupt victuallers. A year later a smaller fleet under a different commander was ordered by Buckingham as Lord High Admiral to pursue the same objectives – intercepting Spanish treasure ships arriving from America and destroying warships anchored at Cadiz. It never reached Cadiz, having been shattered by storms in the Bay of Biscay from whence it limped home.

Charles's foreign policy was largely motivated by his earnest desire to ensure that his only sister and her husband should be restored to their Palatinate realm. When he visited Cecil's fleet at Plymouth in September 1625 he said 'by the grace of God I will carry on war if I risk my Crown ... my brother-in-law shall be restored'.[14] His idea was to exert so much pressure on King Philip IV that he would be compelled to take action over the Palatinate. Buckingham's instructions as Lord High Admiral stated that the fleet had been fitted out to enforce the King's mediation for the Palatinate. But it was by no means clear to the Germans, including Count Mansfeld and Prince Frederick himself, that an attack on Cadiz was likely to be of much help on the Rhine; the 10,000 soldiers shipped in Cecil's fleet would, it seemed to them, have been much more useful in Germany.

The war against Spain, which Charles and Buckingham had initiated, far from enabling them to enlist France as an ally, actually contributed to a war against France as well, even though Charles's young wife was the sister of the French King. The causes of this war were numerous: English warships had been seizing French merchant vessels on the grounds that they were carrying contraband to Spain, and the French retaliated towards the end of 1626 by impounding the entire English merchant fleet of 200 vessels which were employed in carrying wine from Bordeaux. Increasingly angered by the provocative behaviour of his wife's numerous French servants and Roman Catholic priests, Charles had ordered their expulsion in defiance of the terms of the marriage treaty and when a special ambassador was sent to London to deal with this matter the compromise he worked out was repudiated in Paris. Much more important than this personal squabble was the decision taken by Richelieu to build up a large navy, which might endanger English maritime supremacy in the Channel, so threatening the prosperity of English commerce.

Richelieu's reason for refusing to join the anti-Habsburg coalition which Buckingham was trying to construct at this time was because he first wanted to consolidate his own position within France itself. He told Buckingham that 'so long as the Huguenots [the French Protestants] in France are in a state within a state the King cannot be master in his own realm or achieve great things outside it'.[15] There were more than a million Huguenots, some of whom were convinced that they must fight to secure guarantees of their rights amid a Catholic majority. The King and his chief minister were determined that they must be subdued. So hostilities between France and Spain (which had been fighting each other in northern Italy) were brought to an end and in April 1627 Louis XIII and Philip IV ratified a treaty, concluded in secret but soon becoming known, providing for an offensive alliance against England. Charles's reply to this, following the advice of Buckingham, was to assist the French Huguenots, who, centred on the walled and fortified town of La Rochelle, which lay at the head of an inlet in the Bay of Biscay, were in open rebellion against the French King. Charles's hope was that if the Huguenots could hold out against Richelieu and if the French nobles, who were disgruntled at Richelieu's rise to power, conspired successfully against him, the Cardinal would be overthrown, Louis XIII induced to abandon his alliance with Spain and France persuaded to make war on the Habsburgs.

The war against France was directed by the Lord High Admiral himself, who set sail for La Rochelle at the end of June 1627 with a fleet consisting of five squadrons carrying 10,000 soldiers; he was accompanied by the Count of Soubise, the most militant of the French Huguenots. After seeing off the expedition Charles returned to London where he concentrated on obtaining funds to pay the seamen and on collecting reinforcements which were to be sent out to Buckingham when he needed them. Buckingham's orders had been to hand over his soldiers to the Huguenots in La Rochelle, then to sail south to free the English wine fleet and after that raid the Spanish coasts. But the men of La Rochelle did not immediately welcome their saviours. Thereupon Buckingham resolved to capture the isle of Ré, lying west of La Rochelle, which could be used as a base for English warships and a place where reinforcements could be landed if, as Soubise assured him they would, the Rochellois changed their minds and agreed to defy Richelieu.

Although Buckingham succeeded in effecting an unopposed landing on the isle of Ré, he was unable to conquer the island. The French garrison retreated to the town of St Martin, where it occupied the citadel, which was built on rocky ground. The Duke then decided it could not be assaulted, but would have to be starved out. To make sure of his mastery of the island he asked for a reinforcement of 4,000 men to replace his sick and wounded. Charles did his best to comply, but could only produce 400 recruits. Buckingham had to borrow some of his wife's house-keeping money to carry on. In the first week of September, seven weeks after the original landing, 2,000 troops arrived from Ireland. However, the embattled French garrison received supplies and ammunition from small boats that penetrated the English blockading ships. Finally, Buckingham vainly tried to storm the citadel. His losses were considerable. Had he received all the reinforcements and help that he asked for he might have achieved his aims, for the inhabitants of La Rochelle did change their minds, committing themselves to supporting the English and defying Richelieu. But the Duke obtained no further assistance from home.

As has been pointed out, 'there could be no doubt about the genuineness of Charles's intentions, but good will was no substitute for good administration'.[16] He was obliged to tell Buckingham that he 'was much grieved and ashamed that I must make an apology for our slowness here in giving you supplies'. Louis XIII was more efficient. Shiploads of provisions and ammunition were poured into the citadel of St Martin. By the end of October a French relieving army reached the isle of Ré. Buckingham had to abandon it with severe losses. He got back to Plymouth in November just as the reinforcements he had needed arrived there. Later, in reply to a parliamentary remonstrance criticizing the Duke's failure, Charles said: 'And for the isle of Ré, he knew too well it was our own fault at home in not sending timely supplies not his, who in the view of Christendom, did service full of honour there.'

In the spring of 1628 Buckingham's brother-in-law the Earl of Denbigh sailed with three squadrons, mostly manned by mutinous crews with inadequate supplies, to La Rochelle, which was now under blockade by the French royal forces. This expedition failed to give any relief to the Huguenots. The French were building an elaborate dyke or palisade, which was strengthened by a line of sunken ships to protect La Rochelle from an attack by sea, while Louis XIII himself was preparing to assault the town by land once lines of circumvallation had been completed. Moreover, the Spaniards were lending support to the French. They sent warships to La Rochelle, though they arrived too late to be of much help, and earlier their ablest general, Ambrogio Spinola, had arrived there to offer his advice about the blockade. It did not take Denbigh more than eight days to resolve on withdrawal. He came, he saw and he went. The beleaguered men of La Rochelle, left with no wine and little bread, offered to treat for peace, even though in June they received a letter from Charles promising that he would send yet another fleet in a few days to rescue them. But Charles was never reluctant to make a promise, even if he was unable to fulfil it.

On 22 August 1628 Buckingham was assassinated, to his King's deep lamentation. Charles tried to continue the effort to relieve La Rochelle by sending the second Earl of Lindsey, who had been vice-admiral to Denbigh, with a fleet of fireships, but like Denbigh he was baffled by the defences and was also repulsed by French warships and fire from the shore batteries. As they received none of the provisions they were promised, the Huguenots, on the verge of starvation, surrendered. Louis XIII was greeted at the gates of the conquered city by a triumphant Cardinal Richelieu on All Saints Day. The inhabitants were mercifully treated; the Cardinal sent assurances to Charles I that the Huguenots elsewhere would not suffer, provided they did not abuse the royal favour. The siege, which had lasted fourteen months, was a personal victory for Richelieu and a humiliation for Charles.

The Abbé Alessandro Scaglia, an extremely competent diplomatist and peripatetic ambassador for the Duke of Savoy, expressed the opinion when he visited England in 1626 that Charles and Buckingham 'needed someone of greater experience to guide them in foreign affairs, for no one here has any real acquaintance with them'.[17] Charles was obsessed with the desire to see his sister and her husband restored to their possessions in the Palatinate, an almost purely personal ambition. First he had hoped to realize this by an alliance with Spain, but as Rubens, the great Flemish painter and Spanish envoy, explained to his fellow painter, Balthazar Gerbier, who was in Charles's confidence and employment, 'it is most necessary that the English should disabuse themselves of the belief that the King of Spain can settle German affairs absolutely as he pleases'.[18] In fact, the Emperor Ferdinand's army was commanded by the Duke of Bavaria, the very man who had been promised the Electorate previously held by Charles's brother-in-law and whose troops occupied the Upper Palatinate. Rubens told the King himself that 'he must understand once and for all that England was entirely mistaken in supposing that Spain would in any circumstances whatsoever make war on the Emperor, Bavaria or any other Power for the sake of recovering the Palatinate'.[19] It was equally absurd for Charles to assume that if Cardinal Richelieu were overthrown in France because an English fleet had managed to relieve the Huguenots in La Rochelle, Louis XIII, the Most Christian King, would then openly wage war on the Holy Roman Empire in the interests of a German Protestant prince.

It has been argued that Buckingham's scheme for an anti-Habsburg alliance was realistic, but all that Charles succeeded in doing was to drive France and Spain into each other's arms and indeed induce them to discuss plans to invade England or Ireland. England had a population of only about one-sixth of these two nations and no standing army; only command of the sea prevented invasion. After the vast expenditure involved in building, manning and provisioning fleets to fight against Spain and France, and after suffering fiascos in Cadiz and then at La Rochelle Charles had no alternative but to make peace as best he could. A treaty with France was concluded at Susa in April 1629 and with Spain at Madrid in November 1630. Both merely amounted to the restoration of the status quo.

In Germany the balance of power between Catholics and

Protestants shifted with the defeat of the Elector Frederick in Bohemia and the occupation of the Palatinates by Spanish and Bavarian troops. The Emperor Ferdinand II aimed both at a Counter-Reformation and the creation of an Austrian empire. This provoked determined Protestant resistance. First the King of Denmark and then the King of Sweden, Gustavus Adolphus, invaded Germany. But the King of Denmark was defeated, obliging him to withdraw from the contest, while the King of Sweden was killed after two tremendous victories over the Imperial forces. Three days after his death the exiled Elector Frederick, whose hopes had been rekindled by the Swedish triumphs, himself died of plague, leaving his widow, Charles I's sister, petrified with grief. He invited her back to England but she refused to come and bombarded him with pleas for help for her son, Charles Lewis, the disinherited Elector Palatine.

At length Charles came to recognize that he had not the means to give his nephew military aid, but welcomed him and his brother, Prince Rupert, when they visited London in 1636. Charles's purpose now became one of regaining the Palatinate for his nephew by diplomacy or, as Archbishop Laud wrote to the Queen of Bohemia, 'recognized it was better to recover it by treaty than by arms'.[20] But, as Laud confided to his friend, Viscount Strafford, 'For my own judgment, if you will have me speak out, I much fear the regaining of the Palatinate any way. I see no likelihood but force, and I cannot see force enough.'[21] Charles Lewis had to wait until 1648, when his uncle was an impotent prisoner in the Isle of Wight, to secure the restoration of the principality lost by the rashness of his father.

The abject failure of Charles I's foreign policy and foreign wars can be contrasted with the prestige won when Oliver Cromwell was Lord Protector.

9

DIPLOMACY AND WAR – II

Clausewitz said that war is diplomacy carried on by different means. But to be effective in diplomacy, at least in the past, nations needed to be prepared for war. When Oliver Cromwell became Lord Protector he had an experienced army of over 50,000 men and a navy of 160 warships. Thus he was able to negotiate from strength. Three aims, it has been pointed out, directed his foreign policy: religious, commercial and preventive – to stop the Stuarts from regaining the throne. Because of his victories in Ireland and Scotland, the Commonwealth, which was to embrace them both, had impressed the leaders of other nations, who vied for its alliance. Spain, now unquestionably in decline, had been the first country to recognize the Commonwealth. Even before his parliament met in September 1654 Oliver was planning for war.

Before the Protectorate was established, a war – the first war brought about primarily by naval and economic rivalries – had been in progress against the United Netherlands (or the Dutch Republic, as they had become) which had finally wrested their independence from the Spanish empire in 1648. Against all the odds the Dutch had managed to become the foremost commercial power in Europe, to build up a world-wide carrying trade, and to construct a capitalist system, largely based on the herring fisheries in the North Sea. The Dutch were to some extent antagonized by the passage of a Navigation Act in 1651, which required that henceforward goods imported into England, Ireland or the English colonies should only be carried in English ships or ships of the country from which they came. Cromwell had nothing to do with this Act (he was campaigning against Charles II when it was introduced into the House of Commons) and in any case it does not appear to have seriously damaged the Dutch carrying trade.

What precipitated the war, which broke out in 1652, was the searches made by the English navy of Dutch ships accused of carrying contraband, interference with profitable Dutch privateering and, above all, the demand by the English navy that Dutch ships should dip their flags when sailing in waters around the British Isles. The war started when the distinguished Dutch Admiral van Tromp, after provocatively carrying out exercises not far from Dover castle, refused to strike his flag when ordered to do so by the governor. Admiral Robert Blake, a former Somerset shipowner, who had been rejected as a Fellow of Merton College, Oxford, arrived to see what was happening and a confused battle ensued. Cromwell, sent to Dover to report on the action, blamed the Dutch. By the second week of July the two republics were at war. No satisfactory evidence exists to show how Oliver felt about it, but it is certain that before the war ended he was eager for peace; it proved to be a glorious peace.

A far-reaching plan for the amalgamation – or 'coalition', as it was called – of the two republics, which was adumbrated before the war, was not pursued by Oliver, but he does appear to have hoped for an offensive and defensive alliance. But the Dutch did not want it, for they feared it might endanger their independence. That Oliver was anxious for peace with the Dutch and hankered after joint action in the interests of Protestantism is certain and was proved by his private assurances to Dutch ambassadors that extreme demands put forward for a treaty could be modified. In the end the Dutch agreed to acknowledge English sovereignty of the seas, to pay compensation to English merchants whose trade they had injured, and by a secret agreement the province of Holland promised to exclude from authority members of the House of Orange who were related to the Stuarts and had supported them.

Now Oliver, as Protector, with a victorious navy and a well-trained army at his disposal, was determined to exact 'honour in the eyes of the nations about us'.[1] Only two months after the conclusion of the treaty with the Dutch it was decided at a meeting of the Council of State to dispatch a fleet into the

Mediterranean to assert British prestige by punishing pirates and privateers who attacked British shipping. An undeclared war at sea against France was already in progress so the admiral in command, Robert Blake, was instructed to carry out reprisals as well as protecting commerce. At the same time another fleet under Admiral William Penn was ordered to sail to the West Indies, attack the Spanish garrisons there and also seize French ships. Thus Oliver kept his options open between allying with or making war in earnest on France or Spain. The Secretary of the Council of State, John Thurloe, wrote in May 1654 to Bulstrode Whitelocke, who was on an embassy to Sweden: 'All the question is what is to be done with the two Crowns of France and Spain. They both seek our friendship and alliance.'[2] But although the expedition to attack the Spanish West Indies may have been assumed not necessarily to lead to all-out war with the Spanish empire because they lay 'beyond the line', it is hard to believe that Oliver could ever have been confident about that.

The Protector's instructions to General Robert Venables, who was in command of 25,000 soldiers carried by Penn's squadron, were to take on more men from the English colony of Barbados, then to land in Hispaniola (now divided between Haiti and the Dominican Republic), occupy its capital (San Domingo) and Puerto Rico, capture Havana and Cuba and seize Cartagena (in South America) and the Windward Islands – a tall order if ever there was one.[3] The only island that was not mentioned was Jamaica, which was the only island General Venables captured after he had been repulsed at San Domingo. When it was learnt at the Court of Madrid what had happened the Spanish ambassador in London was ordered to leave immediately.

Even before this Oliver had come to realize that an alliance with Spain was out of the question. He had asked for the right of free navigation to the West Indies and the right of English merchants residing or travelling in Spain to practise their own religion and use the English Bible, free from persecution by the Inquisition; the Spanish ambassador in London had told him this was 'to demand the two eyes of my master'. But Oliver did keep the Spaniards on tenterhooks. Before he dispatched Admiral Blake to the Mediterranean he had written a polite letter to King

Philip IV asking that the fleet should be received hospitably in Spanish ports, and in October, when Blake had anchored outside Cadiz, he had been invited by the governor there to enter the harbour and be entertained.[4]

On the same day that the Spanish ambassador left England a treaty of commerce and friendship was signed with France. As the Lord Protector was to explain to his second parliament, the French were not as subservient to the Pope as the Spanish were and were 'able to give us an explicit answer to anything reasonably demanded of them'. He was also satisfied that the French Protestants were allowed to practise their religion without interference and indeed he hoped they would be grateful to him 'and draw them to a dependence upon him' and thus contribute to his claim to be the chief protector of Protestants throughout the world. But he delayed signing the treaty because he learned of the ill treatment of another Protestant people, the Vaudois, who were in the spring of 1655 being expelled from their communes, which lay adjacent to the eastern frontier of France, and were governed by the Regent of Piedmont, who was the aunt of King Louis XIV. The religion of these people had long been tolerated in their communes, but now they were being brutally expelled from them as rebellious heretics. Oliver intervened on their behalf, dispatching an ambassador both to Paris and to Turin, the capital of Piedmont, and it was made absolutely clear to Cardinal Mazarin, Richelieu's successor as chief French minister, that the Protector would sign no treaty unless the Court of France used its influence to secure the restoration of liberty of conscience to the Vaudois.[5] The French exerted the required pressure. Undoubtedly the Vaudois were rescued from devastation by the Lord Protector's good offices.

Besides the treaty that ended the war with the Dutch, treaties of commerce and amity were concluded with Sweden and Denmark. Although Queen Christina of Sweden, daughter of the Protestant hero Gustavus Adolphus, was about to abdicate and declare herself a Roman Catholic, she was an admirer of Cromwell; however, her ministers did not fancy a political alliance. Denmark, which commanded the passage through the Sound into the Baltic, agreed to allow British merchant ships to cross it on the same terms as the Dutch, who were Denmark's allies. That was important because it was the only way in which trading vessels could reach the Baltic sea and bring back timber, hemp, pitch, tar and other naval stores essential to shipping. Oliver told Parliament in September 1654:

> You have the Sound open which was obstructed. That which was and is the strength of the nation the shipping will now be supplied thence. And whereas you were glad to have anything of that kind at the second hand you now have all manner of commerce and as much freedom as the Dutch themselves there and at the same rate and toll.[6]

A commercial treaty was also concluded with Portugal, which had thrown off the yoke of Spain in 1640. It was completed in 1654 but not ratified until 1656, when Admiral Blake arrived with his fleet at Lisbon and made menacing gestures. The treaty allowed English merchants to trade freely in the Portuguese colonies, which included Brazil, and gave England a monopoly of hiring out ships to the Portuguese if their own did not suffice. It was undoubtedly the most advantageous of the commercial treaties negotiated during the Cromwellian Protectorate. Unlike a treaty with Portugal which Charles I had signed in 1642, it was effectual and paved the way for the establishment of a British colony in Oporto and the development of the port wine trade. However, what pleased Oliver most was that the merchants engaged in business with the Portuguese were promised protection from the attentions of the Inquisition and allowed to practise their religion freely.

The Lord Protector outlined these treaties of commerce in his first speech to his parliament and summed up by saying: 'Peace is ... desirable with all men, as far as it may be had with conscience and honour'.[7] Parliament did not know about the two fleets that were soon to set sail with aggressive purposes. Oliver was deeply disappointed by the failure of Penn and Venables to occupy any Spanish West Indian island except Jamaica. He was taken ill and when the two commanders hurried home in June 1655 he clapped them both into the Tower of London and they were never employed again. In writing to the Governor of Barbados he said: 'Our late design miscarried ... through the disposing hand of

God ... for our sins, yet is not this cause the less His, as I verily believe and therefor we dare not relinquish it.'[8]

The Lord Protector then devoted much of his energies to securing, populating and developing the island of Jamaica. He wrote to Vice-Admiral Goodson, who had remained there, telling him that 'seven more stout men-of-war' were on the way to him and to Major-General Fortescue, in command of the troops there, informing him that reinforcements were being sent from Scotland and Ireland and ordering him to fortify the island and raise a force of 500 cavalry ready to attack the Spaniards if they should attempt to recapture the island. He also tried to send colonists there from Barbados, New England and Ireland. It was a disheartening enterprise. One by one the military commanders in Jamaica died, and Major-General Robert Sedgwick, who replaced Major-General Fortescue, wrote to John Thurloe:

> I must profess I am not able to discover or make out to myself what God intends in this business.... Did you but see the faces of this poor small army with us, how like skeletons they look, it would move you to pity, and when I consider the thousands laid in the dust in such a way as God hath visited, my heart mourns.[9]

But Oliver was utterly determined to retain the island, which was ultimately to become a valuable part of the first British empire. He rebuked commanders for the 'unworthy carriage of some of their officers' who 'are upon all occasions ready to provoke' their men 'to discontent'.[10]

The war which followed between Cromwellian England and Spain was declared, or virtually declared, by both sides in October 1655. Had Oliver accepted the fact that the deliberate assault on the Spanish West Indies was certain to lead to full-scale hostilities against the Spanish empire, a resounding victory might have come earlier. For in August 1655, after Jamaica had been invaded, Admiral Blake, who had been cruising off Cadiz, sighted the Spanish fleet sailing westwards and was in a position to fight it. But Blake and his Council of War decided that they had received no permission from Cromwell to do so unless the fleet was bound for the West Indies; they thought that his Highness the Lord Protector did not wish them 'to be the first breakers of the peace'.[11] So Blake sailed to Lisbon and thence returned home. It was rumoured that Blake would be sent to the Tower of London to join Penn and Venables. But it was clearly Cromwell, not Blake, who had missed a golden opportunity.

Several of Oliver's contemporaries questioned the wisdom of his foreign policy. Major-General John Lambert, who was the chief architect of the Protectorate and a leading member of the Council of State, had criticized the decision to attack the West Indies. One argument for it was that the cost of paying off and demobilizing the sailors who had won the war against the Dutch Republic as well as the expenditure involved in laying up the ships would be no greater than the cost of waging war against Spain. Indeed it might be less if Spanish treasure ships were captured. As Oliver himself put it, 'it was told us that this design would cost little more money than laying up the ships and that with hope of great profit'. Lambert questioned this argument. He pointed out that 'whenever you lay down ships the charge will be increased and must be paid'. Moreover, an army had to be sent on board the ships to fight the Spaniards and men could not be spared from the garrisons in Scotland and Ireland. He asserted that the expedition to the far-off places named in the Protector's instructions to Venables would be fiercely resisted and was unlikely 'to advance the Protestant cause or gain riches for us'.[12]

Lambert may have been influenced by the fact that England had a favourable balance of trade with Spain, as it was one of the principal markets for cloth. Lambert was to observe in the House of Commons that 'the most of my poor fortune depends upon the rate [price] of wool'.[13] Though Lambert was opposed to the war with Spain, he does not seem to have wanted to attack France or renew hostilities against the Dutch. Not being a particularly religious man himself, he did not care for wars on behalf of Protestantism. He regarded trading interests as paramount and thought that their enhancement should be the criterion of foreign policy.

Some members of the 'Barebone's Parliament', which was dissolved before Oliver became Lord Protector, thought that 'the seas should be secured . . . in order to prepare for the coming of Christ' and had therefore been opposed to the conclusion of the war against the Dutch. Sir Henry Vane, who had once been an intimate friend of Oliver, said (after Cromwell's death) that he did not understand how the whole state of managing the peace with Holland and the war with Spain 'hath been agreeable at all to the interest of the State but rather to the interest of a single person'.[14] Thomas Scot, a fanatical republican member of parliament, argued that if Oliver had not been in such a hurry to end the Dutch war and had not insisted on aiming at an alliance with the Dutch 'we never bid fairer for being masters of the whole world'.[15]

The attack on the West Indies by troops landed from Admiral Penn's fleet had taken place in April 1655. Clearly Oliver realized by then, if he had not done so earlier, that this must result in war against the whole Spanish empire, for on 2 May Admiral Blake, who was then at Algiers, received a letter from the Protector dated 2 April instructing him to sail to Cadiz and seize the Spanish treasure fleet which was expected to arrive there from South America. In July Blake, who was now off St Vincent, had another letter from Cromwell ordering him to attack, sink or set on fire any Spanish warships that were being sent to the West Indies.[16] It looks therefore that from the outset, whatever Thurloe and members of the Council of State may have imagined, Oliver himself had resolved to make war on Spain, as Queen Elizabeth I 'of famous memory' had done. But he concealed his intentions from Parliament and it was not until the end of November 1655 that war was officially declared on Spain.

Once again Admiral Blake was dispatched with a large fleet to Cadiz. Blake, being in poor health, was given as a colleague Edward Montagu, the future Earl of Sandwich and patron of Samuel Pepys. Oliver was filled with grandiose ideas including the destruction of the Spanish fleet at anchor in Cadiz harbour, the capture of Cadiz itself or the occupation of Gibraltar ('an advantage to our trade and an annoyance to the Spaniard'),[17] but above all he yearned for the capture of Spanish treasure ships called 'the Plate Fleet', which would help to meet the expenses of war. His hopes appeared to have been realized when Captain Richard Stayner, who had been left with eight warships to blockade Cadiz, intercepted part of the Plate Fleet which had arrived unescorted from Havana. The galleons were carrying chests of silver valued at £200,000 and 2 million pieces of eight (Spanish coins) but much of this was lost under the sea during the battle or was embezzled by the victorious English sailors.

Oliver Cromwell ordered the fleet under Blake and Montagu to remain at sea throughout the winter of 1656–7. The great ships – the first-rates – were sent home, but the Protector arranged that Blake was reinforced with two second-rates (fifty to sixty guns) and four fourth-rates (thirty to forty guns). He also saw to it that the fleet received adequate supplies of food and beer. 'No man living,' wrote one who was there, 'remembered so much goods taken out in so short a time without the least damage to the provisions or ships.'[18] Owing to the treaty with Portugal Blake was able to employ Lisbon as a base where the English sailors were hospitably entertained, especially as the Portuguese captains enjoyed some of the beer. Blake's instructions were, as before, to prevent the Spanish fleet from going to or coming from the West Indies and to intercept the Plate Fleet arriving from South America.

The Spanish navy was being blockaded in Cadiz harbour when in April 1657 Blake received the news that the Plate Fleet was sheltering in Santa Cruz harbour in the island of Tenerife in the Canaries. Santa Cruz was protected by a line of forts connected by breastworks. There were guns on the shore and guns on the galleons, while the breastworks were manned by musketeers. But Blake's frigates outgunned the Spaniards so completely that all the sixteen galleons at anchor were sunk or set on fire. Neither Blake's captains nor the government at home were enthusiastic about the destruction wrought at Santa Cruz since none of the silver carried by the galleons was captured. John Thurloe informed Cromwell's last Parliament: 'Though we received no benefit from it, yet certainly the enemy never had a greater loss.' He added piously: 'It is the Lord's doing and the glory is His.'[19]

Oliver had been anxious to justify the war. In the speech with which he opened the second Protectorate parliament he assured his audience that 'your great enemy is the Spaniard ... he is a natural enemy'. 'His design,' Oliver claimed, was 'the empire of the whole Christian world.' He admitted that the trade which

English merchants did with Spain was 'very considerable' – that was why John Lambert and others had been opposed to the war – but English merchants had been denied liberty of conscience and were not even allowed to keep their Bibles in their pockets. Furthermore, Oliver argued that the King of Spain had committed himself to restoring Charles II to the throne; in return Charles was pledged to support 'the Popish interest' in England. 'Can we think,' the Protector asked, 'that the Papists and Cavaliers shake not hands in England?'[20] But of course the Spanish government had not undertaken to give military aid to the exiled King until the war against them launched by Cromwell had begun. In return for this help Charles II had promised to suspend the penal laws against the Roman Catholics in England if he regained the throne, but that was no more than James I and Charles I had guaranteed in the marriage treaties.

Since France had now been at war with Spain for twelve years it was natural that an offensive alliance between the British Commonwealth and the French monarchy should be arranged. The treaty, signed on 23 March 1657, provided that a force of 6,000 soldiers, backed by a fleet, should help carry on the war in the Spanish Netherlands and in return the towns of Dunkirk and Mardyck, when captured, should be handed over to England. Dunkirk, from which pirates and privateers had long operated against English merchantmen, was also valuable, in Thurloe's words, as 'a bridle to the Dutch and a door into the continent'.[21]

To begin with, the English contingent was not employed on the coast but in the interior. Oliver protested indignantly. He told Sir William Lockhart, his ambassador in France, who later took command of the expeditionary force: 'To talk of giving us garrisons which are inland, as caution for future action; to talk of what will be done next campaign – are but parcels of words for children. If they will give us garrisons, let them give us Calais, Dieppe or Boulogne. . . .'[22] The French capitulated. In March 1658 the treaty of alliance was revised: Cromwell sent over two more regiments, and in May Dunkirk was invested. The Spaniards tried to defend it, but were defeated in the battle of the Dunes, in which the English soldiers, fighting on the left of the line, distinguished themselves. On 14 June, seven weeks before he died,

Oliver learned that Dunkirk had been handed over to Lockhart and received congratulations on the campaign from a cousin of King Louis XIV, whom he sent to London as an ambassador extraordinary.

The war against Spain complicated the relations between the Cromwellian Protectorate and the Dutch republic. After they had made their peace with Spain in 1648 the Dutch had developed an extremely valuable trade with Spain, which brought them the bullion they needed to promote their commerce elsewhere. But Oliver insisted on the right of British warships to search Dutch vessels suspected of carrying Spanish goods, though Dutch merchantmen were released when taken into English ports.

Another possible source of friction with the Dutch was the situation in the Baltic. After a decisive Swedish victory over Denmark in 1645 Sweden and Denmark each controlled one side of the Sound, the gateway into the Baltic sea. Sweden was in the process of becoming a Great Power, both politically and economically. The Dutch therefore allied themselves with Denmark. Oliver at one time hoped that King Charles X of Sweden (who succeeded Queen Christina in 1654) would join in a crusade against the Catholic Habsburgs, but when he realized that this was a chimera he still felt that he must rely upon Sweden to ensure that the Dutch and their Danish allies did not gain control of the Baltic and thus block English naval supplies and obstruct English commerce in that sea. When in January 1658 the Swedes and the Danes (backed by the Dutch) were again at war the Lord Protector warned his parliament of the dangers that 'poor Prince', the King of Sweden, faced because 'so many Protestants [that was to say the Dutch and the Danes] are not so right as were to be wished'.[23] 'If they can shut us out of the Baltic [he continued] and make themselves masters of that, where is your trade? Where are your materials to preserve your shipping? or where will you be able to challenge any right at sea or justify yourselves against a foreign invasion of your own soil?'

It was after this passage that Oliver made his famous observation about the need to have available an expeditionary force for a war on the mainland of Europe – which was to be realized when he dispatched the army that gained Dunkirk:

You have accounted yourselves happy in being environed with a great ditch from all the world beside. Truly you will not be able to keep your ditch nor your shipping – unless you turn your ships and shipping into troops of horse and companies of foot; and fight to defend yourselves on terra firma![24]

In fact Charles X defeated the Danes by crossing the Baltic over the ice to lay siege to Copenhagen. Oliver wisely understood that it was to the British interest that neither the Swedes nor the Danes should dominate the entry into the Baltic; he therefore sent ambassadors to both the kings. It was largely through his mediation that a treaty of peace was signed between them, which ensured that the Danes controlled one side of the Sound and Sweden the other. But his hope of constructing a Protestant alliance against the House of Habsburg, in which the Danes and the Swedes would participate, was doomed as a wishful daydream, just as Buckingham's coalition had been.

Oliver Cromwell's foreign policy has usually been described as that of a mixture between a commercial traveller and a Puritan Don Quixote or between a crusader of the Middle Ages and an economic nationalist. That he was a patriotic Englishman who envisaged the Commonwealth he helped to create as a Great Power, developing along the lines laid down by the Tudors Henry VIII and Elizabeth I, has generally been acknowledged, but his materialism has been exaggerated. He was unenthusiastic about the war against the Dutch, England's chief commercial rivals, and the peace that he concluded with them was criticized by contemporaries as being too mild. He had nothing to do with the first Navigation Act aimed against their carrying trade, and during his Protectorate he tried his best to avoid conflict with them. The Dutch for commercial reasons also exercised restraint. It was, as Professor Charles Wilson wrote, 'the first and most remarkable proof that neither conflicting economic ambitions nor the problem of neutral rights need necessarily lead to war if those who held power exercised prudence and restraint'.[25] Cromwell's annoyance with the Dutch, as reflected in the speech just quoted, was because they were in his opinion insufficiently concerned about the threats to Protestantism in Europe.

Again, Oliver's enmity to Spain was mainly inspired by religious considerations, as he himself explained. The opposition to his war against Spain was raised by English merchants who sold cloth to the Spaniards and imported their merino wool. Even though his decision to readmit the Jews into England was partly determined by commercial reasons, he also argued that 'since there was a promise of their conversion . . . that could not be done unless they were permitted to dwell where the Gospel was preached'.[26] The merchants of the City of London were certainly not pleased by that decision.

Although Cromwell's policy in the Baltic may have been based on what have been described as 'worldly motives', he undoubtedly believed that Charles X was a champion of pure religion and a man that had adventured his all against the Popish interest in Poland and made his acquisition still good for the Protestant religion'.[27] Foreign ambassadors in London, whether Protestant or Catholic, found it hard to believe that Oliver meant what he said when he advocated the formation of a league 'against the inhuman cruelties of Popery'. The Swedish ambassador thought it extraordinary that the Protector was determined to keep at peace with the Dutch, who were England's commercial rivals, even though Oliver assured him that 'the Protestant cause and its security were the grounds on which he acted (diplomatically) and to which he would adhere as long as he had anything to say'.[28]

The Commonwealth ruled by Oliver, who had virtually become king in 1657, was recognized throughout the world as a Great Power, which it certainly had not been after the failure of Charles I's wars against Spain and France. The country now had a larger navy than ever before and a standing army. Moreover, in Robert Blake an admiral of genius was discovered in contrast with Sir Edward Cecil, who had no experience of naval warfare when he set out for Cadiz, or the first Duke of Buckingham, a courageous commander but a complete amateur. Oliver had been able to sustain Blake in all his campaigns with adequate provisions and reinforcements, which Charles had failed to do when Buckingham occupied the isle of Ré. During the Protectorate the sailors were better and more regularly paid. The wounded and widows and children of men who lost their lives at sea received gratuities. For the first time they had access to prize money –

indeed Thurloe claimed with obvious exaggeration that after Stayner's capture of the galleons in 1656 'many private mariners' got '£10,000 a man'. Whereas Cecil had been repulsed at Cadiz, Blake by blockading the port reduced the Spanish navy to impotence.

Charles had of course been starved of funds by the House of Commons; on the other hand, Cromwell had benefited from the rise in the yield of Customs duties, which met at least half of the cost of the navy during the Protectorate. It was the victories at sea over the Dutch and the Spanish which sustained Cromwell's foreign policy and enabled him to gain for the Commonwealth the alliance of France, which had a population nearly four times the size of that of England.

Oliver did not make the mistake made by Charles of becoming involved simultaneously in a war against France and Spain. When the Protectorate was established war was in progress not only with the Dutch but also with the French, as Cromwell twice reminded his parliament when he first adressed it in September 1654. The French had concluded an alliance with the Dutch in 1635 and they had assisted the Dutch in operations in the Mediterranean during the Anglo-Dutch war, in response to which Blake had attacked and destroyed a French squadron off Dunkirk in August 1652. But before the Protector dispatched the expedition to the West Indies at the end of 1654 negotiations had been opened with the French government for a treaty of amity and commerce. Unlike Charles, Oliver had no intention of driving France and Spain into each other's arms. He exerted his strength to maintain his authority throughout the world, but never risked going too far. England rapidly lost the prestige he had won for it when Charles I's son came to the throne.

10

HANDLING PARLIAMENTS – I

Although the House of Commons as a separate constitutional assembly dates from the reign of King Edward III in the fourteenth century, it did not become of significant importance until the reign of King Henry VIII, who used it as the instrument with which he reformed the English Church and thus took it into partnership with him. Before then, however, statute laws had often been initiated in the Commons and from the fifteenth century onwards taxation could only be imposed with its consent. The Crown therefore needed to develop a good relationship with the Lower House. That was acquired temporarily; although it was destroyed during the reign of Henry VIII's Roman Catholic daughter, Queen Mary I, it was to some extent regained during the reign of her successor, 'Good Queen Bess'.

The House of Commons had not yet, however, acquired complete liberty of speech nor freedom from arrest for its members. During the reigns of the Tudors the Commons obtained control over its own privileges and received the powers of a law court in ordering its own affairs. In the first half of the sixteenth century it won the privilege of freedom from arrest for its members and was permitted to imprison offenders against its privileges as well as procuring a formal right of freedom of speech.

During the reign of Queen Elizabeth I the gentry of England became highly articulate in the House of Commons, many members showing themselves, though in a confused kind of way, to be more forthright, independent and inquisitive. But the Queen, while she accepted that Parliament was the proper instrument for promoting social and economic reforms and providing her with money, refused to recognize its right to legislate on religious matters (that was the concern of herself and the convocations of the Church of England) or to discuss matters of high policy, including the succession to the throne, unless she gave its members permission to do so. She kept Parliament to short sessions. It was only active for a total period of less than three years during the whole of her reign.[1]

She limited freedom of speech in the House of Commons by warning members that it was not their concern 'to speak there of all causes as they listeth' or 'to frame a form of religion or a state of government, as their idle brains shall seem meetest'. She said no ruler would 'suffer such absurdities'.[2] Sometimes she consulted the Commons, for example over the treatment of her prisoner, Mary Queen of Scots. She answered their grievances, reformed her own household, did not spend money lavishly on herself, and on one occasion remitted a third of the subsidy offered her. When pressed hard, as in her first parliament, she gave way or appeared to give way. In her last parliament she agreed to a demand to abolish oppressive monopolies. But

> time and again she showed her contempt for these little men who dared interfere in the counsels of princes, and it did not help much if that contempt was thoroughly justified. If time and again her gracious speeches poured oil at the end of a session, it is too often manifest that she herself had been responsible in the first place for stirring up the troubled waters.[3]

So writes Professor G. R. Elton in his latest examination of Elizabethan parliaments.

Such was the fragile relationship that had developed between the Crown and Parliament by the beginning of the seventeenth century.

> The Stuarts [to quote Professor Elton again] failed to cope with their parliaments because they were less skilful and less adaptable than Elizabeth, not because their problems were more insoluble or because they were confronted by a new kind of Commons of which the first signs might be conceivably looked for in the four parliaments after 1588.[4]

When King James I came to the throne of England such delicacy vanished. James, who had a hard time as King of the Scots, emphasized that he was a very experienced ruler, who did not need to be taught how to behave; but in fact he had been accustomed in Scotland to deal with a weak and ineffective parliament. He told his first English parliament about 'the blessings which God hath, in my person bestowed upon you all' and added, 'I am the husband and all the whole isle is my lawful wife: I am the head and it is my body. I am the shepherd and it is my flock.'[5] The Commons did not enjoy being lectured in this way or being reminded of the absolute powers of the Crown. They thought that 'the prerogatives of princes may easily and daily grow' while 'the privileges of the subject are for the most part at any everlasting stand'. Sir Robert Philips repeated this in Charles I's parliament of 1628: 'We see in general experience how easily . . . the prerogatives of princes thrive when the liberties of the subjects are at a stand.'[6]

Though Queen Elizabeth had tried to prevent the discussion of matters of state she frequently compromised even over religious questions towards the end of her reign, while admittedly the Commons did not press her too hard because of her age and sex.[7] Now the Commons and the King clashed over a variety of subjects. James wanted a legislative union between England and Scotland. The Commons required the abolition of medieval rights, such as wardships and purveyance, which enabled the Crown to obtain money without parliamentary consent. Parliament rejected the proposal for union, and negotiations for the giving up of feudal rights by the Crown in return for a fixed permanent annual revenue to be voted by the Commons broke down. The only time harmony prevailed was after the failure of the Gunpowder Plot in November 1605, which was followed by the enactment of two statutes penalizing Roman Catholics who did not attend the services of the Church of England.

The King, who was grossly extravagant, asked the Commons for extra large sums of money; the Commons fastened on their grievances both secular and ecclesiastical. James did not gain popularity when he informed Parliament in 1610 that 'the state of monarchy is the supremest thing upon earth: for kings are not only God's lieutenants but even by God Himself they are called Gods'.[8] A parliament summoned by King James in 1614 was a complete failure, although the Commons were promised 'graces' in return for supplies, and it became known to history as the Addled Parliament. Several members of this parliament, who were accused of delivering seditious speeches and disrupting the Commons, were arrested, though released after making submission.

Another parliament was not summoned for seven years when the loss of the Palatinate by the King's son-in-law required naval and military preparations to help him; it was this parliament which clamoured for war against Spain because Spanish troops occupied the Lower Palatinate. The members sought an offensive at sea, the strict enforcement of penal laws against Roman Catholics, who were regarded as Spanish allies, and the marriage of Prince Charles to a Protestant princess. James retorted that they had violated his prerogatives, meddling with matters of state that were none of their concern. When the Commons drew up a protestation he tore out the page in the Commons journal that recorded it and dissolved Parliament. Three years later, after the failure of Charles's visit to Madrid, James called his last parliament and made a complete *volte-face* by seeking its advice; yet when the two Houses petitioned him to end the existing treaties with Spain and promised him assistance 'with our persons and abilities in a parliamentary course' if war broke out, he again told them it was none of their business and that he needed huge sums not vague promises if he were forced into war.[9] Only the intervention of the Duke of Buckingham prevented another rupture between the King and the House of Commons. But until the close of his reign James maintained (with precedent on his side) that the function of Parliament was purely consultative, and he hoped he could obtain his objectives without going to war.

Thus when Charles became King he had no tradition of harmony with Parliament on which he could draw. It has sometimes been argued that his father, though uttering lofty claims for his prerogative powers, had successfully avoided antagonizing his parliaments. But the truth seems to be that James never entirely understood the latent strength of Parliamentarians since the Tudors had used them as the instruments of, or partners in, government. He disliked the way the Commons treated him, as he told his Privy Council in 1610. 'The Lower house ... have imperilled our health, wounded our reputation, emboldened all ill-natured people, encroached upon many of our privileges, and plagued our purse with their delays.'[10]

In theory Charles should have been more capable of handling parliaments than his father had been, for because he had lived all his adult life in England he should not have been misled by analogies with Scottish parliaments. He had often sat in the House of Lords during his father's reign, he had witnessed how James had dealt with his parliaments and he was not, as the Speaker pointed out, 'a stranger to parliaments'.[11] Indeed, he had been instrumental in inducing his father to make concessions to the House of Commons. When he called a parliament soon after his accession the speech he made to it was welcomed as being brief and to the point, contrasting with the loquaciousness of his predecessor. But immediately he asked the Commons to vote him money, 'such supply as the greatness of the work and variety of provision did require'.[12] Neither he nor his ministers explained exactly how much was wanted nor the precise use to which it would be put. In fact, since an undeclared war against Spain was being planned as well as military assistance to Charles's brother-in-law in Germany, Charles was assuming that, as a previous parliament had advocated tearing up the treaties with Spain and was sympathetic to the Protestant cause in Germany, means would be provided for waging war on land as well as on sea. Nevertheless, the majority in the Commons took the view that a vote of two subsidies worth about £160,000 plus the yield from the Customs duties, known as tonnage and poundage, and a vote of £20,000 by the clergy in convocation should suffice for the King's immediate needs.

But what Charles actually required to meet his commitments, which included payment to Mansfeld's worthless army and financial assistance to his uncle, the King of Denmark, amounted to over a million pounds. Furthermore, the Commons refused to vote tonnage and poundage for more than one year after the King's accession because it did not approve of the King also obtaining the yield of a tax on the export of woollen cloth known as the 'pretermitted Customs', which had been levied both by Queen Elizabeth I and King James I and was based on a tonnage and poundage act passed by previous parliaments. It wanted this question cleared up, but in fact the decision to vote tonnage and poundage for only one year had unfortunate consequences for Charles. He sent a message to the Commons thanking them for the subsidies as an earnest of their good will, but disclosing belatedly the extent of his commitments and expressing the hope that they would be 'forward to supply the actions now begun'.[13] Ignoring this message, the Commons turned with enthusiasm to the consideration of religious questions. It ordered the arrest of Richard Montague, an Essex clergyman, because it asserted that his books contained matter offensive to their House, including an attack on the faction he called Puritans who, he said, were worse than Papists. The Puritans in the House were far from pleased when Montague was rescued from their clutches because the King appointed him one of his chaplains.

When Charles's first parliament met in Oxford in August 1625 he again delivered a very short speech asking for further financial aid so that the fleet could put to sea, while Sir John Coke, who was a naval commissioner, assured his fellow members that 'no king loves his subjects, the laws and religion better than he: therefore he leaves it to your choice what to do'.[14] However, the majority in the Commons were not moved by Charles's appeal. One member complained: 'Nothing hath been done. We know not our enemy. We have set up and consumed our own people.'[15] For all that the Duke of Buckingham as Charles's leading minister was blamed implicitly or explicitly. Buckingham was a brave man; he faced both Houses of Parliament in the hall of Christ Church where he ably defended himself and his King. Although he told them that the King had ordered that the penal laws against Roman Catholics would be strictly enforced and defended his far-reaching foreign policy in detail, Parliament was not impressed. The Commons resolved to tell the King that they could not help him now, but might be ready to do so – in the future. In despair Charles dissolved his first parliament. It had been only twelve days in Oxford.

In retrospect it was to be seen that Charles had made two mistakes. In the first place, he had not clarified his foreign policy. His father had always done so and had even consulted Parliament about it, though not guaranteeing to take its advice. Secondly, Charles had assumed that because the House of Commons had clamoured for war against Spain along the lines followed by Queen Elizabeth I it would ensure him of the means to do so. And when he did let the Commons know the full extent of his obligations, he failed to disclose the huge sums that were necessary to fulfil them.

The disastrous failure of the naval campaign against Spain, which led to open warfare between the two kingdoms, left Charles and Buckingham unrepentant. The King summoned a new parliament in February 1626 in the expectation that the Commons would vote financial support for the war effort. Some of the most vociferous critics of the King's policies in the previous parliament had been excluded from the House of Commons by being appointed sheriffs, who could not leave their counties. But a fierce attack on Buckingham was led by his former friend and subordinate Sir John Eliot, who was Vice-Admiral of Devon and a Cornish member of parliament. Eliot, a highly emotional man, had been shocked by what he saw when the English fleet returned to Plymouth laden with sick, starving and half-clothed soldiers and sailors. He put the blame for the catastrophe on his chief, Buckingham. In a speech delivered five days after Parliament met he plainly inculpated the Lord High Admiral without naming him.

In opening the parliament Charles made no attempt to defend the unsuccessful expedition and the fiasco at Cadiz. When Buckingham was censured by name Charles summoned the members of both Houses to Whitehall palace to justify his favourite and leading minister. But Eliot, now the acknowledged spokesman of the Commons, made it crystal clear that they would offer the King no further financial help until their grievances were met; their chief grievance, they thought, was the Duke, who must be punished for his extravagance and incompetence. Charles hit back, giving the warning: 'Remember parliaments are altogether in my power for the calling, sitting and continuance of them; therefore as I find the fruits of them good or evil, they are to continue or not to be.'[16] Buckingham also defended himself before both Houses of Parliament while offering concessions on the part of the King. The Commons remained defiant; they finalized a Remonstrance, insisting upon their right to condemn Buckingham or any other minister, though they refrained from castigating the King himself. Nevertheless, they made it plain to Charles that they would give him no further financial assistance towards the cost of the operations against Spain unless Buckingham had been impeached or dismissed.

In the second week of May the Commons preferred their charges against the Duke before the House of Lords. Charles rather weakly acquiesced in the proceedings in the hope of thereby obtaining the supplies he needed. But when he learned of all the accusations against the Duke, including that of poisoning King James I, and ordered the arrest of Eliot and Sir Dudley Digges, who was if anything more violent in his enmity towards Buckingham than Eliot, both Houses protested vigorously; again weakly Charles released them. Though Eliot had been sent to the Tower of London on the ground that he had committed 'high crimes' against the Crown outside the House of Commons that was a figment of Charles's imagination. For although Eliot's lodgings were searched for incriminating papers and he was examined by the Lord Chief Justice of the King's Bench, nothing 'extra-judicial' could be found against him.[17] At the same time as Eliot's arrest Charles came to the House of Lords in person to defend Buckingham by taking upon himself the blame for the naval calamity.

The Commons paid little attention either to Charles's speech in the House of Lords or to Buckingham's own detailed apologia. They drew up a Remonstrance begging the King to dismiss the Duke, making it evident that they would vote the King no further supplies unless he did so. Charles retorted by dissolving the second parliament and referred the accusations against the Duke to the prerogative Court of Star Chamber. His acquittal by this Court would have prevented any further attempt at his impeachment, but the case did not come to trial because his accusers refused to testify against him.

Meanwhile, the Thirty Years War in Germany, which had broken out after the defeat of Charles's brother-in-law at the battle of the White Mountain, was going badly for the Protestants who were fighting the Holy Roman Emperor. Charles's Danish uncle was decisively beaten at the battle of Lutter in August and King Christian accused his nephew of failing to give him the support he had promised. Charles was driven to desperate measures. He instituted a forced loan, levied on his wealthier subjects, which he hoped would raise the money the Commons had failed to give him. Rich men who refused to pay were sent to prison. When five of them, all knights, demanded that the cause of their imprisonment should be stated, the Court of King's Bench, whose Chief Justice had recently been replaced by the King, ruled that the royal command was sufficient reason. Charles also continued to collect tonnage and poundage, which his first parliament had denied to him for longer than one year. Troops were raised by the imposition of martial law. Soldiers, who were enlisted to sail with the fleet under the Lord High Admiral, were forcibly billeted on unwilling hosts. None of these expedients were welcome or altogether effective. And at the beginning of 1628, after the catastrophe of the Duke of Buckingham's expedition to La Rochelle, Charles was persuaded to release the refusers of the forced loan and to call a third parliament, which met in March.

This parliament was mishandled by Charles. In his opening speech he told the members that they must speedily vote him financial supplies that were required 'for the defence of ourselves and allies', and if that were refused at a time of common danger, 'I must, according to my conscience, take those other courses, which God hath put into my hands for the preservation of that which others, in falling out for particular ends, hazard to lose.' 'I pray you,' he went on, 'not to take this as threatening, for I scorn to threaten any but my equals.'[18] No more provocative words could have been chosen. A lengthy speech by the Lord Keeper, which followed, outlining the dangers to the Protestant cause from the House of Austria and the kingdoms of Spain and France did not persuade the House of Commons, indignant over the violation of the liberties of the people, to do other than concentrate on them. Sir Thomas Wentworth said that Parliament was 'a great physician' capable of mending injuries such as the forced loan and the billeting of soldiers. Of course, he added, Charles himself was not to blame but 'projectors who have extended the prerogative of the King beyond the just symmetry which maketh the sweet harmony of the whole'.[19] The veteran champion of the common law, Sir Edward Coke, agreed. 'The State,' he observed, 'is inclining to a consumption', but it was curable and he would propose remedies for the disease.[20]

The procedure adopted by the Commons to assert their liberties was to vote the King five subsidies worth about £275,000, but not to complete the Bill until their liberties were confirmed by the King. There was much talk about Magna Carta. One member said: 'I shall be very glad to see that good old decrepit law of Magna Carta which hath so kept in and lain bed-rid as it were; I shall be glad I say to see it walk again with new vigour and lustre.'[21] Charles was happy to accept the re-enactment of Magna Carta if no elaborate explanation was agreed upon about what it meant. Sir Thomas Wentworth, however, preferred the introduction of a Bill of Rights invigorating and defining the old laws. But Charles told the Commons that he would govern his people according to the laws and customs of the realm and maintain their liberties without 'new explanations, new interpretations, expositions or additions of any sort'.[22]

The Commons were not prepared to trust Charles's promises, so they drew up a Petition of Right outlining their grievances and appealing to Magna Carta and other medieval precedents, which Charles would be obliged to accept or refuse. In this they obtained the concurrence of the House of Lords, where many of the peers had been alienated from the Crown by the King's dependence on the upstart Duke of Buckingham. Under pressure Charles wriggled. First he told Parliament: 'You will find as much security in his Majesty's royal word and power as in the strength of any law you can make.' Then he gave an ambiguous answer. Finally after an agitation in both Houses he used the words of assent applicable to any private Bill: '*Soit droit fait come est desiré.*' He added, 'I have done my part, wherefore if this Parliament has not a happy conclusion the sin is yours; I am free of it.'[23]

Not content with their success over the Petition of Right, the majority in the House of Commons, led by Sir John Eliot, proceeded to draw up another Remonstrance to the King complaining about many questions ranging from losses of shipping and decay of forts to 'innovations in our holy religion'; it concluded by blaming everything on the excessive power of the Duke of Buckingham. To add weight to their case they delayed sending the subsidy Bill for which Charles had asked to the House of Lords. Naturally the King was infuriated, for the Remonstrance was a wholesale onslaught on all his policies and ministers. Still, as usual, Charles managed to conceal his temper and said he would consider the points of the Remonstrance 'as they deserve'.[24] Of course he perceived the inconsistencies in the remonstrance, which condemned the government for its failures in the wars but reproached him for raising by what they considered to be illegal means – such as the forced loans – the money that they had denied him for the upkeep of the army and the navy. Next the Commons discussed another grievance about the King's collection of Customs duties without legislative authorization. The King then prorogued this obstreperous parliament.

In following year Charles recalled his third parliament, which met in January 1629. Since its last session the Duke of Buckingham had been assassinated, so one major grievance in the Commons vanished. Charles's main reason for summoning Parliament was to procure the legitimization of the levying of Customs duties – tonnage and poundage.[25] The Commons immediately mounted their high horse. Complaints were made about violations of the Petition of Right. Then John Rolle, a member of parliament who was a merchant, informed the House that his goods had been impounded because he had refused to pay Customs duties on them; this was condemned not merely because it was considered that the levy of tonnage and poundage was illegal, but also because it was deemed a breach of the privileges of the Commons. When Charles heard about this he addressed both Houses of Parliament, explaining to them that he had not ordered the collection of Customs duties by exercising prerogative rights, but simply out of necessity while he awaited 'the gift of his people' to enjoy it, following the precedent of its grant by Parliament to other monarchs since the time of Edward IV.[26] But two days after Charles delivered that speech and his Secretary of State moved that the tonnage and poundage Bill should be read in the Commons, the Speaker ruled that they must first discuss higher things – eternal life and their souls. 'I desire first [he said] that it may be considered what new paintings are laid upon the old face of the whore of Babylon to make her seem more lovely and to draw many suitors to her.'[27]

Although Charles continued to send messages to the Commons begging them to pass the Bill about tonnage and poundage, which he needed desperately to pay for the continuing wars against Spain and France, and one member asked his colleagues to 'consider how dangerous it is to alienate his Majesty's heart from Parliament',[28] so indignant were most of the members over the seizure of John Rolle's goods that they procrastinated about the matter, spent much of their time on religious questions and protested, among other things, at the King's |reprieve| of ˌaˌ Jesuit priest, who had been condemned to death, and at his ordering the release of other Jesuits imprisoned at Newgate.

Losing hope of receiving any help from his third parliament, Charles ordered its adjournment after it had been sitting for fewer than six weeks. Then came the dramatic scene famous in the history of English parliaments. The Speaker was held down in his chair while the members voted unanimously, condemning as capital enemies of the kingdom any who introduced innovations in religion or promoted Popery or Arminianism, and anyone who advised the taking or levying of tonnage and poundage without the permission of Parliament. In a third clause they condemned any merchant who paid tonnage and poundage without a grant from Parliament as 'a betrayer of the liberties of England'.

The prorogation of this parliament was followed by its dissolution. Charles then published a declaration to all his loving subjects justifying the dissolution and arguing that Parliament had exceeded its rights and privileges, particularly by examining judges, ministers and public officials and by impugning his own conduct. He then promised to uphold true religion, to safeguard the liberties of his subjects, to enlarge the trade of the kingdom's merchants, and to ensure the defence of the realm.[29] Next he proceeded to make peace treaties with France and Spain and did not summon another parliament for eleven years. That was a longer interval than in previous reigns, but it was not all that exceptional. Queen Elizabeth I, it is true, held parliaments on an average once every five years, but they did not meet for long; King James I, if one leaves out the 'Addled Parliament' of 1610, which accomplished nothing, did not have an effective parliament in session for eleven years.

Yet Charles had started his reign with the best of good intentions towards Parliament. He assumed that because the parliament of 1624 had clamoured for war against Spain the first parliament of his own reign would accept that its constitutional duty was to provide grants of extraordinary supply so that military and naval operations could be conducted successfully. But, as has been noticed already, he committed two serious mistakes: first he did not immediately explain what his aims were and, secondly, he did not state exactly how much help he needed. The prevailing opinion in Parliament was that if the enemy were Spain, war should be waged along the lines followed by Queen Elizabeth's government, concentrating on naval hostilities and subsidizing allies, notably the Dutch, to fight on land. When Parliament failed to provide the funds he needed Charles was driven to the expedients of forced loans, compulsory billeting and martial law, which aroused the anger of rich and poor alike and furnished members of parliament with a host of grievances from their constituents to be aired at Westminster. Then Charles showed himself weak by changing his mind about his reply to the Petition of Right, by allowing the impeachment of Buckingham to go forward, and by making threatening gestures at the outset of the meeting of his third parliament.

On the other hand, clearly the well-to-do gentry, lawyers and merchants, who comprised the House of Commons and had gradually increased their importance at the expense of the House of Lords, were determined to express their opinions about religion and foreign policy, subjects that had been specifically forbidden them by Queen Elizabeth I. As James I was a Calvinist who, despite his devotion to episcopacy, condemned the teachings of Jacobus Arminius, he was not unduly troubled by his parliaments on religious questions. Furthermore, he had consulted them about foreign policy, even though he had not promised to take their advice. Still, the fact was that the Commons were savouring their sense of power. And however tactfully Charles might have handled his parliaments, a Puritan movement was gathering strength which by challenging the Church also challenged the King.

By avoiding wars abroad and by employing expedients suggested to him by his ministers for raising funds, notably ship money to pay for the fleet, Charles became better off financially than he had been at the start of this reign. He benefited from prosperous years in peace. Sir Philip Warwick believed England 'was never master of a profounder peace or enjoyed more wealth or had the power of godliness more visibly in it' than between 1628 and 1638.[30] But just as Charles had been confronted with parliamentary difficulties because of the wars begun at the end of his father's reign, so in 1639 he found he required extra funds to fight effectively against his Scottish subjects, who had signed a National Covenant in defence of their Presbyterian religion. By calling another parliament in England in the spring of 1640 without consulting his Privy Council, Charles hoped he would gain support from his English subjects to resume the war ineffectively begun against the Scottish Covenanters a year earlier, if they did not agree to his terms for a settlement. But the new parliament demanded the solution of their accumulated grievances – which embraced the violation of their privileges, so-called innovations in religion, and the levying of tonnage and poundage and of ship money – before they granted him any subsidies.

Charles soon lost patience, dissolved Parliament and resumed the war against the Scottish Covenanters, who this time decisively defeated him on the river Tyne. Then he summoned a Great Council of Peers at York to ask their advice, but before receiving it he told them he planned to call another parliament in November. It is not clear why after the failure of the parliament held in April of that year (and of the parliament of 1628) to vote him funds he should have imagined that another parliament would do so. But he appears to have hoped that he would obtain public support for resuming the war against the Scots, who after all had long been the enemies of England. Either he was desperate or sanguine – he was usually sanguine. When this parliament met he said: 'It should not be my fault if this is not a happy and good parliament.'[31] One of its members, on the other hand, more accurately surmised that it would be 'a healthy parliament where the subject may have a total redress of all his grievances'. In fact Charles, intimidated, as he revealed in his *Eikon Basilike*, published after his death, by the menacing crowds of Londoners, signed away the life of his champion, the Earl of Strafford, and afterwards gave way to almost everything that a nearly unanimous House of Commons demanded of him.

John Williams, the Bishop of Lincoln, who had been a minister in Charles's government, wrote:

> Parliament . . . is the highest and supereminent Court of the King. . . . And yet in five parliaments which the King called there were distance and discord in them all between him and his people. . . . Our Sovereign had not the art to please: or rather his subjects had not the will to be pleased.[32]

Unquestionably the Commons were eager for greater authority than they had ever possessed before. Once Charles surrendered to them, as he did, the right to continue in session as long as they wished, he was left with no other resource than the use of arms to maintain the Crown's ancient prerogative rights. It is true that before he died he wrote a letter to his eldest son telling him 'not to be averse to or dislike parliament'.[33] King Charles II, a highly intelligent man, realized that the maintenance of his authority rested on his right to call or dissolve parliaments whenever he wished. When his father surrendered that right, his fate was sealed.

11

HANDLING PARLIAMENTS – II

When he came to the throne Charles had acquired a considerable experience of parliamentary affairs. He never missed a day in the House of Lords when his father's last parliament met, he exerted his influence in his Cornish estates to secure the election of members to the House of Commons who were friendly to the Court, and he seconded his friend, the Duke of Buckingham, before Parliament in justifying their behaviour in Spain. Another member of the House of Lords thought 'the Prince his carriage at this Parliament had been [a] little too popular'.[1]

Oliver Cromwell, for his part, had been a member of parliament for more than twelve years before becoming Lord Protector. He first made his mark in Charles's third parliament, witnessing the Petition of Right being passed and agreed to and the pinioning of the Speaker in his chair while the three resolutions about religion and the levying of tonnage and poundage were unanimously proclaimed. After the eleven-year interval between parliaments Oliver was elected as one of the members for the borough of Cambridge largely because his assiduity in local affairs had won him a reputation in the county. He was made a freeman of the borough, a necessary qualification for election, on the payment of one penny to the poor. His colleague was a clerk of the Privy Council named Thomas Meautys. In the election to the Long Parliament the following November Meautys was replaced by John Lowry, a grocer, who was to become Mayor of Cambridge during the civil war. Thus Oliver was a dedicated politician, but hardly a typical back-bencher.

Oliver's speech on 11 February 1629 condemning Richard Neile, the future Archbishop of York, as popishly inclined, which has been assumed to have been his maiden speech, was noted down by no fewer than three of his fellow members whose diaries have survived.[2] In the Long Parliament he again exemplified his animosity against the bishops, favouring a 'root-and-branch' Bill which aimed at their abolition. He became enthusiastic about military preparations as civil war loomed ahead and he contributed £1,000 towards the cost of waging war against the Irish rebels, who had struck against their English masters in the autumn of 1641. For the next five years he was absorbed in fighting the Royalists, but after the surrender of Oxford by them and the subsequent quarrel between a majority in the House of Commons and the New Model Army, which it had created, he had taken sides with the Army, though he had done everything he could to work out a compromise between them, moving backwards and forwards between the House of Commons and the Army headquarters. In May 1647 he told his fellow officers that 'if the authority of Parliament were not respected, nothing can follow but confusion'.[3]

1647 was the critical year during which the divergencies between Parliament and the Army became acute. Once the two Houses voted that all those in the Army who persisted with their petition for the redress of their grievances should be 'looked upon and proceeded against as enemies of the State and disturbers of the public peace' the lines of division were clearly drawn. After the seizure of the King by Cornet Joyce at the beginning of June Oliver was one of the officers who wrote to the Lord Mayor, Aldermen and Common Council of the City of London saying that while they did not desire any alteration of the civil government, they insisted as Englishmen that their just demands should be met. 'A rich city,' they declared, 'may seem an enticing bait to poor hungry soldiers', but they were drawing near to it 'only to ensure the settlement of the kingdom's peace'.[4] Four days later another declaration, drawn up by Oliver's able son-in-law Henry Ireton, entitled 'the Representation of the Army', asked that the House of Commons should be purged of its delinquent and corrupt members and 'those who abuse the State' and that a time should be set for the continuance of this and future parliaments and a redistribution of seats. A charge of treason was appended against Holles and ten other members of the Commons who had condemned the conduct of the Army.[5]

How far Oliver himself agreed with the extreme demands in this declaration is not known. But what is certain is that when the Army headquarters were moved to Reading on 16 July he exerted his influence to persuade the Council of the Army, which included representatives of the private soldiers known as 'Agitators', not to march on London but to aim at reaching 'a general settlement of the peace of the kingdom' in conjunction with Parliament and not to try to get things out of Parliament by force.[6]

Oliver had therefore advanced from the position that the future government of the country should be determined by Parliament alone to the belief that the Army had a right to draw up constitutional proposals and obtain for them the agreement of the existing Parliament and the King. These proposals included the holding of free elections, the redistribution of seats, and biennial parliaments. But the scheme came to nothing. Charles blew hot and cold on it and Holles and his friends did their utmost to defy the Army. In 1648 the whole situation was changed by Royalist risings in the south of England and the invasion by a Scottish army engaged on behalf of the King. In spite of this renewal of the civil war, which ended in August, a majority in the House of Commons tried to negotiate a settlement with Charles, now a prisoner in the Isle of Wight, which might have been successful if Charles had not refused to abandon his personal religion or allow any of those who had fought for him to be punished with the death penalty. Henry Ireton took the view that Charles was irreconcilable and must be brought to justice as a Man of Blood. He drew up a lengthy Remonstrance of the Army in this sense, which was submitted to Parliament on 20 November when its reading occupied four hours.

Meanwhile Oliver, who had returned to England from Scotland after defeating the army of the Engagers, remained in Yorkshire conducting the siege of Pontefract, which still held out for the Royalists. Clearly he knew about the Remonstrance. On the day it was presented to Parliament he wrote to General Fairfax: 'I find a very great sense in the officers of the regiments of the sufferings and ruin of the poor kingdom and in them all a very great zeal to have impartial justice done upon offenders, and I must confess I do in all, from my heart, concur with them.'[7] But five days later he wrote, this time to Colonel Robert Hammond, the Military Governor of the Isle of Wight, where negotiations with Charles were still in progress: 'We in the Northern army were in a waiting posture desiring to see what the Lord would lead us to.'[8] He met the argument that Parliament was the authority in England that must be obeyed by using the justification, which Ireton had also employed in the Remonstrance, that *salus populi suprema est lex* – though his parliamentary colleague, the learned John Selden, thought 'there is not anything in the world so much abused as this sentence' – and Oliver went on to ask 'whether this Army is not a lawful power called by God to oppose and fight against the King'.[9]

In this remarkable letter, which has been variously interpreted by different historians, he did not in fact commit himself to any one course of action; he reminded Hammond that 'our fleshly reasons ensnare us'. What is absolutely certain is that Oliver deliberately procrastinated before returning to London, as General Fairfax finally ordered him to do. He seems to have been reluctant to exert pressure on Parliament until the negotiations in the Isle of Wight failed, and even then he was undecided whether to approve a 'purge' of Parliament or to seek its dissolution and the election of a new one. Before he reached London Henry Ireton and other leading officers, including the former drayman, Colonel Thomas Pride, had acted. On 5 December 1648 the Commons voted that 'the answers of the King to the Propositions of both Houses are a ground for the House to proceed upon for the settlement of the peace of the kingdom'. There was a majority of 129 to 83 in favour of putting the question after an all-night sitting. As soon as the House rose the Army determined to intervene. Colonel Pride began putting under arrest leading members of the majority who had voted for continuing negotiations with Charles when they attempted to return for the next session. This episode in English history became known as 'Pride's Purge'.[10]

Oliver eventually arrived in Whitehall that evening. Clearly he had been disinclined to purge the parliament of which he had been a member for eight years, but he accepted the *fait accompli* as a manifestation of God's will. One historian has written: 'It is inconceivable that he had not been informed of the intention of the Army to put pressure upon Parliament and that he approved of the purge once it had taken place.'[11] Another thinks that 'he could not have known of the plan to purge the House and might have preferred himself to have taken the lead in imposing the Army's wishes from inside the House of Commons.'[12] A third historian, who has examined the question in most detail, considers that 'he balked at the use of force against constitutional authority, but could suggest no alternative which would avoid splitting the Army'.[13] One conclusion that seems reasonable after reading and re-reading Cromwell's letter to Hammond is that Oliver was wrestling with his conscience to find convincing arguments in order to justify abrogating the authority of Parliament.

Such was the complex background to Oliver's handling of parliaments when, first as commander-in-chief of the Army in June 1653 and then as Lord Protector from the end of 1653 until his death, he was compelled to accept the supreme responsibility for political decisions without any longer having the advice of Henry Ireton, who died in Ireland in 1651.

Oliver had first to deal with the 'Rump Parliament', that is to say the parliament which had been elected in the autumn of 1640, had been recruited after the Royalists left the House of Commons and had been purged by Colonel Pride. In September 1651 after his victory at the battle of Worcester Oliver had returned to London, where he lived in the Cockpit (part of Whitehall palace), and was immediately immersed in public affairs. In the act for the abolition of the monarchy passed in 1649 it was 'resolved and declared by the Commons assembled in Parliament that they will put a period to the sitting of the present Parliament and dissolve the same as soon as may possibly stand with the safety of the people'.[14]

The difficulty was that the Rump was the effective government as well as the legislature in the Commonwealth. It is true that the Council of State had many administrative duties, but it contained forty-one members, who had to be split up into a number of committees, while the act that constituted the Council made it plain that it had to take its orders from Parliament.[15] Oliver was unanimously elected to the Council (it was re-elected every year) and as commander-in-chief and a leading member of parliament he was obviously the outstanding figure in the country, but the Rump Parliament prevented him from being administratively supreme by ordering that the chairman of the Council of State had to be changed every month. In his *History* Clarendon wrote perspicaciously that 'from the time of the defeat at Worcester Cromwell did not find the Parliament so supple and so much [ready] to observe his orders as he expected they would have been'.[16]

When in November 1651 the question of setting a date for the dissolution of Parliament was raised the Rump voted by a majority of only 2 (49 to 47) to fix such a date – Oliver was a teller for the affirmative. But a few days later the Rump decided not to dissolve itself for another three years, which was until 3 November 1654. This decision was not to Oliver's liking, for he could see that what the country now urgently needed was an effective executive with clearly defined powers. To obtain it, he thought, was 'a business of more than ordinary difficulty', but he inclined to the view that 'a settlement with somewhat of monarchical power in it' would be best. That was not the opinion of either the republicans in Parliament or of most of Cromwell's officers. Nevertheless, the general feeling in the Army was that a new parliament should be elected to draw up a constitution for the government of the country. So Oliver consulted members of parliament and army officers about what should be done next; for the cumbersome system of a purged parliament (only some seventy members were consistently in attendance), a changing Council of State and overworked committees was hardly suited to the reformist ambitions that the victors in the civil war had anticipated – especially Oliver himself, who after his success at Dunbar had asked the Speaker to 'relieve the oppressed, hear the groans of poor prisoners in England, be pleased to reform all the abuses of all persons', for 'if there be anyone that makes many poor to make a few rich that suits not a Commonwealth'.

In fact the Rump did not manage too badly, but it was unable to reach any major decisions about the Church, plan the reform of the law (except that proceedings should be conducted in English and ordinary writing used instead of court hand) or prevent war against the Dutch Republic breaking out. What really annoyed the Army more than this – after all, these were complicated questions that could scarcely be resolved rapidly – was that Parliament, while raising the pay of sailors, had still failed to meet the long arrears of pay owing to soldiers and was arranging that the size of the Army should be cut down and garrisons disbanded, thus throwing demobilized men on to the labour market where apprenticeship was necessary and unemployment rife. A General Council of Officers, which met in Whitehall during August 1652, presented a petition to the Rump outlining its grievances and asking that speedy consideration should be given to a scheme for the election of future parliaments. Oliver, however, seems to have exerted his influence to persuade the petitioners not to insist upon the immediate dissolution of the Rump.[17] Whatever way Oliver acted that August, when in the following March the Council of Officers, dissatisfied with the response to its petition, wanted to expel the Rump he intervened to prevent it doing so and was said to 'stick close to the House'. So up to that date Oliver was loyal to the parliament which had been purged by the Army three years earlier.

Two problems have to be faced about Cromwell's decision forcibly to dissolve the Rump Parliament, as he did on 20 April 1653.[18] The first is why did he now do this so suddenly after he had exerted all his influence for many months to restrain the Army from taking any more extreme measures against Parliament? The second question is why, defying Oliver's attempts to find an agreed constitutional plan, did the Rump Parliament, after procrastinating for four years about consenting to its own dissolution and the election of a successor, try to rush through a Bill to this effect that April day? The answer to the second question is presumably because it was under immense and imminent pressure from the Army to do so. What the Bill exactly contained is not known. It may have been that at one time the draft Bill contained a clause that existing members had no need to stand for re-election (this had been advocated three times earlier),[19] but if it did, that clause had been dropped. The Rump had already made one concession by agreeing that a general election should be held in November 1653 instead of, as had previously been voted, in November 1654. Possibly the Bill provided that the Rump Parliament should continue sitting and governing the country until, or almost until, a new parliament had actually met. By doing so the members of the Rump would have been able to manipulate the elections in their own favour.

Oliver's personal plan was that the Rump should dissolve itself after appointing a select body of about forty men to govern the realm until they judged the conditions safe for elections to be held for a new sovereign parliament; he evidently received the impression after a meeting in his lodgings on 19 April that the members of parliament who were there, including in all probability his friend Sir Henry Vane the Younger,[20] had agreed to this proposal. What he wanted to avoid was a future constitutional system in which the executive, legislature and, to some extent, the judicature should all be in the hands of parliaments.

> We should then have had [he declared four years later] a Council of State and a Parliament of four hundred men executing arbitrary government without intermission ... one parliament leaping into the seat of another while they left them to warm. The same day as one left the other was to step in. Truly I did think, and do think, that was a foolish remedy.[21]

It is difficult to imagine what Oliver would have thought of the parliamentary system of government in the twentieth century. So pushed on by his two chief colleagues, Major-General Thomas Harrison and Major-General John Lambert, each of whom believed they had been badly treated by the Rump, the commander-in-chief forcibly dissolved the House of Commons and arranged for an assembly, nominated by the Army, to take its place – 'some worthy persons,' he called them, 'to settle the nation'.

The assembly chosen by the Army consisted of 'saints', nearly half of whom were to make their sole appearance at Westminster on this occasion. It contained only a few lawyers and was divided between a majority of moderates and an active minority of radicals, including a dozen or so Fifth Monarchists, that is to say, men who believed it to be their duty to rule the country pending the imminent return of Jesus Christ to the earth. It is not entirely clear what Oliver expected the assembly to do. The suggestion is that he aimed to rally men of experience, all good Christians, behind a programme of measured reform and, after that was accomplished, to organize a return to regular elections. If that was so, he soon became conscious of the gap between the aspirations of the 'saints' and the prejudices of the country gentry. Little light is thrown on his aims in the lengthy speech which he addressed to the assembly on 4 June 1653 with its numerous quotations from the Old Testament: it reads more like a sermon than a political oration. 'It is better,' he told the members, 'to pray for you than to counsel you; to ask wisdom from Heaven for you ... I say it is better to pray than advise.'[22]

Lacking therefore any specific guidance from the commander-in-chief, which it undoubtedly needed, this assembly of 140 Christians at once resolved to assume the title of Parliament and invited Oliver 'to afford his assistance in this House as a member thereof'.[23] The members of this 'Little Parliament' then became extremely zealous. They introduced civil marriages conducted before justices of the peace; they considered the abolition of tithes and lay patronage; they abolished the Court of Chancery and sought the simplification and cheapening of the processes of law; they passed Bills to unite the commonwealths of England, Scotland and Ireland; they set up a High Court of Justice; and they passed an act for the relief of men imprisoned for small debts. But they rejected a scheme for a reformed Church.

Oliver was taken aback by the liveliness of the radical Puritans in the assembly he had created and was disconcerted by its failure to seek his advice, which in his opening speech he had specifically refused to offer it. He told his son-in-law, Charles Fleetwood: 'Fain would I have my service accepted by the saints (if the Lord will), but it is not so.'[24] Thomas Carlyle, one of Cromwell's greatest admirers, thought that 'this Little Parliament in their five months passed various good Acts; chose, with good insight, a new Council of State; took wise charge of the needful Supplies; did all the routine business of a Parliament in a quite unexceptionable or even superior manner'.[25] Its members had in fact followed Oliver's precept to fill their hearts 'with such spirit as Moses had'. Yet Oliver came to regard his establishment of the Assembly of

Saints as a story of his 'own weakness and folly'.[26] He believed that they were endangering 'liberty and property' and that their proposals would have meant 'the subversion of the laws and of all the liberties of this nation, the destruction of the Ministry of this nation, in a word, the confusion of all things, and instead of order to have set up the judicial law of Moses' (hardly surprising in view of his own recommendation of Moses!).[27] He hesitated to dissolve a second assembly by force but fortunately for him, as he later explained, the 'sober men' met early one morning and, led by the Speaker, 'returned their power as far as they could . . . into my own hands'.

Now Oliver, having first followed the advice of Thomas Harrison to create an Assembly of Saints, accepted a constitution known as the Instrument of Government, drawn up by John Lambert, which provided for a balanced authority of Lord Protector, Council of State and triennial parliaments, aiming, as Oliver was to say later, at 'avoiding the extremes of monarchy, on the one hand, and of democracy on the other'. (In fact Lambert and some other officers he consulted had offered to make Oliver king, but this he refused.) In a speech that Oliver as Protector addressed to his first parliament in September 1654 he further justified the new constitution as 'opening a door of hope' to the nation after a long period of 'turnings and tossings' and aiming at 'healing and settling'. He attacked the Levellers, who sought an impossible egalitarianism and also the 'mistaken notion' of the Fifth Monarchists who had exerted so much influence on the Assembly of Saints, but possessed no God-given right to govern. After explaining what the Protectorate had done in domestic matters and foreign policy he emphasized that the members, who had been elected in England and also included thirty from Scotland and thirty from Ireland, were 'a free Parliament'. He concluded by asking the parliament to examine and sanction the Instrument of Government that had brought it into being.

Parliament then naturally proceeded to debate the new constitution, as the 'Court party' pressed it to do.[28] But many of its members, who had served in the Long Parliament which had started the war against Charles I, had become keen republicans, led by Arthur Haslerigg, Thomas Scot and John Bradshaw. They insisted upon the privileges and primacy of the House of Commons and refused to approve without qualification of government by a single person. Instead, these republicans wanted it to be stated that 'the Government should be in the Parliament and people of England and a single person qualified with such instructions as the Parliament think fit'.[29] The debate was hot and furious, often continuing until late in the evening. The dedicated republicans rejected Oliver's arguments that God had chosen him to rule and that 'necessity' required him to do so. The providence of God, they observed, was like a two-edged sword which could be used both ways. It did often permit that of which He did not approve – 'a thief may make as good a title to every purse which he takes by the highways'. And, they said, 'it was an easy matter to pretend a necessity'.[30]

Oliver was disappointed by the behaviour of Parliament and its refusal to accept his arguments for the approval of the Instrument of Government. Eight days after he delivered his first speech he summoned the members to his presence again to tell them plainly that he was 'unwilling to break privileges', but 'necessity hath no law'.[31] He ordered members to sign an agreement that they would be true and faithful to the Lord Protector and Commonwealth and would not attempt to alter 'the government as it is settled in one single person and a Parliament'. About a hundred eventually refused to sign, including Haslerigg and Scot, but the rest of them fell with a good will to tearing the Instrument to pieces. The Protector's powers and income were restricted, the ordinances passed by him and the Council of State, including that for the reform of the Chancery court, were questioned or suspended, and it was laid down that the ultimate decisions on peace and war were to be determined by Parliament.

What irked Oliver most was Parliament's resolutions about religion and the responsibility for the militia.[32] The Instrument of Government stated that all who professed faith in God by Jesus Christ should be tolerated so long as they did not disturb the public peace or 'practise licentiousness'. Parliament, however, demanded the right to restrain 'damnable heresies' and to condemn any man who 'maintained anything contrary to the fundamental principles of doctrines publicly confessed' without seeking the Protector's consent. The Commons exemplified their position on religion by dispatching the Serjeant-at-Arms to arrest John Biddle, a Unitarian, and, after examining him, ordered his imprisonment. Oliver stopped Biddle's trial when it seemed likely that he would be sentenced to death under the Blasphemy Act of 1648 and had him sent instead to confinement in the Scilly Isles. Three years later Biddle was set free and wrote to thank Oliver for allowing him ten shillings a week when he was in prison.

Oliver told a committee which came to talk about the religious clauses they wanted inserted in the Instrument that he disliked them so intensely that he refused to discuss them.[33] As to the militia, the House voted on 20 January 1655 that 'it was not to be raised, formed or used without the consent of parliament'.[34] The Lord Protector retorted that 'if the power of the militia should be yielded up at such a time as this ... what would become of us all?' Two days later he dissolved Parliament, thus preventing it from presenting him with its revised constitution and allowing him, as one member wrote, 'to rule ... under his own Instrument of Government unsupported even by the semblance of a Parliamentary sanction'.[35]

Here the parallel between Oliver's and Charles's handling of Parliament is striking. Charles, although he gave way to the Long Parliament on most questions had, like Oliver, refused in March 1642 to yield over the militia. When he was asked to hand over its control to Parliament for a limited period Charles had answered: 'My God! Not for an hour. You have asked that of me was never asked of any king.'[36] Similarly, until he was defeated in the civil war and was a helpless prisoner, Charles had refused to make any concessions over religion because as Supreme Governor of the Church of England he did not consider that religious questions were the concern of Parliament any more than Elizabeth I had done. As has been noticed, he even regretted his political concession of agreeing to the exclusion of the bishops from the House of Lords. Like Oliver also, he took the view that so long as people accepted the fundamental beliefs of Christianity he had no quarrel with them. In the last resort Charles and Oliver were both certain that they could not govern without having the power of the sword in their hands and that it was not the business of the House of Commons to determine questions of theology. Finally, in the speech which he made in dissolving his first Protectorate parliament Oliver argued that 'though some may think it a hard thing without Parliamentary authority to raise money upon this nation it could be necessary to do so in order to ensure the safety of the good people of this nation'.[37] Was that not what Charles might have claimed during his 'eleven years tyranny'? Was not necessity the tyrant's plea?

Oliver's justification for dissolving his first parliament was that he had not intended it to be a constituent assembly occupying all its time in amending the Instrument of Government but a legislature making 'good and wholesome provisions for the good of the people of these nations'. After the dissolution John Thurloe wrote that the parliament had not presented a single act to the Protector and had not voted money for the payment of the Army, which had been obliged to go on free quarter, much to the public discontent.[38] These two omissions during the time that Parliament sat, Oliver contended, had encouraged the Royalists and the Levellers to resume their plots to destroy the Commonwealth government. His two-hour concluding speech emphasized the depth of his disappointment. Though he asserted that he had carefully avoided encroaching on parliamentary privilege, he once again appealed to the argument that the necessities which drove him forward were 'of God's imposing', for 'all our histories' were 'but God manifesting Himself' and in the future 'if the Lord take pleasure in England' He will 'do us good', 'bear us up', and enable us to overcome our difficulties. Thus the Protector told his audience, 'I think it is my duty to tell you that it is not for the profit of these nations nor for the common and public good for you to continue here any longer.'[39]

After the dissolution the wheel turned full circle. The plots about which Cromwell had spoken were genuine enough. To cope with them Oliver raised a 'standing militia of horse' under the command of major-generals whom he entrusted to police the country. The invention of this scheme, as of the Instrument of Government, has been attributed to John Lambert. Oliver was not a constitutional innovator and was, as has been seen, indifferent about forms of government. The major-generals banned horse races, kept close watch on inns and taverns (shutting down many of them), and largely superseded the justices of the peace. To pay for them a discriminatory tax of 10 per cent, called the decimation, was levied on former Royalists. Other taxes, as with Charles, were exacted without parliamentary consent. When a merchant refused to pay Customs duties he was arrested and then intimidated into submitting after his lawyers had been sent to the Tower. The Lord Chief Justice resigned rather than try the case. Understandably the leading republicans regarded this arbitrary government as reminiscent of Charles I's despotism when he too collected taxes without parliamentary consent on the ground of necessity. Major-General Edmund Ludlow, a consistent republican, when he was asked why he refused to acknowledge the legality of the Protectorate government, replied: 'Because it seems to me to be in substance a re-establishment of that which we all engaged against and had with a great expense of blood and treasure abolished.'[40]

Just as Charles had been obliged to call a parliament in 1640 in the hope that it would pay for his war against the Scottish Covenanters, so Oliver very reluctantly summoned his second Protectorate parliament in the summer of 1656 to persuade it to vote funds to meet the cost of the war against the Spaniards. The major-generals of the horse militia promised him a co-operative parliament. The election results, on which the major-generals exerted all their influence, were not unfavourable to the Court party, but Cromwell and his allies were taking no chances. The Council of State vetted the results and excluded a quarter of the 400 members elected by English constituencies. Over a third of the remaining members had been in the Army, the sixty members nominally representing Scotland and Ireland were virtually hand-picked by the Government, and the boroughs were manipulated to elect Cromwellians. Moreover, a protest was organized at the exclusion of some of the English county members and when it was rejected a number of other members voluntarily withdrew from the House. Thus the second Protectorate parliament, like the first, was subjected to discipline and a new 'rump' parliament was brought into being, which should in effect have been Oliver's ideal assembly.

When Oliver addressed this parliament in a lengthy speech he outlined the dangers with which the Commonwealth was confronted, their chief enemy being Spain, which had adopted the cause of Charles II and was allegedly supported by Roman Catholics in England, who were described by him as 'Spaniolized'.[41] The Papists and the Cavaliers, he said, shook hands in England. He reminded his audience that immediately the last parliament had been dissolved a rising had taken place, which was so widespread that it needed the introduction of the major-generals of the horse militia, whose operations he commended. Furthermore, he said, the Levellers and Fifth Monarchy men by their attacks on the Protectorate had emboldened their foreign foes, thus creating 'a complication of interests'. Oliver begged Parliament to accept liberty of conscience for all Christians who did not 'make religion a pretext for arms and blood'. He advised it also to undertake what he called 'the reformation of manners', which the major-generals had attempted to improve, and also to set about the reform of the criminal law so that men should not 'lose their lives for petty matters' while abominable murderers escaped scot-free. And he ended by asking for a grant of money, particularly to pay for the war against Spain, since the huge capital assets that the government had acquired by dismantling the Church of England and the Stuart monarchy had by then been exhausted.

On Christmas Day 1657 (the Puritans did not approve of 'this foolish day's solemnity', but nevertheless the attendance in the Parliament was thin) Oliver's brother-in-law, John Desborough, brought in a Bill to continue the 'decimation' which paid for the horse militia. For some days Parliament was diverted from this question by considering the appropriate punishment of the Quaker James Nayler for blasphemy and by answering a message from Cromwell questioning their right to act as a judiciary. However, on 7 January 1657 several members, who were not army officers, objected to the decimation tax on Royalists as being contrary to an Act of Oblivion passed in 1652 and as constituting a dangerous precedent by singling out one section of the community as subject to discriminatory taxation. One such member condemned the Bill as setting up a new militia, raised with a tendency to divide this Commonwealth into provinces; a power too great to be bound within any law; in plain terms to cantonize the nation, and prostitute our laws and civil peace, to a power that was never set up in any nation without dangerous consequences.[42]

Feelings ran so high in a fairly crowded House that eventually the whole system of government by the major-generals was abandoned by Cromwell, who was placated by a vote of £400,000 to help pay for the war against Spain. At last he felt convinced that he had found a friendly parliament willing to co-operate with him on legislative reforms.

This parliament went much further in its affability. It decided in March 1657 by a majority of two to one to invite Oliver to assume the title and office of king. Moreover, a new constitution was drawn up, aimed at superseding the Instrument of Government and creating a Cromwellian constitutional monarchy complete with Upper and Lower Houses, a Privy Council, a fixed revenue and a confession of faith. The draft constitution none the less stressed the powers and privileges to be exercised by Parliament and asserted its right to be consulted on questions of war and peace, while the powers of the Council were reduced; and it laid down that its acceptance did not involve the dissolution of the existing assembly. After several conferences Oliver refused the Crown not because he was opposed in principle to accepting it (he was never didactic about forms of government, being opposed to the Stuarts, not to monarchy) but because he feared that the rank-and-file of his Army would not stand for it, and without the Army he could not rule the country.[43]

Although Oliver therefore refused the Crown an elaborate investiture under the new constitution was held on 26 June 1657 to which the Master of the Ceremonies invited foreign ambassadors. Before the ceremony the Lord Protector gave his assent to a 'humble additional and explanatory Petition and Advice' of which the most important proviso was that the House of Commons should have the ultimate right to decide whether members were entitled to sit or not.[44] Oliver then, clad in a mantle of state lined with ermine, entered Westminster Hall where the Speaker presented him with a Bible and a sword and administered an oath of office. His installation was greeted with loud huzzas and the blast of trumpets. The Commons then adjourned while the Protector began his task of choosing members of the new Upper House.

When the two Houses of Parliament met on 20 January 1658 all the members who had been excluded or withdrew from the Commons after the general election of 1656 were now able to take their seats. At the same time most of the peers who had been nominated and accepted the invitation of the Lord Protector to join the Upper House – about forty in number, of whom twenty-one were army officers and the rest chiefly officials and friends of Oliver – had vacated seats in the Lower House. Thus the complexion of the second Protectorate House of Commons was completely changed. Oliver did not realize this, or pretended not to realize that this was the case, although John Thurloe certainly did.

The Lord Protector opened the proceedings with a short exhortation, which was more or less a sermon based on the text 'Mercy and truth are met together, righteousness and peace have kissed each other.' But on 25 January he delivered a much longer speech in which he discussed foreign policy and warned his listeners of the dangers to the nation from abroad and at home; he also asked for funds for the army as it was five or six months behindhand in pay; and he warned them of the perils of disunion. But the members of the Commons, led once again by Sir Arthur Haslerigg (who had refused a seat in the Upper House) and Thomas Scot, turned immediately under their direction, as they had done in 1654, to nothing but constitutional issues.

A long debate opened on the question whether the Upper House should be called the House of Lords (as Cromwell called it) or the Other House. The Commons were evenly divided about the matter, but the tactics of Haslerigg and Scot were clearly designed to destroy the Other House altogether and to overthrow the Protectorate, as they were to succeed in doing after Oliver's death. Haslerigg said that the lords nominated by the Protector aimed 'to invade the liberties of the free-born people of England', which were 'inherently' in the Commons, and he of course refused to betray the liberties of the people of England.[45]

In barely a fortnight it dawned on Oliver that the parliament was not doing anything that he had hoped for from it. He reminded members of the House of Commons that it was they who had invited him by their Petition and Advice to undertake the government of the country (first as King, the office which he had refused, and then as Protector) and that he had told them then that he could not do so unless there were some other persons that might interpose between him and the Commons, who had 'the power to prevent tumultuary and popular spirits'. By going back on what they had agreed to as a constitutional settlement and had discussed in detail with him they had now created confusion, tried to estrange the Army from him, and had encouraged Charles II to invade the country. Therefore he dissolved Parliament and exclaimed, 'Let God judge between me and you', to which the republicans cried, 'Amen.'

Oliver did not publish a declaration, as he had been expected to do, explaining why he had so quickly and suddenly dissolved his second parliament. But clearly he was afraid that the out-and-out republicans, both in the Commons and the independent congregations, were stirring up trouble for him in the City of London and in the Army.[46] A petition had in fact been signed by 2,000 Londoners demanding, among other things, a one-chamber parliament and its regular meetings. He also believed that since the Commons had been questioning the validity of the Petition and Advice, on which his authority was founded, it was hopeless to expect he would be granted the additional financial assistance he needed to carry on the war against Spain and to pay the garrisons in England, Scotland and Ireland. Thus he felt convinced that the stability of his government was in imminent danger of being undermined.

It was rumoured during the last months of Oliver's life that a new parliament would be called. His son, Henry, wrote to Thurloe on 31 March 1658: 'Parliaments are so casual that one would not profane them by overfrequency; and yet, on the other side, to raise money without them is a condition from which I pray God to keep us.' When Richard Cromwell succeeded his father as Lord Protector he was obliged to call a parliament because the state was some £2 million in debt, but its members were once again in no hurry to discuss the matter. In fact the two Cromwells, like

Charles I, summoned their parliaments largely for financial reasons, not in order to legislate. And although Oliver expressed his anxiety for legal reforms he was glad to be rid of the Assembly of Saints because 'it flew at liberty and property' and preferred religious anarchy to the mildest form of order. His two Protectorate parliaments displeased him because they occupied so much of their time debating constitutional questions. There is some slight evidence that if Oliver had called another parliament he would have received an offer of the Crown from it since the restoration of the monarchy would be the only means of ensuring political stability in the nation.[47]

When Oliver first sat in the Long Parliament he was eager to pare down the powers of the monarchy, as exercised through the royal prerogative, and to give Parliament the right to veto ministerial appointments and to govern the Church. He accepted the plea of necessity put forward by his leader, John Pym, to justify the denunciation of Charles's government in the Grand Remonstrance of 1641. Yet by 1647 he had come to believe that Parliament's power had become too absolute and that this endangered public liberties as much as did an autocratic king. The New Model Army was estranged from the Long Parliament when its leaders proclaimed that the Army was the enemy of the State and Oliver, though a member of parliament, sided with the Army. The Long Parliament, he insisted towards the end of his life, had assumed supreme authority and sought to be executive, legislature and judiciary all rolled into one. After he became Protector he thought that the parliamentary regime envisaged by his republican opponents was arbitrary and that his own government, subject to checks and balances by the Council of State and triennial parliaments, was not: he was, he claimed, 'a child in swaddling clothes'.[48]

The question remains whether either Charles or Oliver could have been more effective statesmen if they had handled their parliaments differently. Elizabeth I was good at delivering golden speeches, but she managed without a parliament for much of her reign. When her Parliament became obstreperous, as it did towards the end of her reign, she was an aged virgin Queen governing a country which had been victorious in war. Her critics in the Commons were willing to bide their time. King James I had made more provocative speeches than his son was to do, but at least he and his Parliament had been thrown into unison after the Gunpowder Plot and, on the whole, he managed to avoid tricky issues – moreover his theological views were Puritanical. During the reigns of Elizabeth and James the members of the Commons were beginning to relish their growing strength and gradually acquiring supremacy over the House of Lords. Although some modern historians have written about the rise of a revolutionary party or an opposition party during James I's reign, in fact neither a formed opposition nor a formed Court party existed. And as late as the autumn of 1641 the Commons actually sent a distinguished theologian to the Tower of London for remarking privately that there were two sides in the House of Commons. Certainly until a genuine division of opinion disclosed itself in the debate on the Grand Remonstrance the criticisms in the Commons of Charles's policies – particularly his fiscal policies – had been virtually unanimous. However tactfully Charles might have behaved, as was revealed during the struggle over the Petition of Right, he would surely have found it impossible to please his parliaments.

As for Oliver, unlike Charles, he did deliver lengthy speeches to his parliaments, defending his actions in detail. But during the previous hundred years the Commons had become more and more constitutionally-minded. They had realized the value of the rights they had acquired in voting taxation and initiating legislation. In addition to this, they had won the right to vet their own membership and to enjoy the privileges of freedom of speech and freedom from arrest when in session. The victory of the Long Parliament in the civil wars gave the republicans, who were certainly a small minority before 1648, stronger convictions. Though Oliver as Lord Protector was not wedded to any particular form of government, as he disclosed when he was offered kingship, yet as a former member of parliament himself he accepted that a periodical meeting of representatives of the people in the shires was essential to public welfare. But his parliaments failed to do what he thought they ought to do, that is to say, introduce legal reforms, uphold liberty of conscience and vote money for the support of his foreign policy. So he lost his temper with them and dissolved them. As far as their handling of parliaments was concerned, there is little to choose between Charles and Oliver as statesmen.

One can reflect that King Charles II was more successful than either of his predecessors in dealing with parliaments, for two reasons.[49] The first was that he recognized from the outset that his authority to call, adjourn or dissolve them, whenever he wished, gave him the whiphand over them; the second was that he was able to establish a Court party in the House of Commons which consisted not merely of Privy Councillors and other officials, such as had served Queen Elizabeth I, but was a genuinely devoted Royalist party – the Tories – who triumphed at the end of his reign. But of course Charles II, like Oliver Cromwell, then had the backing of an army, much smaller than his, but highly efficient. Without it the King could not successfully have defied the Exclusionists, who wanted to prevent his Catholic brother following him on the throne and were, like the republicans during the Protectorate, advocating constitutional changes never achieved before.

12

CHARACTERS IN CONTRAST

During his youth when Charles was Prince of Wales he was, as has been noticed, shy, grave and sweet and willing to take advice. But after he became King he submitted himself to rigorous self-discipline and self-control. Sir Philip Warwick wrote:

> His deportment was majestic, for he would not let fall his dignity.... His conversation was free, and the subject matter of it ... was most commonly rational or if facetious, not light ... there were few gentlemen in the world that knew more of necessary learning than this prince did.[1]

Though he seldom, if ever, lost his dignity or temper, his gravity, delicacy and retiring nature struck some people as arrogance, and his chilly reserve and aloofness often created a poor impression on those who met him. John Williams Archbishop of York, who knew him well, said that he treated people with little grace. He could, however, be tender and compassionate, as Oliver Cromwell realized when he saw him with his children.

One of Charles's outstanding characteristics was his sanguine nature. Sir Henry Slingsby, a Yorkshire baronet, who fought for him at the battle of Naseby, wrote: 'No perils ... would move him to astonishment; but that he still set the same face and settled countenance upon what adverse fortune soever befell him; and was neither exalted in prosperity nor dejected in adversity.'[2] The Scottish theologian, Alexander Henderson, who tried to convert him to Presbyterianism in Newcastle, confirmed what Slingsby said. 'Never,' he wrote, 'man saw him passionately angry or extraordinarily moved either with prosperity or adversity.'[3] After he became a captive of the Parliamentarian army he was described as being 'very pleasant and merry' and even when he was a close prisoner in the Isle of Wight he was said to be 'patient and cheerful'. To the end his motto was *Dum spiro spero* (while I live I hope).

Such self-control and confidence in the righteousness of his cause tended to make him obstructive at critical moments in his life. For example, when Cromwell and Ireton offered him the *Heads of the Proposals*, which would have enabled him to regain his Crown, he insisted: 'You cannot do without me: you will fall to ruin if I do not sustain you.' Sir John Berkeley, who thought Charles wrong to reject these terms, could only say to his master: 'Your Majesty speaks as if you had some secret strength and since Your Majesty hath concealed it from me, I wish you had concealed it from these men too.'[4] Earlier, after the battle of Naseby, which was Charles's most devastating defeat in the civil wars, the King complacently moved off to enjoy the hospitality of the Marquis of Worcester, one of the wealthiest men in England, at Raglan castle and, as Lord Clarendon wrote, 'amused himself with forming a new army in counties which had been vexed and worn out with the oppression of his own troops'.[5] And when his commander-in-chief, Prince Rupert, advised him to make peace he retorted: 'I must tell you that God will not suffer rebels to prosper, or His cause to be overthrown.'[6]

Such was Charles's obstinacy and optimism. Yet when it came to the crunch he was irresolute. Four months after he came to the Isle of Wight he decided to escape from his imprisonment; then, discovering minor obstacles in the way, he dropped the attempt and even as late as October 1648, when Berkeley had received clear warnings that the King was to be brought to trial and begged him to escape in order to save his life, Charles refused. By the time he did try to escape at the end of that year he was too stringently guarded in Carisbrooke castle to be able to join a ship which awaited him. Another earlier instance of his irresolution occurred when he fled from Oxford in 1646, apparently making for London, but after he arrived at an alehouse in Hillingdon he changed his mind and took a circuitous route to Newark, the headquarters of the Scottish army, having contemplated on his way north an escape from England by sea. Again, after he managed to get away from Hampton Court palace in 1647, he wandered as far as an inn in Bishop's Sutton in Hampshire, after losing his way in Windsor forest, before he made up his mind where to go and what to do next. Clarendon noted in his *History* that it was then 'generally believed that he had not within himself at that time a fixed resolution what he would do'.[7]

Charles's indecision and obstinacy revealed an inability to adjust himself to circumstances, which is the hall-mark of a statesman. It has rightly been observed that he 'combined a rigidity of mind and a lack of warmth and generosity to all but his family and a few friends'.[8] He had not the flexibility and political wisdom of Elizabeth I, nor the shrewdness and accessibility of his father. What mattered to him was the technical merit of his case and he found it easier to talk of reasons for doing nothing than to think what was best to be done. 'It was,' it has been contended, 'Charles's habit to meet difficulties with neatly arranged phrases rather than prompt recognition of unpleasant facts.'[9] Clarendon put it very clearly, writing that

> he was very fearless in his person but in his riper years not enterpris-
> ing. He had an excellent understanding, but was not confident of it,
> which made him oftentimes change his own opinion for a worse and
> follow the advice of men that did not judge as well as himself. This
> made him more irresolute than the conjunction of his affairs would
> admit: if he had been of a tougher and more imperious nature he
> would have found more respect and duty.[10]

Towards the end of his life, after the collapse of his last negotiations with Parliament, Charles recognized his own want of self-confidence and his irresolution, for he said: 'I wish I had consulted nobody but my own self, for then when in honour or conscience I could not have complied, I could early have been positive; for with Job I could willingly have chosen misery than sin.'[11]

The Roman Catholic historian John Lingard noted in Charles a habit of duplicity which had marked his conduct since his first entrance into public life.[12] Certainly his tergiversations over the Petition of Right induced members of parliament to be suspicious of his trustworthiness. Once the civil war broke out, Charles tried to enlist both the Scots and the Irish to fight for him and gave diametrically opposite promises to them. He aimed to gratify the Irish by sending over the Roman Catholic Earl of Glamorgan to offer them far-reaching pledges. Glamorgan in fact concluded a secret treaty with the Irish Catholics without informing the Marquis of Ormonde, who was the King's official Lord Lieutenant in Ireland and was of course a Protestant. After Charles lost the war he tried to play off the Independents, headed by Cromwell and Ireton, against the Presbyterians.[13]

Another instance of his duplicity is to be found at the very beginning of the civil war. He then allowed Prince Rupert to launch his belated attack on London at the time he was engaged in peace negotiations with the Parliamentarian leaders and had agreed to a 'cessation of arms'. Finally, when he was a prisoner in the Isle of Wight and was given a last chance to reach an agreement with Parliament he revealed his attitude of mind clearly. He told the Earl of Lanark: 'Many things may be freely offered to obtain a treaty that may be altered when one comes to treat; and there is a great difference between what I will insist on and what I will permit for the obtaining of peace.'[14] Unquestionably Charles believed that his devious means of securing his restoration to power were justified by the ends. He exemplified what Voltaire made Moses say: 'It is not the business of a ruler to be truthful but to be politic.'

Both Lord Clarendon and Sir Philip Warwick thought that the King was insufficiently energetic and resolute and that if he had only acted firmly, he could have crushed the rebellion immediately it began. But his trouble was that he was extremely sensitive about levying war on his own subjects. After his side had obtained an advantage in the first big battle of the war at Edgehill his chief military adviser, Lord Forth, urged him to thrust the cavalry on a forced march upon London so that the capital city could be seized before the Parliamentarian army could get back to ensure its defence. Charles, however, had been so shocked by the deaths incurred in the battle – including those of his general-in-chief, his standard-bearer and a young cousin – that he rejected the idea, hoping that he could gain his capital without shedding blood. It was for the same reason that when during the following year it looked as if he were winning the civil war he refused to storm Gloucester, one of the few towns in the west of England held by the Roundheads, preferring to offer the garrison generous terms if it would surrender. Then he settled down to a leisurely siege which gave ample time for a relieving force to reach the city from London. This episode was a military turning-point in the war. In his *Eikon Basilike* Charles wrote, 'I never had any victory which was without sorrow because it was on mine own subjects' and he instructed his son to use clemency in order to heal wounds.[15]

Undoubtedly Charles was sincere in his reluctance to take extreme measures in the civil war and wanted to avoid unnecessarily provoking ordinary citizens. Yet he was inconsistent, for he invited both Irish Catholics and Scottish Protestants to enter England and fight his English subjects. Indeed it was when his schemes to bring Irish (and French) troops into England were revealed, because his private papers were discovered by the Parliamentarians after the battle of Naseby, that his bad faith alienated more of his subjects from him. After patiently negotiating with Charles for many months Oliver Cromwell reached the conclusion that the King 'was so great a dissembler and so false a man that he was not to be trusted'.[16]

Although previously blaming their grievances on Charles's 'evil counsellors', several of the nobility who had met him – and many of the minor gentry who had not – gradually came to condemn him personally for their grievances, yet his sensitivity, refinement and courage in adversity could be attractive to those who served him. It is remarkable that one of the men who tried hardest to help him escape from his imprisonment in the Isle of Wight, Henry Firebrace, had fought against him in the civil war, while one of the grooms of the bedchamber appointed by Parliament to replace Charles's own trusted courtiers, James Harrington, 'passionately loved his Majesty' and was distraught when the King was executed.[17]

It has been argued that Charles only became deeply religious when his fortunes faded. But nearly all those who knew him intimately testified to his constant faith and prayer. Like his father, he studied theology and, as has been noticed, debated capably with an eminent and learned Presbyterian minister. It was his trust in a beneficent deity that gave him the fortitude with which he faced his trial and execution. Charles would never have admitted that he was dishonest or hypocritical. He took it for granted that his double-dealing was justified by his conviction that he had been chosen by the Almighty to care for the welfare and liberties of his people. He did not regard himself as, or aspire to be, a despot, but a loving father. At the beginning of the civil war he declared: 'I will either be a glorious king or a patient martyr.'[18] Indeed he deliberately chose to be a martyr during his last months on earth.

So in spite of all his shortcomings, his lack of enterprise, his futile deceitfulness and his failure to be ruthless as a military commander, the Royalists who were true to him treasured his memory. To Sir Philip Warwick he was

> a prince of most excellent temper and strength of understanding and regularity of affection, having no transports into vice, but endowed with habits of knowledge and piety and so unapt to have made any invasion upon the liberty and property of his subjects but as some rude attacks of a popular faction seemed to force him to defend his sovereignty.[19]

To Edward Hyde Earl of Clarendon he was 'the worthiest gentleman, the best master, the best friend, the best husband, the best father and the best Christian that the age in which he lived had produced'.[20] But Clarendon confessed that he was not the best king, while Archbishop Laud called Charles 'a mild and gracious prince', but had to admit he knew 'not how to be, or be made great'.[21]

As Charles was a hereditary king, it is natural enough that light can be thrown on his character by noblemen and courtiers who knew him personally as well as by the insights that can be derived from letters that he wrote to his wife and son, the future Charles II, which have survived. But for Oliver less evidence is available. Most observations about his character come from his enemies, not only from the Royalists whom he conquered but from men who were estranged from him once he assumed the Protectorate. A few letters to his wife and children are revealing, but even his dedicated Secretary of State, John Thurloe, discussed in his voluminous correspondence his master's policies, not his behaviour.

One characteristic stands out: he was a highly emotional man; in times of trial he could not be restrained from tears. Easily touched by the distress of others, he could show sympathy and at times be unexpectedly pitying, as was shown, for example, in the letter he wrote to his brother-in-law Valentine Walton, whose son was killed at the battle of Marston Moor: 'There is your precious child full of glory to know sin nor sorrow any more. He was a gallant young man, exceeding gracious. God give you his comfort.'[22] He was shattered when his own son, also named Oliver, died early in the civil war and his grief over his daughter Elizabeth's sufferings from cancer contributed to his own death. His steward, John Maidston, wrote of him: 'He was naturally compassionate to objects in distress even to an effeminate measure; though God had given him a heart wherein was left little room for fear but what was due to himself . . . yet he did exceed in tenderness towards sufferers.' To Charles also 'a tender and compassionate nature' was attributed.[23] Yet he and Oliver spent five years watching men die on battlefields.

Oliver's emotions could be aroused easily in other ways than compassion, as when he gave the orders that resulted in the massacre of Irishmen at the siege of Drogheda or when in a fury he put an end to the Rump Parliament and to his second Protectorate parliament. His hysterical exaltation in battle showed him at his worst. Whereas on the field he took his decisions rapidly, exploiting mistakes made by the enemy (as with Lord Byron's premature charge on the Royalist right wing at the battle of Marston Moor or the Duke of Hamilton's over-extension of his invading army at the battle of Preston or David Leslie's cramping of his left wing at the battle of Dunbar), in politics he was less decisive. Invariably he spent a long time in contemplation before reaching a crucial conclusion. It took him several months before resolving to leave the Parliament to join the Army in 1647, and it was nearly two years after the battle of Worcester before he decided forcibly to dissolve the Rump Parliament. He had deliberately delayed his arrival in London at the time of Pride's Purge. In every case he awaited God's guidance. Finally, after a majority in the Parliament of 1657 voted to offer him the title of king, he occupied five weeks in mulling over the arguments for and against acceptance, but in the end insisted that as 'every man' had 'to give an account to God of his actions' he must have 'the approbation of his conscience' and felt that what was not 'of faith' was 'a sin', so he refused the honour.[24] Andrew Marvell put his hesitations poetically:

> And knowing not where heaven's choice may light
> Girds yet his sword and ready stands to fight.

Oliver has often been accused of being an opportunist, of dealing with each situation as it arose, perceiving the necessity but not the consequences. Opportunism is hard to define: most men can be described as opportunists. Certainly, as Guizot, who was once Prime Minister of France, remarked, 'Cromwell was not a philosopher; he did not act in obedience to systematic and pre-meditated views; but he was guided in his government by the supreme instinct and practical good sense of a man destined by the hand of God to govern.'[25] What also may be stated is that Oliver reacted sharply to changing circumstances: for example, he wanted to rule with the aid of parliaments, but when he discovered that members were more concerned with constitutional subtleties than legislative reforms he discarded them. Likewise, when he first began negotiating with Charles 'he thought he was the uprightest and most conscientious man in the three kingdoms', but within two years he described the King as 'the most hard-hearted man that lives on earth'. Again, at one time when he was critical of his superior officer, the Earl of Manchester, he exclaimed (according to Manchester) that he hoped 'to live to see never a nobleman in England'; yet after he became Lord Protector he nominated his own House of Lords and tried to persuade Manchester and other members of the nobility to serve in it.

In public life Oliver was impressive. His earliest biographer, Samuel Carrington, wrote:

> The generosity, courtesy and affability of his Highness did so super-abound as that no one person ever departed from his presence unsatisfied, for he received the petitions of all men, he heard their

grievances and his charitable memory was so retentive as that he never forgot their requests but made it his chief object to have them in mind and most tenderly provide for them.[26]

The foreign ambassadors in London were satisfied with the courteous and considerate way in which he treated them when he granted them interviews. Sir Philip Warwick, when he first saw Cromwell in the House of Commons, noted his poor clothes and excited manner, but came to admire his 'great and majestic deportment and comely presence'.[27] Oliver had, it has been observed, a very masculine personality (unlike Charles), 'with an appeal for women to whom he was unfailingly courteous'.[28] For example, he treated the Marchioness of Ormonde, the wife of Charles's Lord Lieutenant in Ireland, with kindness, not seeing why she should want for food or money because her husband was a Royalist commander. After the death of John Lilburne, who had become one of Oliver's fiercest critics, he granted his widow Elizabeth the continuance of the pension he had paid to her husband plus arrears, and arranged for her to obtain possession of his family property in Durham.

Oliver was undoubtedly a Puritan in the modern sense of the word. As has been noticed, he told the Army Council in 1647: 'It is the general good of all the people in the kingdom we ought to consult. That's the question: what is for their good, not what pleases them '[29] He condemned drunkards and 'whoremasters' and reproved his daughter Bettie for her vanity and 'carnal mind' and asked his wife to tell her 'to turn to the Lord' instead of being 'cozened with worldly vanities and world company which I doubt she is too subject to';[30] still, she was his favourite daughter. Conscious of the temptations of power, he acknowledged once

that the glories of the world had so dazzled his eyes that he could not discern clearly the great works the Lord was doing: and said that he was now resolved to humble himself and desire the prayers of the Saints that God would be pleased to forgive his self-seeking.[31]

Oliver Cromwell's assumption of the Protectorate modified his Puritan austerity. When he lived in Drury Lane he entertained his friends with bread, cheese and ale, but after he became Protector he enjoyed his sherry and roast beef and liked to smoke a pipe.

Often he drank wine with his fellow officers – in fact he seems to have been less abstemious than Charles. Richard Baxter, the distinguished Presbyterian minister, who disliked him, thought he 'was pious and conscionable in the main course of his life till prosperity and success corrupted him'.[32] At the marriage of his youngest daughter, Frances, there was mixed dancing continuing through the night until five o'clock in the morning. And when his third daughter, Mary, was married at Hampton Court the ceremony was conducted by an Anglican clergyman according to the form in the Book of Common Prayer, which the Puritans in the Long Parliament had abolished in favour of a Presbyterian directory. Mrs Lucy Hutchinson, a typically straitlaced Puritan, thought Cromwell's younger daughters were insolent fools and his son, Henry, 'a debauched ungodly cavalier'.[33]

Oliver's religious beliefs of course lay at the root of his character. He looked to God for inspiration in all he did, and if he did not receive it, he was perplexed. He conceived the kingdom of God, it has justly been said, in terms of its people being given liberty of conscience and the redress of civil and social wrongs. He regarded the possession of private property as the basis of civil liberty. The English people, he was convinced, had been singled out by the Almighty as a Chosen People; that is why he aimed 'to make the name of Englishmen to be as much feared as ever the name of *civis Romanus*'. Indeed, as Clarendon wrote, 'his greatness at home was but a shadow of his greatness abroad'. At home, in spite of his ruthlessness in warfare and the part he played in Charles's execution, he was, again as Clarendon observed, 'not a man of blood'. Invariably he did his best to see that those who opposed him after he became Protector and had to be dismissed from office did not suffer unduly. For instance, when he cashiered John Lambert, who evidently resented the fact that Oliver had been empowered by the Petition and Advice to nominate his own successor, he assured the major-general that 'until he should be provided with other employment suited to his merits he should continue to enjoy the pay of a lieutenant-general'. So it was thought to be a good thing to be 'Lambertised'.[34]

A word that was used about Oliver not by his friends but by his adverse critics was magnanimity. Clarendon spoke of his 'personal courage and magnanimity' and Lucy Hutchinson also wrote of 'his personal courage and magnanimity' which upheld him against all his enemies and malcontents. One doubts if magnanimity meant quite the same in those days as it does now. But like Sir Winston Churchill, the most magnanimous of all English statesmen, who had to accept enormous sacrifices of human life in wartime, Oliver Cromwell sympathized deeply with individual sufferings and want. Just as Churchill invited Neville Chamberlain to join his War Cabinet, Fairfax, after Cromwell failed to persuade him to retain his command in 1650, was offered a place in the Council of State.

Another word that may be applied to Oliver is fatalism. So often what he had striven after turned out entirely differently from what he had expected, above all in the behaviour of his parliaments. He had not set out to become a military dictator, as was clear after he dissolved the Rump, and was to deny that he had done so. Ten years before he attained the peak of his authority he told his fellow officers that he was persuaded by his conscience that their purpose must be to achieve the peace and safety of the people. 'It remains only that God show us the way and lead us in the way, which I hope He will.' In his last speech to Parliament he claimed to have 'attained mercy and truth, righteousness and peace' following in 'those footsteps God had laid for us'.[35] It was a fateful conclusion.

The impression of Cromwell's greatness fastened itself on several of his contemporaries even when they thought him wicked or bad. The Royalist Sir Philip Warwick concluded: 'I will say no more but that verily I believe he was extraordinarily designed for extraordinary things.'[36] The republican Lucy Hutchinson wrote: 'To speak the truth ... he had much natural greatness and well became the place he had usurped.'[37] Lord Clarendon thought he had some virtues which caused the memory of some men in all ages to be celebrated'.[38] John Milton, who became disillusioned with the Protectorate towards its end, wrote of Oliver's 'rare and all-but-divine excellence'.[39] Sir John Reresby, who fought for the King and was imprisoned by General Fairfax, believed that 'had his cause been good, he would have ranked as one of the greatest and bravest men the world ever produced'.[40]

A notable difference that can be seen between Oliver Cromwell and Charles I is in the records of their health. Oliver was constantly ill after the civil wars ended. He contracted malaria and dysentery in Ireland, where he was, he said, 'crazy in his health' and nearly all his officers were sick 'fitter for the hospital than the field'. In Scotland during the winter of 1650 and the early spring of 1651 he was taken seriously ill, and not until June was he able to write that 'the Lord had plucked him out of the grave'. In the winter of 1655 he was again ill and sent for a surgeon from Paris to ask his advice about his bladder; in the winter of 1656 another surgeon dressed a boil on his breast, and his health remained poor throughout the whole of that winter – he had a heavy cold and was ill of the stone. During the next winter he was again ill with catarrh. In February 1658 he suffered from sleeplessness and was reported to have been given opiates. On the other hand, Charles, in spite of his weakness as a child, of which the only remnant was his stutter, by taking regular exercise and never over-exerting himself was always in excellent health, which helped him to face the slings and arrows of outrageous fortune with equanimity. He never agonized, as Oliver did, over taking political decisions.

But what they had in common was constant appeals to their consciences: what a modern historian has dubbed their 'super-ego'.[41] Charles's conscience would not allow him to betray his supporters – except the Earl of Strafford – or commit him to the permanent destruction of the episcopacy. In general 'his tender conscience made him choose the softer way'.[42] Oliver prided himself on ridding the Church of scandalous ministers and 'profaneness, disorder and wickedness in high places'.[43] His conscience was invoked to prevent all that and he appealed to the consciences of others to approve of what he had achieved. 'The mind is the man,' he claimed, 'and if that be kept pure, a man signifieth somewhat.'

Yet whatever their consciences dictated, both Charles and Oliver also appealed to over-riding necessity in acquiring what they needed in the way of arms and money. Oliver did not attribute these necessities to God, for that would have been sinful, but thought that all of his actions had been 'in order to the peace and safety of the nation'. Charles aimed to perform his duty as a king so as 'to govern God's people for His honour and their safety'. In his last days on earth he declared: 'Neither liberty nor life are so dear to me as the peace of my conscience, the honour of my crown and the welfare of my people.'[44] Oliver saw himself 'as being set on a watch-tower to see what may be for the good of these nations and what may be for the preventing of evil'.[45] Both, then, were conscientious men who felt assured that they were divinely inspired in their decisions and actions and were convinced that they had no other end in view than to fulfil God's purposes and confer blessings on those committed to their care.

13

REVOLUTIONARY TIMES

Charles I and Oliver Cromwell lived in a time of revolution: Charles was its victim and Oliver its instrument. But what sort of a revolution was it? During the past hundred years professional historians have held divergent views. It has been called a Puritan revolution, a Puritan rebellion, a great rebellion and, generally, simply *the* English revolution; yet one or two scholars have even questioned whether it was a revolution at all. Certainly if by a revolution is meant, in the words of an American historian, 'a sweeping fundamental change in political organization, social structure, economic property control and the predominant myth of a social order'[1] then clearly the events in England during the middle of the seventeenth century can scarcely be described as revolutionary; for in spite of the sale of all the Crown and Church lands, the confiscation of some Royalists' lands and heavy taxation imposed on the properties of other Cavaliers, so far as the spread of wealth between social groups was concerned England in 1660 was to be barely distinguishable from England in 1640.[2] Compared with the Reformation the sixteenth century, the industrial revolution of the eighteenth century, the establishment of the trade union movement and the Labour party at the end of the nineteenth century, and the introduction of the Welfare State and dissolution of the British empire in the middle of the twentieth century, the civil wars and their aftermath were of no such enormous historical significance.

This revolution was simply a political revolution sparked off by religious passion. It is true that the preconditions of the political revolution were social and economic. The dissolution of the monasteries, the closure of abbeys and the sale of chantries enabled King Henry VIII to confer financial advantages by selling most of them off to pay for foreign wars and so benefiting the landed gentry and rising middle classes, including lawyers and merchants. On the other hand, partly because of inflation (the price revolution of the sixteenth century), partly because of incompetent estate management and partly owing to the urge for peers to indulge in lavish building and conspicuous consumption, the aristocracy's wealth and influence declined, allowing political and social power increasingly to fall into the hands of the squirearchy. Thus the House of Commons now became more important than the House of Lords; a contemporary statement that has frequently been quoted was that the House of Commons could in the reign of James I buy the House of Lords three times over. A solid class of lesser landowning gentry had risen on the ruins of the old aristocracy. At the same time, because the monarchy experienced financial difficulties owing to the costly wars against Spain, it had been obliged to sell off lands, which constituted capital assets, in order to make ends meet. Even then the Crown was forced to come to the Commons to ask for subsidies or to borrow money from Customs farmers and the City of London. In Charles's case he felt compelled to levy taxes without the consent of Parliament, thereby arousing widespread discontent throughout his kingdom which was reflected in petitions presented by members of parliament as soon as they were called to Westminster. The monarchy and the aristocracy having been weakened, members of the Commons could and did relish their growing strength.

It must not, however, be forgotten that peers were still looked to for leadership by the Commons. The Earl of Essex was appointed to command the Parliamentarian army; after another army was formed in East Anglia, in which Cromwell served, the Earl of Manchester became its general. The Earl of Warwick was put in charge of the navy when it revolted against Charles. Noblemen like the Earls of Bedford, Pembroke, Salisbury and Northumberland, Lord Saye and Sele and Lord Grey of Groby all sided against the King. Altogether some thirty peers supported the Roundheads at the outbreak of the civil war. No class divisions determined the character of the armies once hostilities began. The gentry were split right down the middle with fathers and sons, brothers and cousins fighting on opposite sides. Even the so-called 'middling people' were divided in their allegiance,[3] while many of the yeoman farmers, the backbone of England, were chiefly concerned with trying to keep the war out of their own counties and were to attempt to do so by arming themselves with clubs.

Oliver Cromwell was a fairly typical member of the rising squirearchy. Both the uncle after whom he was named and his father had profited from the purchase of the properties of abbeys and nunneries and were prominent in the local affairs of Huntingdonshire. But Oliver's father died when he was fairly young so that he was obliged to look after a widowed mother and six sisters. Consequently, for a time he was relatively badly off. Nevertheless he was elected a member of parliament when he was twenty-seven, and a few years later received a useful inheritance from an uncle. The fact that he was able to lay out between eleven and twelve hundred pounds, as he told his friend, Oliver St John, on 'the business of Ireland and England'[4] shows that he was fairly affluent. King Charles I, for his part, had managed comfortably enough after he dissolved Parliament in 1629 by continuing to levy tonnage and poundage and by reviving ship money as well as using other ingenious expedients, but as soon as he involved himself in war against the Scottish Covenanters he was compelled to rely on a parliament to vote him supplies unless the Scots meekly gave in. Thus it was Charles, not Oliver, whose financial needs shaped his future career.

Some historians have insisted that the English revolution, as they call it, was part of a general crisis that afflicted the whole of Europe in the mid-seventeenth century.[5] Crisis is a word that can be lavishly applied, but one fact is clear. Much of the unrest was a result of demands for heavy taxation by governments committed to warfare.[6] To that extent the long-term causes of the civil war in England certainly had much in common with outbreaks elsewhere. Lately another interpretation of the causes of the civil war has been advocated. The common people, it has been pointed out, were angered by enclosures, disafforestation and the drainage of the fens, which led to much rioting. Whether these riots can be called 'the intrusion of the popular element into national politics' can be questioned, but clearly this unrest lent fuel to the country gentlemen who came to Westminster to express the grievances of the communities they represented.[7]

When the Long Parliament met in November 1640 it consisted mainly of reasonably well-to-do gentlemen like Oliver Cromwell. It did not contain a revolutionary party and had no intention of overthrowing the monarchy or abolishing the House of Lords. It simply wanted to air its accumulated woes, both secular and religious, and exact remedies for them. The House of Commons received something like front-bench leadership from John Pym, an experienced politician with a morbid dread of Popery.[8] Men like Edward Hyde, John Culpeper, Viscount Falkland and George Digby, who were all to become Royalists in the civil war, were alike critical of the government's recent actions, particularly its financial methods. But if one man can be picked out as the principal agent of a revolution against the Crown it was not John Pym but Alderman Isaac Penington.[9]

Penington was about the same age as Pym. He was a wealthy merchant, who made his money by trading in Europe and Asia and was the warden of the Fishmongers Company, although he does not appear to have had anything to do with fish. A zealous Puritan – a Presbyterian and therefore hostile to episcopacy – he had a town house in Coleman Street, a country house in Buckinghamshire, and owned a brewhouse and inn in Whitefriars where he and his wife entertained the kind of clergy of whom they approved. Elected as one of the four members of parliament for the City of London, he soon became prominent in the Long Parliament by agitating for the abolition of all bishops and the rest of the hierarchy of the Church of England – 'root-and-branch' – and advocated the suppression of idolatry and superstition by law. His value to the Parliamentarian cause once civil war loomed up was because he acted as an intermediary between the Commons and the City in borrowing money and by overthrowing the Royalist Lord Mayor and getting himself elected in his place.

On 11 December 1640 Penington presented a 'root-and-branch' petition to the House of Commons, said to have been signed by 15–20,000 Londoners, which bore witness to the strength of the Puritan movement there. The question of root-

and-branch was temporarily postponed because John Pym had decided to concentrate his opposition to the government by impeaching the Earl of Strafford for high treason on the grounds that he was the chief of Charles's 'evil counsellors'. Under the impulse of this threat two of Charles's leading ministers fled the country. Charles intended to do his best to defend Strafford and hoped to save his life (execution was the punishment for treason) just as he had saved the life of a Jesuit priest, John Goodman, in January 1641 by reprieving him from a death sentence imposed under an Elizabethan act of parliament. But in the following April, after the Commons had resolved to secure the condemnation of Strafford not by impeachment but by a Bill of Attainder, which needed to be passed by the King and both Houses of Parliament, another petition from the City was presented to the Commons signed by 20,000 Londoners demanding Strafford's death. This was followed in the first week of May by demonstrations in Westminster, first by substantial citizens and then by ordinary 'mechanic folk', baying for Strafford's blood. They 'cried to every Lord as they went in and out [of the Upper House] in a loud and hideous voice' for 'justice against Strafford and all traitors'.[10] The Bill of Attainder had been duly passed by the House of Commons on 21 April. On 1 May Charles had told the House of Lords that he would not assent to the Bill, but would debar Strafford from office for life, and begged the Lords to find some way of getting him out of his difficulties because his conscience was troubling him.

This feeble plea cut no ice. The Lords were unimpressed by Charles's anxiety over his conscience, but felt that it exonerated them from saving the life of a fellow member. The menacing crowds continued their demonstrations outside the Houses of Parliament and placards were posted up vilifying any who voted against the Bill of Attainder. On 8 May the House of Lords passed the Bill by 26 votes to 19 (the total membership of the House was 150). Most of the peers who might have voted against the Bill were said to have 'absented themselves upon pretence (whether true or suppositious) that they feared the multitude'.[11] Next day Charles signed the Bill after receiving a letter from Strafford absolving him from the promise the King had given him that he should not suffer in life, honour or estate. Immediately after this Charles gave his assent to another Bill which laid down that the parliament could not be dissolved without its own consent. Thus Charles's betrayal of Strafford was the catalyst that paved the way to civil war.

Charles had never really liked Strafford. As has been noticed, he did not care for confident men. But until the end of his own life Charles's overworked conscience smote him for shedding the blood of an innocent man. In his *Eikon Basilike* he wrote:

> I never thought anything, except our sins, more ominously presaging all these mischiefs, which have followed, than these tumults in London and Westminster soon after the convening of this Parliament, which were like a storm at sea ... like an earthquake shaking the foundations of all. . . . Indeed nothing was more to be feared, and less to be used by wise men, than these tumultuous confluxes of mean and rude people, then to dictate, at last to command and overawe Parliament.[12]

After yielding other concessions to Parliament, particularly that no taxation could be levied without its consent and that all prerogative courts should be abolished, Charles left London for Scotland in August 1641 in the evident hope that once peace had been concluded with the Covenanters he could win support there against the English parliament which had been humiliating him. When he returned to London at the end of November he had a pleasing reception and was entertained at a banquet by the Lord Mayor and Aldermen, though John Venn, a close colleague of Isaac Penington, had done his best to prevent it. At the banquet Charles told his audience that the tumults and disorders before he left for Scotland had been carried out by 'the meaner sort of the people' while the main part of the City was loyal to him. He was soon to be disillusioned.

The month of December 1641 saw the climax of the political drama. On the 1st Charles was presented with the Grand Remonstrance by the Commons, a revolutionary document and programme (at any rate from the King's point of view) to which he gave a restrained and temperate answer. Then Penington introduced into the Commons another monstrous petition, this time demanding the exclusion of the bishops from membership of the House of Lords and requiring the control of the militia, meaning the armed forces of the kingdom, by Parliament. Next the Grand Remonstrance was printed, published and distributed as an appeal to the general public against the monarchy. Seeing that the City was seething with excitement, Charles retorted by dismissing Sir William Balfour, whose sympathies lay with the majority in the House of Commons, from his command of the Tower of London and replacing him with Sir Thomas Lunsford, a rough character trusted by the King. On 23 December a new Common Council dominated by Puritans was elected in the City. On the same day Penington produced yet another petition, this time signed by 30,000 people, again calling for the abolition of the episcopacy and protesting at Balfour's dismissal. On Boxing Day the Lord Mayor warned the King that he could not answer for the public safety unless Lunsford was removed. Though Charles complied, on the following three days further demonstrations by citizens of London and apprentices took place with shouts of 'No bishops!: No popish Lords!' The mob even invaded Westminster Abbey. Twelve bishops were prevented by violence from entering the House of Lords.

The majority in the Commons had come to regard the London citizens as their 'surest friends' and Pym said: 'God forbid that the House of Commons should proceed in any way to dishearten people to obtain their just desires in such a way.'[13] Evidently the London mobs were easily swayed. In 1647 and 1648 they were to cry out for the reinstatement of Charles I on his own terms and in 1660 they were to clamour for 'a free parliament' which signified the restoration of Charles II. It is on no account clear why they should have been so eager for the execution of Strafford or so worked up about whether the bishops should be members of the House of Lords unless inspired by parliamentary Puritans. Without their intimidation Strafford might not have lost his life nor the King his authority.

Oliver's antagonism towards the bishops, which had first been emphasized in his maiden speech in the Commons, points to affinities with John Pym and Isaac Penington. Pym, it is true, regarded himself as an orthodox Christian and not a Puritan, which he considered to be an opprobrious term. He believed that life was a struggle between good and evil, that evil was represented by Anti-Christ, and that Anti-Christ was the Pope. After Charles came to the throne Pym thought that a conspiracy to introduce 'Arminianism' – disguised 'popery' – had been sanctioned by the King under the influence of clergymen like Roger Manwaring, whom Pym vainly tried to impeach. When Penington introduced his first petition from the City of London aiming at overthrowing episcopacy Pym favoured its committal, and although his original belief was that the episcopate could be reformed by depriving the bishops of their legislative and judicial powers, when Oliver Cromwell and his friends Sir Henry Vane and Sir Arthur Haslerigg persuaded Sir Edward Dering to introduce a root-and-branch Bill in May 1641 Pym voted for its second reading. Oliver and another friend of his, the reverend Hugh Peter, the adventurous son of a Cornish merchant, who, among other exploits, helped to found Harvard university, used to meet regularly at the Star Inn in Coleman Street. Peter was a friend of John Goodwin, the Puritan vicar of St Stephen's church in Coleman Street;[14] it is likely enough, therefore, that Oliver was also a friend and ally of Penington. Pym, however, was not an enthusiast for root-and-branch, which he regarded as a divisive issue in the Commons. An ordinance abolishing the episcopacy was not passed until October 1646.

The final debate on the Grand Remonstrance at last split the Commons asunder. What was called 'an episcopal party' emerged, consisting of members who spoke vehemently against it and did not want it rushed through. But Oliver thought the arguments in its favour were so clear that the outcome of the debate was assured. Nevertheless, the debate lasted from twelve noon till two o'clock the following morning when the Remonstrance was carried by 159 votes to 148; the minority wanted to record their protest and urged that it should not be published, but Oliver, according to Edward Hyde, said that if it had been rejected 'he would have sold all he had the next morning and never seen England again'. Thus he identified himself with the political revolutionaries. Years afterwards he was to claim that although the revolution was not caused by disputes over religion, it 'was not the first thing contended for . . . [but] God brought it to that issue at last'.

But did not the revolution, that is to say the civil war, arise over religion in the beginning? Most members of parliament in 1642 agreed that the main questions before them were the preservation of religion and the future government of the Church.[15] During the debate on the Grand Remonstrance 'the episcopal party' strongly objected to all the bishops in the Church being accused of superstition and ecclesiastical tyranny: they resolved that they would 'no longer be baffled by such a rabble of inconsiderable persons set on by a juggling Junto'.[16] On the opposing side Pym and Cromwell maintained that it was high time 'to deal plainly with the King and posterity . . . since all projects have been rooted in Popery'.[17] The accusation that 'idolatrous and Popish ceremonies had been introduced into the Church by the command of the bishops' remained an integral clause in the Grand Remonstrance. Most of those who voted against the Remonstrance became Royalists. When Charles summoned the Short Parliament in April 1640 no Royalist party existed; now it had been created, though many Royalists went reluctantly to war simply because they saw 'King Pym' as a greater threat to their liberties than King Charles.

Charles supposed that if he withdrew from London the violence would subside: he could 'allay the insolency of the tumults'.[18] He hoped to save the Church from destruction and denied that he had started the civil war. He might well have argued that Penington had begun it when in the spring of 1641 he had manipulated the crowds which had so menacingly demonstrated against Strafford and the bishops.

Under the impulse of his Queen, before he left his capital he tried to arrest five members of the House of Commons and accuse them of treason. Penington was not one of them but it was he who, after receiving a warning of Charles's intentions, appears to have hidden them in his house in Coleman Street. Frustrated in his counter-attack Charles later admitted that he had behaved unconstitutionally, but he had been driven to extremities. So he left London and proceeded slowly to York, whence he carried on negotiations with Parliament. The terms demanded from him were too radical for his acceptance and both sides prepared for civil war.

Which side started the war is a hard question to answer. Charles, when he saw off his wife Henriette Marie at Dover towards the end of February 1642, knew that she was going to pawn the Crown jewels, buy munitions and seek aid against the Parliamentary leaders. It has been argued that the withdrawal of his accusations against the five members of the Commons whom he had attempted to arrest, plus his agreement to the exclusion of the bishops from the House of Lords, which he gave that February, formed a mere smokescreen covering his real purpose of regaining his full authority by force.[19] On the other hand, the passage of an ordinance by Parliament at the beginning of March seizing control of the militia, thus arming themselves for 'their necessary defence', was also a first step towards war. Indeed, Oliver Cromwell was at the forefront of such military preparations, for only one week after Charles left London he moved in the House of Commons that a committee should be appointed to consider means to put the kingdom into 'a posture of defence'. Against whom? – obviously the King. The Earl of Northumberland, one of the peers who took up arms against Charles, was to declare in 1648 that 'not one in twenty of the people of England are yet satisfied whether the King did levy war against the Houses first, or the Houses first against him'.[20]

Nearly all the constitutional changes sought by Parliament had been settled before Charles went to the north of England. The prerogative courts had been abolished, unparliamentary taxation repudiated and the holding of parliaments regularly guaranteed. Henceforward, apart from control over the militia, the principal demand that the Parliamentarian leaders insisted upon was Charles's agreement to the dismantling of the Church of England set up by the Tudors, but that was the one concession that he refused to grant. As he told his Queen, he was ready to abandon to Parliament control over the armed forces, but in the words of his father, 'No bishop, no king.' Charles created the impression that he intended to defend the existing order in the Church through thick and thin.

To Oliver too at the outset of the civil war religious questions were at the forefront of his mind. He was convinced that Charles had been involved in a popish conspiracy: two of his ministers, Cottington and Windebank, who fled the country after the meeting of the Long Parliament, were thought with some justification to have been crypto-Catholics; the influence of Charles's Roman Catholic Queen and the papal agents who came to her Court were believed to have been paramount; Charles's reprieve of the Jesuit (Goodman), his refusal to send away a papal agent (Count Rosetti) when asked to do so by Parliament and the outbreak of rebellion by Irish Roman Catholics all added fuel to the flames of fury against Catholic 'innovations' lit by Puritan preachers throughout the kingdom.[21] Oliver was a leading advocate of the abolition of episcopacy. When it was suggested that elected committees should govern the Church instead of the bishops, he denied that 'a parity [equality] in the Church' meant 'that we must at last come to a parity in the Commonwealth'. Oliver was no democrat at any time.

Apart from his animus against the bishops, in what sense can Oliver be called a revolutionary? His most recent biographer has called him a 'conservative revolutionary', but that surely is a contradiction in terms.[22] Another modern historian has stated that he was not a committed revolutionary and that 'his real achievement was his defeat of army radicalism and the restoration of the supremacy of the gentry in English political life'.[23] Certainly he came to make high claims for the Army when he and Henry Ireton became disillusioned with the Long Parliament that had started the war. He accepted the contention that the New Model Army was no 'mere mercenary army hired to serve any arbitrary power of a State, but called forth and conjured by several declarations of Parliament to the defence of their own and the peoples' just rights and liberties'. They might be soldiers, Oliver declared, but they were also Englishmen, who desired the peace of the kingdom and the liberties of the subject for which Parliament had invited them to fight.[24] In the twentieth century army chiefs in Africa and Asia have often made the same sort of claims, namely that the services are justified in overthrowing the rule of corrupt politicians.

What the rank-and-file of the New Model Army wanted once

the first civil war had been won was the right to petition Parliament about their grievances.[25] In April 1647, when Parliament aimed to demobilize the armies, dispatch an expeditionary force to Ireland, and deprive Oliver of his military rank, the pay of the infantry was twenty weeks in arrears and that of the cavalry fifty-five weeks in arrears. No indemnity had been promised for unlawful acts committed during the war and no provision made for the widows and orphans of soldiers killed in action. The Agitators in the New Model Army were chiefly concerned over their material worries, not over the need for radical political reforms.

Most of the democratic ideas expounded in the debates conducted in the Army Council at Putney in the autumn of 1647 were put forward by John Wildman, John Lilburne's deputy as Leveller leader, the author or part author of a radical constitution called the *Agreement of the People*, who had not served in the Army, and Colonel Rainsborough, who was not a Leveller though he sympathized with their views. What motivated the unruly soldiery was their conviction that the majority in the House of Commons, led by Denzil Holles and other Presbyterian notables, was treating them unfairly and not giving them their deserved rewards. This discontent among the Parliamentarian soldiers was not confined to the New Model Army, but prevailed in other armies in the north and west of England and among scattered garrisons. It has been estimated that altogether in the spring of 1647 Army arrears amounted to £2½ million, equivalent to about the total annual state expenditure.[26] If so, it was no wonder mutinies were common. They would have occurred without being influenced by the propaganda of the Levellers. 'No one need doubt,' Professor J. P. Kenyon has written, 'that if the Long Parliament had settled its [the New Model Army's] arrears of pay and carried through its scheme of demobilization no more would have been heard of the Levellers or the *Agreement of the People* and very little of Oliver Cromwell.'[27]

Furthermore it has to be remembered that it was Lord Fairfax, the commander-in-chief of the New Model Army, who was responsible for the suppression of the mutinies that followed the King's execution in 1649. The notion that Fairfax was a marionette, manipulated by Cromwell and Ireton, will not stand up to serious examination. And the idea that Cromwell frustrated a social revolution is far-fetched.

Of course a wide variety of revolutionary thoughts were adumbrated during the Interregnum, some of which were to find expression during the reigns of King William III and Queen Anne, though these were political and religious rather than social and economic. Otherwise, what the English revolution achieved was limited.

During the Protectorate Oliver Cromwell was absorbed in a struggle to establish order and peace at home and win prestige abroad. Not unnaturally he felt that the Levellers, the Fifth Monarchists, the Quakers and other extremist groups and cranks (whose often comical notions have been elaborately investigated during the twentieth century)[28] were a threat to his objectives. Yet in his maturity he became more and more convinced of the importance of liberty of conscience for all Christians so long as they did not provoke disorder. So he always tried to unravel divergent beliefs, as the founder of the Society of Friends, George Fox, bore witness. The great Victorian historian Gardiner wrote that Oliver 'was marvellously tender to fanatics and fools'. By his toleration and magnanimity he fostered dissent, so that even after the Anglican Church was re-established in 1660 nonconformity could not be repressed. And out of nonconformity concepts of political liberty burgeoned. Only to that extent was Oliver the agent of a lasting revolution, though Charles, obstinate to the last, was undoubtedly its victim.

14

Epilogue:
DEPARTURE

Charles had been contented enough when the Army sent him to Hampton Court palace, where he was able to play tennis and billiards and hunt in the park. As has been noticed, he was visited there not only by Cromwell and Ireton but also by their wives. The officer in charge of him was Oliver's cousin Edward Whalley, a fair-minded man, although Sir Philip Warwick, then the King's secretary, thought him to be 'a crack-brained fanatic'.[1] Hampton Court was the largest of the royal palaces, containing 1,500 rooms. Whalley told General Fairfax that he 'could no more keep the King there if he had a mind to go than a bird in a pound'.[2] Charles, however, had given his oath that he would not try to escape.

On 1 November 1647 Oliver had been taking part in the debates in the Army Council at Putney, where the future government of the kingdom was earnestly discussed. Distrust of Charles was obvious. Oliver recognized that it was generally questioned whether the liberty and safety of the country required the continuation of the monarchy and the House of Lords and that a strong case was being made out for Charles's deposition. But at that time Oliver was certainly not contemplating the trial and execution of the King. When Major-General Harrison asserted that Charles was 'a man of blood' and ought to be arraigned for his life, Oliver answered that there had been several cases 'in which murder was not to be punished'. Henry Ireton supported him, urging that they ought not to adopt any unlawful way of bringing a wrongdoer to justice.[3]

Evidently Oliver derived from what he heard in these debates in the Army Council a belief that some of those participating in them, who had put forward a republican and democratic constitutional scheme which would have brought the monarchy to an end, were even prepared to assassinate Charles. It was a highly dubious assumption. For John Lilburne, the Leveller leader who had initiated a radical movement when he published a large petition to Parliament in March 1647, was not only perfectly clear that Charles ought not to be put on trial until a new constitutional scheme had been agreed upon, but had actually attempted to reconcile the Army, in which he had been a lieutenant-colonel, with the King, and was even prepared to accept a constitutional monarchy. Why then did Oliver after these debates were over send an urgent message to his cousin Whalley, to the effect that Charles was in danger of assassination by the Levellers, and why did Whalley show this letter to the King, as he did? Thereupon Charles broke his parole in a devious way, which enabled him to claim that he was justified in doing so, and that very night escaped from Hampton Court.

As usual, Charles had not made up his mind where he was going. Apparently his first idea was to find his way to London and appeal to Parliament to help him against the Army, but soon he realized that this was dangerously impracticable. Instead, accompanied by his loyal servants Jack Ashburnham and John Berkeley, who had both been earlier ordered by Whalley to leave Hampton Court, he set out for Southampton. From there Berkeley wanted him to sail to Jersey, but Ashburnham advocated the Isle of Wight, where a young officer, Colonel Robert Hammond, who was a nephew of one of the King's former chaplains, had just been appointed governor by General Fairfax. Ashburnham had recently met Hammond and received the impression that he was disgusted with the Army's treatment of the King.

With Charles's permission Ashburnham and Berkeley sailed to the Isle of Wight to interview the young governor and then brought him back across the Solent to see the King, who was by no means pleased but, as usual, took the situation calmly, saying that 'it was too late to boggle'.[4] It has been suggested both then and now that somehow Oliver had manipulated this escape by Charles to the Isle of Wight and that he himself visited the island either before or after Charles went there. But the evidence for this is negligible.[5] Thomas Hobbes, the famous philosopher, who tutored Charles I's eldest son, wrote in his *Behemoth*, an account of the Long Parliament, that Oliver's intention in frightening the King from Hampton Court was

> to let him escape ... whither he pleased beyond the sea.... The going into the Isle of Wight was not part of Cromwell's design, who neither knew whither nor which way he would go; nor had Hammond known any more than other men if the ship had come to the appointed place [Southampton] in due time.[6]

The reason why Charles refused to go abroad and preferred to stay in what he believed was a safe place in his dominions was that at Hampton Court he had been negotiating with Scottish commissioners in the hope that they would undertake to send an army into England in order to enforce his restoration to his throne. On his first evening in Carisbrooke castle in the Isle of Wight he wrote to the English Parliament offering terms for a settlement, agreeing to abandon his control of the militia and his right to appoint ministers of state without Parliament's approval, and to allow Presbyterianism to be the national religion for three years; but he refused to consent to the permanent abolition of the bishops or to confirm the sale of their lands.

To Charles's proposals Parliament retorted by passing four Bills. If Charles accepted them, he would be permitted to treat on constitutional reforms. Charles refused to give his assent to the four Bills and notified Parliament of his decision on 28 December 1647. On Boxing Day he had signed an engagement with the Scots commissioners by which they agreed to be satisfied with the imposition of Presbyterianism in England for only three years, while exempting Charles and his household from becoming Presbyterians themselves; during these three years an assembly of divines, including members nominated by the King, would settle the future of the Church. Meanwhile, Charles undertook to do his best to suppress the Puritan sects. In return the commissioners promised to dispatch an army to invade England, which, if victorious, would restore Charles to most of his constitutional rights. How Charles managed to reconcile this agreement with the promise he had given to the leaders of the English army during the previous spring that he would not 'engage our people in another war' or a letter he wrote to Parliament before he left Hampton Court in which he said he aimed 'to avoid effusion of more Christian blood' is obscure, but presumably he satisfied his conscience with the thought that any commitments were justified if they led to his liberty and reinstatement in the authority conferred on him by God.

Much has been made by latter-day historians of the party known as the Levellers who, headed by John Lilburne, were at this time putting forward proposals for political, social and economic reforms. They were given their name, it seems, either by Charles or by Oliver, because they advocated manhood suffrage. In fact they certainly did not envisage anything like the suffrage that exists in the modern democratic world. One of these Levellers, who took part in the debates at Putney, agreed that apprentices, servants and those who received alms should not have the right to vote.[7] The Levellers do not appear to have had more than a few thousands of followers, who were chiefly concentrated in London. They did not emerge until the spring of 1647 and two years later they had practically vanished from the public stage. Their influence upon the rank-and-file of the Army was sporadic and has been exaggerated: most soldiers were much more concerned with their own treatment by the government than with constitutional niceties, although naturally they felt resentful 'towards the Army's detractors inside and outside Parliament'.[8]

Whatever the precise strength and influence of the Levellers were, they made a profound impact on both the Cromwellians and the Royalists. Oliver temporarily came to terms with them by withdrawing his opposition to the appointment of the only field officer friendly to them, Colonel Thomas Rainsborough, as Vice-Admiral of the navy. He replaced Admiral Batten, who had gone over to the other side, while Sir John Berkeley, who arrived from the Isle of Wight in November 1647 to deliver letters from Charles to Cromwell and Ireton, was warned that although they had pacified the Levellers for the time being they were so dangerous that the King should escape abroad if he valued his life. It looks indeed as if Oliver would have been thankful – as Thomas Hobbes believed – if Charles had fled the country.

Before Charles escaped from Hampton Court he had left a

message for Colonel Whalley assuring him that it was not the
letter from Oliver that had persuaded him to do so, but because
he was 'loath to be made a close prisoner upon pretence of
securing my life'.[9] In fact he *had* been panicked by fear of
assassination, as he later confessed both to Colonel Hammond
and to his own companions. By then Oliver had given up any hope
of concluding an agreement between the Army, Parliament and
the King. On 2 January 1648, after Charles had rejected the four
Bills, Oliver voted with the majority in the House of Commons
that no further addresses should be made to the King. He
observed that Parliament should not 'teach the people any longer
to expect safety and government from an obstinate man whose
heart God had hardened'.[10] He at once wrote to Colonel Hammond warning him that the Commons were fully aware of 'the
King's dealings' and advising him to watch out for any 'juggling'
and be sure to keep Charles secure. Charles had in fact already
signed his engagement with the Scots, which made him 'patient
and cheerful'.[11] With the coming of spring the second civil war
broke out.

While the war was in progress Charles was kept a close prisoner in the Isle of Wight at Carisbrooke castle. The one attempt
he made to escape, as he had done from Hampton Court, was
frustrated because he was unable to thrust his head through a
barred window from which it was only a drop of five feet to the
ground. Despite this mishap and some minor annoyances such as
the dismissal of his chaplains, including Colonel Hammond's
uncle and even his barber (which decided Charles to grow a
beard), he soon reverted to his usual placid self. He enjoyed his
food, his meals consisting of sixteen courses. He took walks,
played bowls when it was not raining, read books (mainly theological but including Spenser's *Faerie Queen*), wrote letters and
drafted or revised the *Eikon Basilike*. The monotony was varied by
planning further escapes, which came to nothing since Hammond had received reinforcements from General Fairfax which
enabled him to strengthen the guards around the castle. Even the
news of the defeat of the Scots by Oliver in the battle and rout of
Preston did not rattle Charles unduly. When he told Hammond
that it was 'the worst news ever came out of England' and

Hammond remarked that the Scots under the Duke of Hamilton, had they won the war, would have controlled the thrones of England and Scotland, Charles replied: 'You are mistaken. I would have commanded them back with the wave of my hand.'[12] On the surface Charles had good reason for his continued cheerfulness since in spite of his engineering the second civil war a majority in both Houses of Parliament repealed the vote of no addresses passed in January and voted to reopen negotiations with him.

These negotiations were to take place at Newport, a prosperous market town with plenty of inns, soon to be overflowing with soldiers, where Charles set up a miniature Court. Restrictions on his movements were lifted and Charles ordered several new riding suits for the occasion. He arrived early in Newport to await the parliamentary delegation. Yet before the negotiations began he did not think much good would come of them: he feared, rightly as it turned out, that it would be 'a mock treaty'.[13] Still, he was delighted to get away from his confinement in the castle and be treated, so far as the ceremonies went, like a king again.

The commissioners, who included Oliver's old friend Sir Henry Vane and his leading opponent in the Commons, Denzil Holles, were instructed merely to reiterate the proposals for a settlement which the King had previously rejected first in Newcastle and then at Hampton Court. Charles had to conduct all the negotiations himself; his courtiers watched what went on but were not allowed to take any active part in the proceedings. Charles began by stipulating that nothing to which he agreed should have any validity until a complete understanding had been reached on every point. Once again the question of religion was the chief stumbling block, but Charles also could not stomach an extensive demand for the punishment of many of the Cavaliers who had fought for him in the civil wars. And although he repudiated the arrangements made by the Marquis of Ormonde with the Irish Catholics, Charles had secretly sent him a message to ignore his concessions in Newport – a typical example of his duplicity. Soon Charles was confirmed in his conviction that the negotiations would lead nowhere, but he deliberately spun them out by offering large sacrifices of his rights in the hope that if the

commissioners were persuaded that he would deny them nothing
– or practically nothing – he would not be guarded so carefully at
Newport and thus would be able to escape abroad. On 9 October
1648 he explained to Sir William Hopkins, his host:

> Notwithstanding my too great concessions already made I know that
> unless I shall make yet others which will directly make me no king, I
> shall be at best but a perpetual prisoner ... my great concession this
> day [this was to surrender control of the militia for twenty years] was
> merely in order to my escape of which, if I had not hope, I would not
> have done.[14]

The period of negotiations was twice extended but, as Charles
foresaw, nothing came of them in the end. On 25 November he
bade farewell to the commissioners with these words: 'I thank
God I have made my peace with Him and shall without fear
undergo what He shall be pleased to suffer men to do unto me.'[15]
In the previous week he had urged his friends in Newport to
organize his escape, but he had left it too late, for by now the Army
under the inspiration of Ireton had resolved to intervene: a
lengthy Remonstrance to the House of Commons that was delivered in the name of General Fairfax and the Council of Officers
demanded that 'the capital and grand author of our troubles, the
Person of the King may be speedily brought to justice for the
treason, blood and mischief he is guilty of'. At the same time
Ireton wrote to instruct Colonel Hammond to ensure that
Charles did not escape from his custody.

Oliver was then in Pontefract, but had been closely following
the negotiations in Newport. In writing to Hammond on 6
November he showed his distrust of the King; using his most
involved prose style, he said that he hoped that their experiences
of the Lord's favour 'will keep their hearts and hands from him
[Charles] against whom God hath so witnessed' and warned
Hammond against 'snares'. And, as has already been noted, he
told Fairfax (on 20 November 1648) that impartial justice should
be done upon offenders. Henry Ireton was determined that the
negotiations at Newport should fail, although the majority of the
members of the House of Commons, who wanted them to succeed, postponed consideration of the Army's Remonstrance,

which, it voted, was 'tedious'. When Fairfax notified the Commons that he was intending to advance on London, they sent him a message prohibiting him from doing so.

Meanwhile Cromwell, like Ireton, had come to the conclusion that the transactions in Newport endangered the safety of the realm. He called Charles's proposals, reasonably enough, 'a ruining hypocritical agreement' and convinced himself that the King – once again he called Charles 'the man against whom the Lord hath witnessed' – must be brought to justice. Furthermore, since the majority in the Commons were desirous of coming to terms with Charles, he changed his mind about the relationship between the Army and Parliament, about which he had been so positive during the debates at Putney the year before. With some hesitation therefore he suggested that the Army was 'a lawful power' called by God to fight the King, and that this authorized it to act in the interests of the nation as a whole. In fact Oliver gave his tacit consent to what his son-in-law, with the help of Colonel Pride, was about to do at Westminster.

The Army marched into London on 4 December; on 5 December the Commons defiantly voted that the King's answers were 'a ground to proceed upon for the settlement of the peace of the kingdom'. While both Ireton and his father-in-law would apparently have approved of the dissolution of the Long Parliament rather than its purge by Colonel Pride, they accepted it, which meant that they conferred upon the minority left in the House of Commons the badge of 'moral righteousness', so paving the way for the trial and execution of the King.[16]

Of course it must not be forgotten that Lord Fairfax, not Oliver Cromwell, was in command of what had been Parliament's army. Fairfax was no weakling, though he has often been pictured as acting under Ireton's thumb. When the Army Remonstrance, drawn up by Ireton, was submitted to the Council of Officers under the chairmanship of Fairfax, he insisted that before it was presented to Parliament the Army itself should send its own proposals to the King in the Isle of Wight for the future settlement of the country. But these proposals were such that they would have deprived Charles of all real power. In the middle of November he rejected them out of hand. Thereupon Fairfax agreed to

forward the Remonstrance to the Commons, which required that
the King should be brought to justice, led his army up to London
and dispatched Colonel Isaac Ewer, the very man who presented
the monster Remonstrance to the House, to escort Colonel Hammond to Army headquarters should he refuse to put the King
under close arrest without the authorization of Parliament. To
prevent the Levellers, now headed by John Lilburne in person,
who had been released from prison in August 1648, from trying to
stir up trouble in the Army, Fairfax had agreed to their being
consulted about the contents of the Remonstrance and, on
Oliver's suggestion, meetings were arranged between Ireton,
Lilburne and other officers, politicians and Puritan clergy to
discuss a future constitution, based on Ireton's *Heads of the
Proposals* and Wildman's *Agreement of the People*. It is perfectly
clear that Fairfax had derived the impression that what Ireton had
in mind was simply the deposition of the King and possibly his
succession by one of his younger sons.

Charles had therefore not only refused to agree to all the
demands put forward by the Parliamentary delegation at Newport
but also to those sent to him by the Army. On 27 November Ewer
took Hammond away from the Isle of Wight and accompanied
him to Fairfax's headquarters at Windsor. Two days later another
colonel with cavalry reinforcements arrived at Newport with
orders from Fairfax to the officers left in charge by Hammond to
escort Charles back to Carisbrooke castle. By then Charles had
abandoned all thoughts of escape, even saying grandly that he had
given his parole not to do so – Charles's parole was a flexible
instrument. He resigned himself to his fate.

Once again he believed he was threatened with assassination when he was brought away from Carisbrooke and un-
ceremoniously dumped at Hurst castle in Hampshire under
the care of a governor with a stern look and a bushy beard.
Here he was kept for three weeks in rooms which were so dark
that they had to be lit by candlelight in the daytime and with
only a causeway on which he was allowed to take walks for
exercise. It was while he was there that Pride's Purge took
place. Those members who were left in the House of Commons voted that no more addresses should be made to the King

and annulled the vote that authorized the negotiations with him at Newport.

From Hurst castle Charles was removed to Windsor after one or two futile attempts to escape on the way there. While he was back in his usual apartments in the castle Cromwell and Ireton – not Fairfax – wrote to the governor of the castle and to Major-General Thomas Harrison giving them detailed orders to take the utmost care of Charles and the few servants who were still with him, and telling them to prevent any Royalists or other local inhabitants from visiting the castle. There Charles remained over Christmas. When he learned that he was at last to return to London he said thankfully: 'God is everywhere alike in wisdom, power and goodness.'[7] Ever optimistic, he imagined that he would be allowed to plead his cause before Parliament.

On Boxing Day Oliver was present in the attenuated House of Commons where an ordinance establishing a special court for the trial of the King was under discussion. Oliver then stated: 'If any man moved upon this design that he should think him the greatest traitor in the world, but since Providence and necessity had cast them upon it, he should pray God to bless their counsels, though he was not provided on the sudden to give them counsel.'[8]

The ordinance was passed without a division, but the few members left in the House of Lords rejected it; so the Lower House resolved on 4 January 1649 that 'the Commons of England in Parliament assembled, being chosen and representing the people, have the supreme power in the nation' and two days later passed an act to set up a high court of justice, naming 135 commissioners to be judges and jurors at the trial of King Charles.

One may pause to reflect on the psychology of the two men. Charles, always resilient, felt that, as with Job in the Old Testament, he had been obliged to submit to a series of misfortunes, but was convinced that in the end God, who had chosen him to rule his people for their own good, would redeem him. Oliver was momentarily hesitant. He accepted that it was necessary to put Charles on trial, but it was significant that he himself was not able to offer his counsel on the matter because God had given him no guidance.

Already during the first half of December Oliver had shown his anxiety that the trial of Charles, 'the man against whom God had witnessed', should be legitimate and conclusive. He attempted to persuade the Duke of Hamilton, who had led the army of the Scottish Engagers into England and after he was captured had been imprisoned in Windsor castle, to bear witness to the King's complicity in the second civil war, but he had steadfastly refused. Oliver would also have liked more of the members of parliament who had absented themselves after Pride's Purge to have returned, and later in the month he consulted two eminent lawyers and, most significantly, the Speaker of the House of Commons in the hope that they would think of 'means to make the trial of the King acceptable to some at least of the absent members'. He also urged – in contrast with Ireton – that other Royalist offenders should be put on trial before the King in the expectation that they would provide damaging evidence against Charles. So he wanted justice to be done and to be seen convincingly to be done.

On 19 January Charles was driven by coach from Windsor to London and next day his trial opened in Westminster Hall.[19] The Court had been in session since 8 January. John Bradshaw, a stern republican who had recently been appointed Chief Justice of Chester, was chosen to preside over the proceedings, Oliver St John, who had been Cromwell's friend and associate over the years, and other distinguished judges having refused the invidious task. After the charge was read out accusing Charles of 'having traitorously and maliciously levied war against the present Parliament and the people therein represented' Charles naturally refused to recognize the legality of the court. Equally naturally, Oliver had anticipated his doing so. When Colonel Algernon Sidney, who had fought with him at the battle of Marston Moor, told him that the King could be tried by no court and that no man could be tried by that court, Oliver retorted, 'I tell you we will cut off his head with the Crown on it.' For he was fully aware that in spite of his own efforts the court established by the vote in the purged House of Commons and with fewer than half of the commissioners nominated to serve being present (General Fairfax was conspicuously absent, having attended just one preliminary meeting) was little more than a façade. In that court, such as it was, in Westminster Hall Charles and Oliver confronted each other for the last time.

On the first day, when Charles was brought into the court to be charged with high treason 'in the name of the good people of England', Lady Fairfax, the wife of the commander-in-chief, who sat wearing a mask in one of the galleries, called out: 'Not half, not a quarter of the people of England; Oliver Cromwell is a traitor!'[20] Few, except perhaps Oliver himself, knew who she was or even heard what she said. Charles denied the competence of the court and its right to impeach him, just as the Commons seven years earlier had not recognized the King's right to impeach five of its members, and he therefore would not plead. Evidence, that was in a way superfluous, was given to prove that the King had started and taken an active part in the war 'traitorously against his people'. Charles insisted that the court had no jurisdiction and that the House of Commons, which created it, had never been a court of law. He exclaimed that he 'did not value the charge a rush', but stood for 'the liberty of the people of England'. On 27 January the president of the court, Bradshaw, clothed in red, began to pronounce judgment. But before he began Charles, though still denying the competence of the court, asked because of

> the desire that I have for the peace of the kingdom and the liberty of the subject, more than my own particular ends, makes me now at last desire, that having something to say that concerns both, before sentence be given, that I may be heard in the Painted Chamber before the Lords and Commons.[21]

In this plea Charles was being consistent. For five years, while he was in exile from his capital, he had aimed to state his case before Parliament.

The court withdrew to consider Charles's request. Though it is not certain what happened during the adjournment, it appears that Oliver strongly resisted Charles's appeal and after half an hour drove Bradshaw and the commissioners back into Westminster Hall. Bradshaw then spoke for forty minutes before calling on the clerk to read out the sentence of death by beheading. Charles remained calm, but was denied leave to speak again. The death warrant was signed by only 59 of the 135 original commissioners, Oliver's signature coming third after those of Bradshaw and Lord Grey of Groby, elevated no doubt because of his rank.

It is beyond question that Oliver had determined that Charles should be tried for his life and was resolved that, once the verdict was reached, the execution should be promptly carried out. Before the second civil war started and Oliver set out for Wales to fight the Royalists there he had attended meetings of a Council of War at Windsor, where he had asked his fellow officers to examine their consciences and consider their duty. It was then resolved 'that it was our duty, if ever the Lord brought us back again in peace, to call Charles Stuart, that man of blood, to an account for that blood he had shed, and mischief he had done to his utmost against the Lord's cause and people in these poor nations.'[22]

There is no reason to suppose that since that time Oliver had changed his mind about the necessity of bringing Charles to trial as a war criminal. The evidence that Oliver only wanted to threaten Charles with death in the hope that he would at last concede all the demands made upon him by the purged Parliament and the Army is flimsy in the extreme, depending on a letter written by an obscure Royalist and the speculations of the French ambassador in London.[23] Unlike Charles, Oliver had no confidence in his mastery of elaborate political manoeuvres and negotiations. Once he had made up his mind – or once he felt certain that he had received guidance from God about what he ought to do – he carried out his decisions forcibly. He was always to maintain that in the King's trial justice had been done.

As to Charles, he was resolute that he could not live with the title of King if it meant he could not use his reason or act as his conscience dictated. Like Oliver, he believed in his cause with deep religious fervour. In his *Eikon Basilike*, which has been called 'a textbook on the right way to die',[24] he wrote: 'If I must suffer a violent death with my Saviour ... it is but mortality crowned with Martyrdom.'[25] And before his death he declared: 'I go from a corruptible to an incorruptible Crown where no disturbance can be, no disturbance ... in the world.'[26]

William Juxon, the erstwhile Bishop of London, who was

allowed to attend Charles on the scaffold, where he was executed on 30 January 1649, was told by Charles that what he had intended to say at his trial was this: 'I cannot submit to your pretended authority, without violating the trust which I have received from God for the welfare and liberty of my people.'[27] In the end, therefore, he deliberately sought martyrdom. By his death he saved the monarchy.

The day after Charles was executed his head was sewn back onto his body, which was embalmed. Permission was refused for its interment in King Henry VII's chapel in Westminster Abbey, where his father had been buried. Instead Charles's friends, led by the Duke of Richmond, took the coffin by coach from St James's palace to St George's chapel in Windsor castle, where it was lowered into a vault near the coffins of Henry VIII and his third wife, Jane Seymour. The cost of the funeral was £500. It was snowing in Windsor at the time so that, Sir Thomas Herbert wrote, 'the black velvet-pall was all white (the colour of innocency) . . . so went the white King to his grave in the 48th year of his age'.[28]

Oliver Cromwell, who survived Charles by nearly ten years, died in his bed in Whitehall palace on 3 September 1658. His body was embalmed and later taken secretly by night to Henry VII's chapel, where Charles's burial had been banned. The coffin that was carried in the Lord Protector's funeral procession, resplendent in pageantry, on 23 November 1658 carried only an effigy. The cost of the funeral was £60,000. After the Restoration Oliver's corpse was dug up and carried to Tyburn; there on 30 January 1661, the anniversary of Charles's execution, it was hung on a triple gallows along with the carcases of Henry Ireton and John Bradshaw. At sunset the carcases were cut down, beheaded by the Common Hangman, and then buried beneath the gallows. Oliver's head was put on a pole on the roof of Westminster Hall. It was blown down some time at the end of the seventeenth century, picked up, and after many adventures is now interred beneath the chapel of Sidney Sussex College in Cambridge, where Oliver had been a Fellow Commoner for a year.

The crowd outside Whitehall palace had watched Charles's execution with dejected faces and in silence. Oliver was said to have died in deeper silence than any king. 'There is not a dog that wags his tongue so great a calm are we in,' wrote John Thurloe afterwards.[29] So Charles and Oliver both left the earth in silence; and both, as faithful Christians, were convinced that they were on their way to paradise.

BIBLIOGRAPHICAL NOTES
AND REFERENCES

Until recently there were few scholarly biographies of Charles I, but in the last twelve years three have been published: John Bowle, *Charles I* (1975); Pauline Gregg, *King Charles I* (1981); and Charles Carlton, *Charles I: the Personal Monarch* (1983). Professor Bowle, as he told me, was chiefly interested in Charles as a connoisseur. Professor Carlton's biography is a psychological study, which contains a number of inaccuracies and misprints. To my mind Pauline Gregg's biography is the best and most reliable: it is only marred by an eccentric system of references.

Many biographies of Oliver Cromwell are extant. I find Sir Charles Firth's biography, first published in 1901 and many times reprinted, is still the best. Wilbur Cortez Abbott, *The Writings and Speeches of Oliver Cromwell* (1929–47), indispensable for its documentation, is also in effect a full biography, but some of its argument is justly criticized by Robert S. Paul in his *The Lord Protector: Religion and Politics in the Life of Oliver Cromwell* (1955), which I consider to be the second best biography. Charles I's letters and speeches are scattered; Sir Charles Petrie, *The Letters, Speeches and Proclamations of King Charles I* (1935) is only a small selection. His letters and speeches deserve scholarly compilation and collation, such as his proclamations have recently received.

The following are the most up-to-date surveys of the period under discussion:

G. E. Aylmer, *Rebellion or Revolution?: England 1640–60* (1986)
B. Coward, *The Stuart Age* (1980)
Derek Hirst, *Authority and Conflict: England 1603–1658* (1986)
J. P. Kenyon, *Stuart England* (1978, since revised)
Ivan Roots, *The Great Rebellion 1642–60* (1983)
J. S. Morrill, *Seventeenth-Century Britain 1603–1714* (1980). This contains a comprehensive bibliography; Dr Aylmer's book includes a dated table of events.

The following abbreviations are used in the references under chapter headings which are listed below:

Abbott = W. C. Abbott, *The Writings and Speeches of Oliver Cromwell* (1929–47)

Ashburnham = *A Narrative by John Ashburnham of his attendance on King Charles the First* (two vols, 1830), vol. II; this also contains the memoirs of Sir John Berkeley.

Burton = *Diary of Thomas Burton Esquire, member of the Parliaments of Oliver and Richard Cromwell* (ed. J. T. Rutt, four vols, 1828)

Cal. Cl. S. P. = *Calendar of the Clarendon State Papers* (four vols, 1869–1932)

C.S.P. (Dom) = *Calendar of State Papers (Domestic)*

C.S.P. (Ven) = *Calendar of State Papers (Venetian)*, both published by the London Record Office

Carlton = Charles Carlton, *Charles I* (1982)

Carlyle = Thomas Carlyle, *Oliver Cromwell's Letters and Speeches, with elucidations* (ed. S. C. Lomas, 1904)

Clarendon S. P. = *State Papers collected by Edward Earl of Clarendon* (three vols, 1767–86)

Eikon Basilike = *Eikon Basilike* (ed. P. A. Knachel, 1966)

Firebrace = C. W. Firebrace, *Honest Harry, the biography of Sir Henry Firebrace 1619–1691* (1932)

Gregg = Pauline Gregg, *King Charles I* (1981)

Paul = Robert S. Paul, *The Lord Protector* (1955)

Stevenson = G. S. Stevenson, *Charles I in Captivity* (1927)

Warwick = Sir Philip Warwick, *Memoirs of the reign of Charles I* (1813)

Woodhouse = A. S. P. Woodhouse, *Puritanism and Liberty* (1938)

Notes to Chapter 1

1 cit. D. Harris Willson, *King James VI and I* (1956), pp. 109–10.

2 Some biographers have asserted that Charles and Oliver played with each other as children. John Buchan, *Oliver Cromwell* (1934), p. 61 wrote: 'It is a pleasant and by no means fantastic thought that there [at Hinchingbrooke] he [Cromwell] may have met and played with the delicate little boy who was Prince Charles.' By p. 72 this becomes a fact: 'The new king, the thin little boy with a Scots accent whom he

[Cromwell] had played with . . .' But royal parents saw little of their young children, who were assigned to governors and governesses. Charles spent much of his childhood under the care of Sir Robert and Lady Carey in his apartments in Whitehall while his father went hunting outside London. There is no positive evidence that Charles ever went to Hinchingbrooke.

3 Charles to Henry Vane the Younger, 2 March 1646, endorsed by Charles 'a true copy'. Cal. Cl. S.P., I, p. 305. Charles to Henriette Marie, 15 April 1646. Clarendon S.P., II, p. 230.

4 Charles to Henriette Marie, 10 June 1646, J. Bruce, *Charles in 1646* (1856), pp. 45–6.

5 Charles to Henriette Marie, 31 Aug. 1646, ibid., p. 62.

6 Henriette Marie to Charles, received 29 Nov. 1646, Clarendon S.P., II, p. 292.

7 Charles to Lord Digby, 26 March 1646. Petrie, *The Letters, Speeches and Proclamations of King Charles I* (1955), p. 176.

8 Charles to Henriette Marie, 12 March 1646, Bruce, op. cit., pp. 23–4.

9 Charles to Henriette Marie, 3 March 1646, ibid., p. 21.

10 Carte MSS xx, f. 630, cit. S. R. Gardiner, *History of the Great Civil War* (1893), III, p. 239.

11 Cromwell to Fairfax, 21 Dec. 1646, Abbott, I, p. 420.

12 Cromwell to Fairfax, c. 11 March 1647, p. 430.

13 Gardiner, op. cit., p. 226.

14 Skippon, Cromwell, Ireton and Fleetwood to the Speaker of the House of Commons, 17 May 1647, Abbott, I, p. 446.

15 ibid., p. 442.

16 John Rushworth, *Historical Collections* (1721), VI, p. 513; Stevenson, p. 54.

17 Sirrahniho (John Harris), *The Grand Design*, 8 Dec. 1647, E 419.

18 George Joyce to an unknown officer from Huntingdon, *Clarke Papers*, I (1891), pp. 119–20. Sir Charles Firth thought the recipient was Major Scroope, but that was a guess.

19 ibid., p. 118; Add MSS 31116, f. 624.

20 Ashburnham, p. cxxxviii.

21 Stevenson, p. 57.

22 ibid., p. 77.

23 Newsletter, 8 June 1647, E 393.

24 Stevenson, p. 58.

25 Fairfax, Cromwell and other officers to the Lord Mayor Aldermen and Common Council of London, 10 June 1647, Abbott, 1, p. 459.

26 ibid., p. 460.

27 ibid., pp. 460–1.

28 Clements R. Markham, *The Great Lord Fairfax* (1870), p. 286 notes 1 and 2.

29 Abbott, I, p. 460.

30 Edward Hyde to Lord Hopton, 9 June 1647, Clarendon S.P., II, p. 395.

31 Charles to the Scottish Commissioners, 22 Oct. 1647, ibid., p. 381.

32 Ashburnham, p. cxl.

33 ibid., pp. cxl–cxli.

34 ibid; p. cxliii.

35 ibid., pp. cxlviii–cxlix.

Notes to Chapter 2

1 *The Memoirs of Robert Carey* (ed. F. H. Mares, 1972), pp. 68–9.

2 Warwick, p. 62.

3 Professor Carlton in his biography of *Charles I* (1983) writes (p. 7) of 'the lack of a satisfactory relationship with his mother' and states that 'Henry did not like Charles, whom he used to tease without mercy'. Pauline Gregg writes (p. 23) of Charles's 'close and deeply affectionate relationship with his mother' and states that Prince Henry 'expended thought and care on his delicate younger brother'. I think Pauline Gregg's opinion is a more accurate interpretation of the known facts. A biography entitled *Henry Prince of Wales and England's Lost Renaissance* by Roy Strong was published in 1986. Sir Roy writes that Henry was 'taciturn and withdrawn' but also states that 'he revelled in public appearances', which Charles certainly did not.

4 Harleian MSS 6986 f. 159, cit. E. Beresford Chancellor, *The Life of Charles I 1600–25* (1886), p. 25.

5 Warwick, p. 65.

6 Chancellor, op. cit., pp. 13–14 gives various versions of this anecdote.

7 C.S.P. (Dom) 1611–18, p. 273. The chaplain's name was Dr George Carleton.

8 Godfrey Goodman, *The Court of James the First* (1839), I, pp. 225–6.

9 G.P.V. Akrigg, *Jacobean Pageant* (1962), p. 208.

10 ibid., p. 229.

11 Lawrence Stone, *The Crisis of the Aristocracy* (1965), p. 450.
12 *The Political Works of James I* (ed. C. H. McIlwain, 1918), p. 12.
13 J. R. Tanner, *Constitutional Documents of the Reign of James I* (1930), p. 15.
14 Cit. D. H. Willson, *King James VI and I*, p. 132.
15 C.S.P. (Ven) 1619–21, p. 688.
16 Abbott, I, p. 10.
17 The story told by some of Cromwell's biographers that he was frequently birched by Dr Beard is deduced solely from the frontispiece to *The Theatre of God's Judgements Displayed*, which was first published in 1597, two years before Oliver was born.
18 M. M. Knappen, *Two Elizabethan Puritan Diaries* (1933), p. 9.
19 Samuel Carrington, *History of Oliver, late Lord Protector* (1659), p. 4.
20 John Buchan, *Oliver Cromwell*, p. 64.
21 Carlyle, I, p. 42.
22 Warwick, p. 65; F. N. L. Poynter and W. J. Bishop, *A Seventeenth-Century Doctor and his Patients* (1950), p. xxi. Symcotts took the degree of M.D. at Cambridge in 1636, but settled in practice in Huntingdon before then. He is known to have treated Cromwell as late as 1642.
23 Mayerne wrote 'Mons. Cromwell valde melancholicus', ibid., p. xxi.
24 Oliver Cromwell to Mrs St John, 13 Oct. 1638, Abbott, I, pp. 96–7.
25 cit. C. H. Firth, *Oliver Cromwell* (1929), p. 39.
26 For a critical up-to-date account of Cromwell and the rioting in the Fens, see Keith Lindley, *Fenland Riots and the English Revolution* (1982).
27 Abbott, I, pp. 67 seq.
28 ibid., I, pp. 131–2.

Notes to Chapter 3

1 Speech at Reading, 16 July 1647, Woodhouse, p. 420.
2 ibid., p. 174.
3 Owen C. Watkins, *The Puritan Experience* (1972), p. 7.
4 Richard Sibbes, *The Bruised Reed and Smoking Flax* (1934), p. 15.
5 Timothy, I, v. 15.
6 Charles Harvey, *A Collection of Several Passages* (1659), pp. 5–6.
7 cit. J. B. Black, *The Reign of Elizabeth 1558–1603* (1958), p. 16.
8 cf. Conrad Russell, ed., *The Origins of the Civil War* (1973), p. 19.

9 *Clarke Papers*, II, pp. 162–4.

10 Abbott, I, p. 80.

11 ibid., pp. 61–2.

12 ibid., p. 128.

13 ibid., p. 123.

14 *Table Talk* (ed. 1927), p. 20; cf. Patrick Collinson, *The Religion of Protestants* (1967), p. 70, who writes: 'The Elizabethan and Jacobean bishops were the poor relations of their predecessors.'

15 Epistle to the Ephesians, II, v. 8–9.

16 John F. H. New, *Anglican and Puritan* (1964), pp. 12 seq.

17 E. C. E. Bourne, *The Anglicanism of William Laud* (1947), pp. 60–1.

18 New, op. cit., p. 15.

19 Conrad Russell, 'The Parliamentary Career of John Pym', *The English Commonwealth* (1979), pp. 151 seq.

20 Abbott, I, pp. 340, 360, 375.

21 ibid., p. 519.

22 ibid., p. 542; Paul, p. 138.

23 ibid., p. 696.

24 Speech of 4 July 1653, Abbott, III, p. 53.

25 Burton, I, p. xxv.

26 Letter from Bristol, 14 Sep. 1645, Abbott, I, p. 377.

27 Abbott, III, p. 62.

28 Letter of 19 Oct. 1649, ibid., II, p. 146.

29 Letter of 26 Dec. 1656, ibid., IV, p. 368.

30 R. T. Petersson, *Sir Kenelm Digby* (1656), p. 251.

31 S. R. Gardiner, *Commonwealth and Protectorate* (1903), II, p. 100.

32 New, op. cit., p. 28.

33 *The History of the Rebellion and Civil War in England* (ed. W. D. Macray, 1885), IV, p. 42.

34 *Memoirs and Reflexions upon the Reign of Charles I* (1701), pp. 67–8.

35 cit. John Bowle, *Charles I* (1975), p. 127.

36 Charles to Henderson, 19 May and 6 June 1646, Cal. Cl. S.P., I, pp. 319 and 321; Henderson to Charles, 17 June 1646, ibid., p. 321; G. Burnet, *Memoirs of . . . the Dukes of Hamilton* (1852), p. 356.

37 Charles's third answer to the propositions at Newcastle, 12 May, 1647. S. R. Gardiner, *Constitutional Documents of the Puritan Revolution* (1906), pp. 311 seq.

38 Charles to Henriette Marie, 28 May 1646, J. Bruce, op. cit., p. 42.

39 Charles to Henriette Marie, 30 Nov. 1646, ibid., pp. 79–80.

40 Charles to Jermyn, Culpeper and Ashburnham, 21 Nov. 1646, Clarendon S.P., II, p. 396.

41 Charles to the Bishop of London, 30 Sep. 1646, ibid., p. 266.
42 Charles to Henriette Marie, 16 Oct. 1646, Clarendon S.P., II, p. 278.
43 D. Wilkins, *Concilia* (1737), iv, p. 471.
44 Charles to Jermyn, Culpeper and Ashburnham, 22 July 1646, Clarendon S.P. II, p. 242.
45 Charles to the Prince of Wales, 22 March 1646, Petrie, op. cit., p. 175; the same to the same, Stevenson, p. 271.
46 Gregg, p. 280.
47 Woodhouse, p. 97. I have altered the word 'moral' to 'mortal'.
48 *Eikon Basilike* (ed. 1879), p. 37.
49 *Eikon Basilike* (ed. P. A. Knachel, 1966), pp. 188 seq.
50 Caroline Hibbard, *Charles I and the Popish Plot* (1983), p. 22.
51 *The Anglicanism of William Laud* (1947), p. 58: 'The Puritans were not interested in toleration: what they demanded was to impose on everyone else the form of worship which they believed to be the only one compatible with God's word.' Laud undoubtedly found double predestination distasteful, but did not object to members of the Church of England believing in it, ibid., p. 61. For the opposite view that Laud was the innovator see Nicholas Tyache, apud *The Origins of the English Civil War* (ed. Russell 1973), pp. 119 seq.

Notes to Chapter 4

1 cit. Violet A. Rowe, *Sir Henry Vane the Younger* (1970), pp. 238–9.
2 Abbott, I, pp. 644, 678; II, pp. 405, 643.
3 Lucy Hutchinson, *Memoirs of the Life of Colonel Hutchinson* (ed. C. H. Firth, 1885), II, p. 202.
4 Abbott, II, pp. 329, 412.
5 ibid., II, pp. 405, 103; I, p. 416.
6 Antonia Fraser, 'Bess and Old Noll', *Horizon*, XIII, no. 4 (1971), pp. 106 seq.
7 W. H. Dawson, *Cromwell's Understudy* (1938), pp. 129, 278.
8 Abbott, II, pp. 248–50; I, pp. 382, 333.
9 George Bate, *Elenchus Motuum Nuperorum in Anglia* (1685), pp. 190–1 cit.; Roy Sherwood, *The Court of Oliver Cromwell* (1977), p. 135.
10 Roy Sherwood, op. cit., chs 4 and 6.
11 *The Diary of John Evelyn* (ed. E. S. de Beer), III, p. 229.
12 ibid., p. 97.
13 Lucy Hutchinson, op. cit., I, p. 119.
14 Stevenson, p. 49.

15 Warwick, pp. 64–5.

16 Lucy Hutchinson, loc. cit.

17 Stevenson, p. 260.

18 Carlton, p. 6.

19 Roy Strong, *Van Dyck: Charles I on Horseback* (1970), p. 42.

20 H. Trevor Roper, *The Plunder of the Arts in the Seventeenth Century* (1970), pp. 28 seq.

21 Beresford Chancellor, op. cit., p. 31.

22 ibid., p. 50.

23 Gregg, pp. 70–1, but see L. Stone, *The Crisis of the Aristocracy*, p. 660, who describes her as 'a dreadful old baggage'. She was buried in Westminster Abbey, having died in 1639 at the age of sixty-three.

24 Chancellor, op. cit., p. 91; Gervase Huxley, *Endymion Porter* (1959), p. 85.

25 cf. Caroline Hibbard, op. cit., p. 214 seq.

26 Quentin Bone, *Henrietta Maria* (1972), p. 173.

27 Charles to Henriette Marie from Oxford, 11 April 1646, Cal. Cl. S.P., I, p. 311.

28 Charles to Henriette Marie from Newcastle, 24 June 1646, Bruce, op. cit., 52.

29 ibid., pp. 76–7.

30 Henriette Marie to Charles, 26 Nov. and 30 Nov. 1646; Bruce, op. cit., p. 96; Clarendon S.P., II, p. 297.

31 Gregg, p. 389.

32 cit. Firebrace, pp. 52–3.

33 Charles to Mary [Lee?] 13 Feb, 1648, cit. J. D. Jones, *The Royal Prisoner* (1965), p. 142. This letter is in the Cambridge University library, Add MSS 7311. I interpret it as meaning that Jane Whorwood was already in the Isle of Wight then and may have been involved in Charles's first attempt to escape on 20 March. In April she was certainly in London obtaining files and nitric acid with which to remove bars from the window through which the King next intended to escape. Having hired a ship to take the King to Holland, she arrived back in the Isle of Wight on 13 May. The second attempt to escape was on 24 May.

34 Firebrace, p. 292.

35 Charles to Jane Whorwood, 26 July 1648, Firebrace, pp. 293–4.

36 Charles to William Hopkins, 13 Aug. 1648, ibid., p. 333.

37 Charles to Hopkins, ibid., p. 337.

38 Charles to Hopkins, 9 Oct. 1648, ibid., pp. 344–5.

39 Jane Whorwood to Hopkins, 23 Nov. 1648, Firebrace, pp. 151–2.

40 ibid., p. 184.
41 Gregg. p. 443.
42 *Eikon Basilike*, p. 40.

Notes to Chapter 5

1 cf. Roger Lockyer, *Buckingham* (1981), ch. 6.
2 *Dictionary of National Biography*, sub Thomas Howard quoting Clarendon.
3 Peter Young in his book on *Edgehill* (1967), p. 72, writes that 'strategy, one might almost say, had not yet been invented', but in his book on *The English Civil War*, written in collaboration with Richard Holmes (1974), the word is often used.
4 F. J. Varley, *Cambridge during the Civil War* (1935), p. 79.
5 *Commons Journals*, II, p. 720.
6 Abbott, I, pp. 189–90.
7 Peter Young and Richard Holmes, op. cit., p. 55.
8 cf. F. T. R. Edgar, *Sir Ralph Hopton: The King's Man in the West 1642–52* (1968), chs IV and V.
9 The story of Charles's 'grand strategy' originated with S. R. Gardiner and was based on a report received at second-hand by the Venetian representative in London; see my *English Civil War* (1974), p. 79. It is reiterated in Young and Holmes, op. cit., p. 98, but they admit that no written document exists to substantiate it.
10 ibid., p. 149.
11 Charles had been assured by the Earl of Leven that he would not take up arms against him again and the Duke of Hamilton had told Charles that the Scots would not enter the war. The Marquis of Montrose had warned both the King and the Queen of the likelihood that the Covenanters would do so, but was not believed. H. L. Rubinstein, *Captain Luckless* (1970), p. 157; Veronica Wedgwood, *Montrose* (1966), p. 53; Patrick Morrah, *Prince Rupert of the Rhine* (1976), p. 126.
12 Harleian MSS 7379, f. 96.
13 Sir Edward Walker, *Historical Discourses upon Several Occasions* (1705), p. 85.
14 The original of this famous letter is in the Victoria and Albert Museum. It has often been reprinted, e.g. in Morrah, op. cit., p. 148. Peter Newman, *The Battle of Marston Moor* (1981), pp. 40–1, defends Charles's writing of this letter and argues in contrast with most other historians, that it was a letter 'of information' and not an order to fight

at all costs. But it can hardly be claimed that the letter was a model of lucidity.

15 Charles I to Rupert, 3 Aug. 1645, Cal. Cl. S.P. iv, p. 74.

16 Richard Bulstrode's account in Young *Edgehill*, p. 267, and Young's comment, ibid., p. 124.

17 ibid., p. 125.

18 For a detailed account of Charles's tactics before and during the battle see Margaret Toynbee and Peter Young, *Cropredy Bridge, 1644* (1970).

19 Letter to Prince Rupert from Evesham, 12 July 1644, ibid., p. 125.

20 Young and Holmes, op. cit., p. 212.

21 I have discussed Rupert's career as a soldier in my book, *Rupert of the Rhine* (1976) chs 3–6.

22 cf. B. N. Reckitt, *Charles the First and Hull* (1952), ch. VII.

23 Carola Oman, *Henrietta Maria* (1936), p. 132.

24 *Eikon Basilike*, p. 34.

25 Young, *Edgehill*, p. 138.

26 ibid., p. 273.

27 Walker, op. cit., p. 34.

28 *Eikon Basilike*, p. 120.

29 Ashburnham, p. 130.

30 Charles to Rupert in April 1643, B. Warburton, *Memoirs of Prince Rupert and the Cavaliers* (1849), II, p. 167.

31 Clarendon, *History of the Rebellion* (ed. Macray), IV, p. 490.

Notes to Chapter 6

1 Abbott, I, p. 205.

2 See David Underdown, *Revel, Riot and Rebellion* (1985); John Morrill, *The Revolt of the Provinces* (1976); R. Hutton, *The Royalist War Effort* (1981).

3 B. Whitelocke, *Memorials* (1702), p. 72.

4 Cromwell to the Mayor of Colchester, 23 March 1642, Abbott, I, p. 221.

5 Cromwell to Harrison, 3 May 1651, Abbott, IV, pp. 411–12.

6 Morrah, op. cit., p. 75.

7 Abbott, I, p. 258.

8 ibid., p. 264.

9 ibid., pp. 277–8.

10 ibid., p. 272 quoting C. H. Firth, 'The Raising of the Ironsides', *Transactions of the Royal Historical Society*, xiii (1899), p. 53.

11 *Documents relating to the quarrel between the Earl of Manchester and Oliver Cromwell* (ed. J. Bruce, 1875) pp. 78 seq.; *Camden Miscellany*, viii (1883).

12 Clive Holmes, *The Eastern Association in the English Civil War* (1974), pp. 73 seq.

13 Abbott, I, pp. 251–2.

14 Peter Young and Richard Holmes, *The English Civil War* (1974), p. 157.

15 Abbott, I, p. 272.

16 Cromwell to John Cotton, 2 Oct, 1651, Abbott, II, p. 483.

17 Peter Young, *Marston Moor* (1970), p. 123.

18 H. C. B. Rogers, *Battles and Generals of the Civil Wars* (1968), pp. 149–51.

19 Accounts by Scoutmaster-General Watson and Thomas Stockdale, cit. Young, *Marston Moor*, pp. 232–7; Peter Newman, op. cit., p. 68.

20 Cromwell to Lenthall, 14 June 1645. Abbott, I, p. 360.

21 Cromwell to Lieutenant-Colonel Burgess, 29 April 1645, ibid., p. 345.

22 Abbott, II, p. 253.

Notes to Chapter 7

1 Gregg, pp. 207–8.

2 C. S. P. (Dom) 1653–4, pp. 298, 315.

3 Carlton, p. 158 quoting S.P., 16/198/9.

4 Gregg, p. 208.

5 Abbott, III, p. 179.

6 Carlton, p. 158.

7 The index figure for wheat from the tables compiled by Phelps Brown and Hopkins in *Economica*, Nov. 1956, are 1629:547; 1630:759; 1631:1055.

8 T. G. Barnes, *Somerset 1625–40* (1961) ch. VII; Paul Slack, 'Books of Orders: the Making of English Social Policy', *Transactions of the Royal Historical Society*, vol. 30 (1980), p. 1 seq.; Brian Quintrell, 'The Making of Charles I's Book of Orders', *English Historical Review* (1980).

9 Kevin Sharp, 'The Personal Rule of Charles I' in *Before the English Civil War* (ed. Howard Tomlinson, 1983), pp. 60–1.

10 Keith Lindley, *Fenland Riots and the English Revolution* (1982), pp. 23 seq.

11 ibid., p. 95.
12 William Dugdale, *History of imbanking and drayning of divers fens and marshes* (1662), p. 460.
13 Lindley, op. cit., p. 23.
14 Gregg, p. 224.
15 Maurice Ashley, *Financial and Commercial Policy under the Cromwellian Protectorate* (1972), p. xii.
16 M. V. C. Alexander, *Charles I's Lord Treasurer* (1975), ch. 7.
17 F. C. Dietz, *English Public Finance 1658–1641* (1932), ch. XI.
18 Barnes, op. cit., p. 143.
19 The best discussion of these ordinances is that by Ivan Roots in *The Interregnum* (ed. G. E. Aylmer 1972), ch. 6.
20 Carlyle, II, p. 358.
21 See F. A. Inderwick, *The Interregnum: studies of the Commonwealth legislation, social and legal* (1891).
22 Thurloe to Whitelocke, 7 April 1654. S. Bischoffshausen, *Die politik des Protectors Oliver Cromwell in der auffassung und thätigkeit seines Ministers des Staats Secretärs, John Thurloe* (1899), p. 178.
23 Laud to Wentworth, 22 Aug. 1635, *Laud's Works*, VII, p. 273.
24 Laud to Wentworth, 19 Dec. 1637, ibid., p. 391.
25 See supra, p. 55.
26 G. E. Aylmer, *The State's Servants* (1973), pp. 165–6.
27 *Thurloe State Papers*, VII, p. 807.
28 Aylmer, op. cit., passim.
29 Aylmer, *The King's Servants* (1961), pp. 171–2.
30 Roy Sherwood, *The Court of Oliver Cromwell* (1977), chs 4 and 5.
31 Aylmer, *The State's Servants*, p. 341.
32 Maurice Ashley, *Cromwell's Generals* (1954), p. 90.
33 Sherwood, op. cit., pp. 37–8.

Notes to Chapter 8

1 Henry Kamen, *The Iron Century* (1971), p. 79.
2 Professor J. H. Elliott has written copiously on the decline of Spain, e.g. in vol. IV of the *New Cambridge Modern History* (1971), ch. XV. He emphasizes the 'crumbling of the foundations of Castile's primacy' as an important factor in reducing Spanish power, and most recently in his *Olivares: The Statesman in an Age of Decline* (1986), ch. III he also writes of 'a moral failure', notably in the Court of Philip III. But basically broader economic causes were clearly the most significant; they may not have been obvious to the governments of

other European nations which, like that ruled by the Lord Protector, remained impressed by the safe arrival of the Spanish treasure fleets from America.

3 H. Trevor-Roper, 'Spain and Europe 1598–1621', *New Cambridge Modern History* (1970), p. 280.

4 Carlyle, II, p. 516.

5 Roger Lockyer, *Buckingham* (1981), p. 137.

6 ibid., p. 164.

7 Carola Oman, *Elizabeth of Bohemia* (1938), p. 172 note 1.

8 John Hacket, *Scrinia reserata* (1682), p. 183.

9 Gordon Albion, *Charles I and the Court of Rome* (1935), p. 54.

10 Quentin Bone, *Henrietta Maria* (1972), p. 22.

11 Lockyer, op. cit., pp. 236–8.

12 Letter to Sir Thomas Roe, cit. Oman, op. cit., p. 290.

13 *Debates in the House of Commons in 1625* (ed. S. R. Gardiner, 1873), pp. 31, 78.

14 S. R. Gardiner, *History of England* (1882), VI, p. 7.

15 Lockyer, op. cit., p. 237.

16 ibid., p. 399.

17 Harleian MSS 6988, f. 42.

18 H. G. R. Reade, *Sidelights on the Thirty Years War* (1942), p. 78.

19 ibid., p. 439.

20 Laud to the Queen of Bohemia, 25 June 1636, *The Works of William Laud*, VII, p. 261.

21 Laud to Wentworth, 26 April, 1637, ibid., p. 342.

Notes to Chapter 9

1 Carlyle, II, p. 357.

2 Bischoffshausen, op. cit., p. 184.

3 Abbott, II, pp. 534–7.

4 Cromwell to Philip IV, 5 Aug. 1654, F. P .G. Guizot, op. cit., p. 474.

5 Bordeaux to Brienne, 26 Aug. 1655, Guizot, op. cit., p. 512. Christopher Hill, *God's Englishman* (1970), p. 165, writes that Cromwell made 'diplomatic capital' out of the massacre of the Vaudois. 'It gave him,' he adds, 'just the lever he wanted for putting pressure on France.' To my mind that puts Cromwell's motives upside down.

6 Carlyle, II, p. 359.

7 ibid., p. 357.

8 Abbott, III, p. 874.

9 *Thurloe State Papers* IV, pp. 451–8.
10 Cromwell to the Chief Commander in Jamaica, 17 June 1656, ibid., p. 129.
11 J. R. Powell, *Robert Blake* (1971), pp. 271–2.
12 *Clarke Papers*, III, pp. 207–8.
13 Burton, I, p. 127.
14 ibid., III, p. 490.
15 ibid., p. 112.
16 Powell, op. cit., pp. 265, 268.
17 Cromwell to Blake and Montagu, 28 April 1656, Abbott, IV, p. 149.
18 *The Letters of Robert Blake* (ed. J. R. Powell, 1937), p. 455.
19 Commons Journals, VII, p. 41, cit. Powell, op. cit., p. 305.
20 Carlyle, III, p. 519.
21 Bischoffshausen, op. cit., pp. 205 seq.
22 Cromwell to Lockhart, 31 Aug. 1657. Carlyle, III, p. 140.
23 ibid., III, p. 168.
24 ibid., III, p. 148.
25 Charles Wilson, *Profit and Power* (1957), p. 81.
26 Abbott, IV, p. 53.
27 ibid., IV, p. 714.
28 Bonde's farewell interview with Cromwell on 25–6 July 1656, ibid., IV, p. 214.

Notes to Chapter 10

1 A. G. R. Smith, *The Government of Elizabethan England* (1967), p. 26.
2 J. E. Neale, *Elizabeth and her Parliaments 1584–1601* (1957), p. 249.
3 G. R. Elton, *The Parliament of England 1559–81* (1986), p. 329.
4 G. R. Elton, *England under the Tudors* (1974), p. 466.
5 W. Notestein, *The House of Commons 1604–10* (1976), p. 126.
6 *The Commons Debates for 1629* (ed. W. Notestein and F. Relf, 1921), p. 216 quoting Grosvenor's diary.
7 W. Notestein, op. cit., p. 23.
8 Speech of 21 March 1610, ibid., p. 278.
9 R. E. Ruigh, *The Parliament of 1624* (1971), p. 126.
10 Notestein, op. cit., p. 21.
11 *Debates in the House of Commons in 1625* (ed. S. R. Gardiner, 1873), p. 3.
12 Speech of 18 June 1625, ibid., p. 1.

13 Message of 8 July 1625, ibid., pp. 56–9.

14 Speech of 4 Aug. 1625, ibid., p. 76.

15 The speaker was Sir Francis Seymour, ibid., p. 78.

16 H. Hulme, *The Life of Sir John Eliot* (1957), p. 122.

17 ibid., pp. 141 seq.

18 *Commons Debates 1628* (1977), II, p. 3.

19 ibid., p. 60.

20 ibid., p. 64.

21 Cobbett, *Parliamentary History of England* (1807), pp. 335–6.

22 Hulme, op. cit., p. 221.

23 Conrad Russell, *Parliaments and English Politics 1621–1629* (1979), p. 383.

24 ibid., pp. 384 seq.

25 Professor Russell, ibid., p. 396, writes: 'Anyone who wishes to maintain that Charles was a natural enemy to Parliament must produce a better explanation of the recall of Parliament in 1629 than has yet been heard.' But the reader of the *True Relation* in *Commons Debates for 1629* (ed. W. Notestein and F. H. Relf, 1921) pp. 4 seq, does receive the distinct impression that after Charles had consented to the Petition of Right he assumed that the Commons would vote him tonnage and poundage, the collection of which had been rendered difficult because merchants said it was illegal.

26 ibid., pp. 10–11.

27 ibid., p. 129.

28 ibid., p. 27.

29 The King's declaration, 10 March 1629. S. R. Gardiner, *The Constitutional Documents of the Puritan Revolution* (1901), pp. 83 seq.

30 Warwick, p. 46.

31 Gregg. p. 320.

32 John Hacket, *Scrinia reserata* (1693), pt. II, p. 8.

33 Stevenson, p. 273.

Notes to Chapter 11

1 The Earl of Kellie to the Earl of Mar, May 1624, cit. Gregg, p. 97.

2 *Commons Debates for 1629*, pp. 192–3 and note.

3 Speech at Saffron Walden, 16 May 1647, *Clarke Papers*, I, p. 72.

4 Abbott, I, pp. 459–61.

5 ibid., p. 467.

6 Woodhouse, pp. 412–13.

7 Cromwell to Fairfax, 20 Nov. 1648, Abbott, I, pp. 690–1.

8 Cromwell to Hammond, 25 Nov. 1648, ibid., p. 698.

9 ibid., p. 697.
10 David Underdown deals comprehensively with this episode, *Pride's Purge: Politics in the Puritan Revolution* (1971).
11 Abbott, I, p. 708.
12 C. V. Wedgwood, *The Trial of Charles I* (1964), p. 43.
13 Underdown, op. cit., p. 150.
14 Gardiner, *Constitutional Documents*, p. 386.
15 ibid., p. 384.
16 Clarendon, *History of the Rebellion*, XIV, pp. 1–3.
17 Austin Woolrych, *Commonwealth to Protectorate* (1982), pp. 41–2 refutes Gardiner's and Firth's statements about Cromwell's attitude to the petition, but admits that 'Gardiner was probably right all the same in sensing Cromwell's restraining influence'; Blair Worden, *The Rump Parliament* (1966), p. 307, accepts that Cromwell exerted his influence to modify the officers' demands.
18 The most up-to-date and comprehensive investigation into these problems is to be found in Blair Worden's and Austin Woolrych's books cited in note 17 above.
19 Worden, op. cit., pp. 212, 221, 266. Dr Worden states that the recruiting scheme was never incorporated into the Bill framed by the committee set up in September 1651 and intermittently debated by the Rump until its dissolution.
20 There is no clear evidence that Vane attended the meeting, but Cromwell's behaviour towards him the next day is circumstantial evidence, cf. Violet A. Rowe, *Sir Henry Vane the Younger* (1970), pp. 188–9.
21 Abbott, IV, p. 487.
22 Carlyle, II, p. 291.
23 Burton, I. p. i.
24 Cromwell to Fleetwood, 22 May 1653, Carlyle, II, p. 307.
25 ibid., pp. 311–12.
26 Abbott, IV, p. 489.
27 ibid., loc. cit.
28 Burton, I, p. xxi.
29 ibid., p. xxv.
30 ibid., p. xxx.
31 Carlyle, II, p. 386.
32 Gardiner, *Constitutional Documents*, pp. lviii–lx.
33 Burton, I, p. lxxiv.
34 ibid., p. cxxii; Carlyle II, p. 420.
35 Burton, I, pp. cxxxv–cxxxvi.

36 Gregg, p. 350.
37 Carlyle, II, p. 425.
38 *The Protectorate of Oliver Cromwell and the State of Europe* (ed. R. Vaughan, 1839), I, p. 118.
39 Carlyle, II, pp. 424 seq.
40 *Memoirs of Edmund Ludlow* (ed. C. H. Firth, 1894), II, p. 11.
41 Abbott, IV, pp. 260 seq.
42 Burton, I, p. 315.
43 cf. Hugh Trevor-Roper, 'Cromwell and his Parliaments', *Religion, the Reformation and Social Change* (1967), p. 383.
44 Gardiner, *Constitutional Documents*, p. 459 seq.
45 Burton, II, p. 437.
46 Abbott, II, p. 733–4.
47 Austin Woolrych writes: 'If Cromwell had lived to meet the Parliament that he intended to call later in 1658, it might well have been as generally favourable as Richard's Parliament was to prove.' *The Interregnum* (ed. G. E. Aylmer, 1972), p. 187.
48 Abbott, IV, p. 488.
49 cf. Maurice Ashley, *Charles II* (1971), chs. 14–16.

Notes to Chapter 12

 1 Warwick, p. 65.
 2 cit. Peter Young, *Civil War in England* (1981), p. 15.
 3 cit. Hugh Ross Williamson, *Charles and Cromwell* (1946), p. 147.
 4 *Memoirs of Sir John Berkeley* (1699), pp. 31 seq.
 5 Clarendon, *History of the Rebellion*, IV, p. 47.
 6 cit. Gregg, p. 398.
 7 Clarendon, op. cit., p. 192.
 8 Mary Coate, 'Charles I and the Kingship' apud *King Charles I*, Historical Association pamphlet no. 11.
 9 Gardiner, *The Great Civil War 1645–7* (1983), p. 83.
10 Clarendon, op. cit., p. 190.
11 Warwick, p. 326.
12 John Lingard, *A History of England to 1688* (1820), VI, p. 142.
13 Charles to Digby, 26 March 1646, Petrie, op. cit., p. 176.
14 Charles to Lanark, 26 Nov. 1647, G. Burnet, *Memoirs of James and William Dukes of Hamilton* (1855), p. 416.
15 *Eikon Basilike*, p. 170.
16 cit. Roger Howell, *Cromwell* (1977), pp. 106–7.
17 cit. Richard Ollard, *The Image of the King* (1979), p. 27.

18 Burnet, op. cit., i, p. 10.

19 Warwick, p. 1.

20 Clarendon, op. cit., IV, p. 492.

21 Laud, *Works*, III, p. 243.

22 Cromwell to Walton, 5 July 1644, Abbott, I, p. 288.

23 *Thurloe State Papers*, I, p. 766; Clarendon, op. cit., IV, p. 489.

24 Abbott, IV, pp. 522–4.

25 Guizot, *Cromwell and the English Commonwealth* (trans. A. R. Scobie, 1854), II, p. 94.

26 Samuel Carrington, *The History of the Life and Death of his most Serene Highness Oliver Late Protector* (1659), p. 266.

27 Warwick, p. 249.

28 A. L. Rowse, *Discourses and Reviews* (1975), p. 223.

29 *Clarke Papers*, I, p. 209.

30 Cromwell to his wife Elizabeth, 12 April 1651, Abbott, II, p. 405.

31 Ashburnham, pp. clxxxiii–clxxxiv.

32 cit. Abbott, IV, p. 880.

33 Lucy Hutchinson, op. cit., II, pp. 202–3.

34 W. H. Dawson, *Cromwell's Understudy*, pp. 227–8, 276.

35 Abbott, IV, p. 729.

36 Warwick, p. 248.

37 Hutchinson, op,. cit., II, p. 202.

38 G. D. Boyle, op. cit., p. 283.

39 John Milton, *The Second Defence of the People of England* (1806 edition), p. 433.

40 *Memoirs of Sir John Reresby* (ed. Andrew Browning, 1936). p. 22.

41 Carlton, p. 344.

42 Clarendon, *History of the Rebellion*, IV, p. 490.

43 Abbott, IV, pp. 273–4.

44 *Eikon Basilike*, p. 195.

45 cit. Paul, p. 377.

Notes to Chapter 13

1 S. Neumann, cit. Lawrence Stone, *The Causes of the English Revolution 1529–1642* (1972), p. 48.

2 ibid., p. 49.

3 John Morrill (ed.), *Reactions to the English Civil War* (1982), pp. 50 seq., Brian Manning, *The English People and the English Revolution* (1976), p. 243.

4 Cromwell to St John, 11 Sept. 1643, Abbott, I, pp. 258–9.

5 R. B. Merriman, *Six Contemporaneous Revolutions* (1938); *Crisis in Europe 1560–1660* (ed. Trevor Aston, 1965) pp. 5 seq.

6 Charles Wilson, *Taxation and the Decline of Empire: an Unfashionable Theme* (1963).

7 See David Underdown's brilliant book, *Revel, Revolt and Rebellion* (1985), and John Morrill, *The Revolt of the Provinces* (1976).

8 Barry Coward, *The Stuart Age* (1980), p. 165; Conrad Russell, 'The Parliamentary Career of John Pym', loc. cit., p. 151.

9 For Penington and his activities see Valerie Pearl, *London and the Puritan Revolution* (1961), pp. 176–206, 210–21, 260–3.

10 ibid., pp. 216–17; Firth, *The House of Lords during the Civil War* (1910), p. 86.

11 ibid., p. 89.

12 *Eikon Basilike*, p. 14.

13 Pearl, op. cit., p. 230. The view that Pym was a 'moderate', first expounded by J. H. Hexter, has never convinced me. As Lotte Glow wrote in her article 'Pym and Parliament: the Methods of Moderation', *Journal of Modern History*, vol. XXVI (1964), 'Pym himself came to see that the war needed to be intensified after the failure of the Oxford peace negotiations. . . . We can follow closely Pym's shift towards the radicals.'

14 ibid., p. 184.

15 Fletcher, *The Outbreak of the English Civil War* (1980), p. 416.

16 Quoted from Sir Edward Nicholas, 'History of the Long Parliament' in *The Journal of Sir Simonds D'Ewes* (ed. W. H. Coates, 1942), p. 186, note 21.

17 ibid., p. 184, note 14.

18 *Eikon Basilike*, p. 53.

19 Fletcher, op. cit., p. 229.

20 Gardiner, *History of the Great Civil War* (1891), III, p. 560.

21 cf. C. Hibbard, *Charles I and the Popish Plot*.

22 cf. Roger Howell, *Cromwell* (1977), p. 166.

23 Conrad Russell, ed., *The Origins of the English Civil War* (1973), p. 3.

24 Abbott, I, p. 459.

25 Mark A. Kishlansky, *The Rise of the New Model Army* (1979), p. 3.

26 J. S. Morrill, 'Mutiny and Discontent in English Armies 1647–9', *Past and Present*, no. 56 (1972), pp. 49 seq.

27 cit. Kishlansky quoting from *The Times Literary Supplement*, 1 June 1978.

28 See *inter alia* B. S. Capp, *The Fifth Monarchy Men* (1972);

Christopher Hill, *The World Turned Upside Down* (1972); Keith
Thomas, *Religion and the Decline of Magic* (1971); J. Frank, *The Levellers*
(1969).
29 A useful analysis of the debate by historians on 'the English
revolution' is to be found in F. D. Dow, *Radicalism in the English
Revolution* (1985) ch. 1. I accept the views of those academic historians
whom she calls conservative revisionists, but this does not mean that I
(or, I imagine, anyone else) deny that extremely radical ideas were put
forward during the Interregnum.

Notes to Chapter 14

1 Firebrace, p. 49 note.
2 *Moderate Intelligencer*, 2 Sep. 1647, cit. Firebrace, p. 49.
3 Meeting of Council of Officers at Putney on 11 Nov. 1647, Abbott,
I, p. 551.
4 Ashburnham, p. clxxvii.
5 The evidence that Cromwell visited the Isle of Wight comes from
Mercurius Melancholicus, a Royalist news-sheet covering 4–12 Sep.
1647. Cromwell visited Lilburne in the Tower of London on 6 Sep.;
on 9 Sep. he was at Putney; on 14 Sep. he was attending the House of
Commons. It is extremely unlikely that he could have found time to go
to the Isle of Wight and back between these dates. G. M. Young wrote,
that 'just before Christmas Cromwell paid a flying visit to the Isle of
Wight to stiffen Hammond's principles' (*Charles I and Cromwell*
(1935), p. 98,) but did not give his authority. During the last week
before Christmas Cromwell was at Windsor.
6 Thomas Hobbes, *Behemoth* or *The Long Parliament* (1889), p. 143.
7 The Leveller concerned was William Petty. Woodhouse, p. 83.
The question of what the Levellers meant by manhood suffrage has
been elaborately discussed by C. B. Macpherson, *The Political Theory of
Possessive Individualism* (1962) and by Peter Laslett and other critics of
Macpherson.
8 The organization of the Levellers in London was described by one
of their opponents, George Masterson, an account confirmed by
Lilburne. Norah Carlin, 'Leveller organization in London', *Historical
Journal* (1984), pp. 955–60.
9 cf. Mark A. Kishlansky, *The Rise of the New Model Army*, pp. 180
seq. Austin Woolrych has some criticisms of Kishlansky, but accepts
that the Leveller influence on the Army has been exaggerated. 'Putney
Revisited', loc. cit. pp. 99 seq.

10 Abbott, I, p. 575.

11 Cal. Cl. S.P., I, p. 410.

12 Edmund Ludlow, *Memoirs* (1698), I, p. 262.

13 J. D. Jones, *The Royal Prisoner* (1965), p. 109.

14 Charles to Hopkins, 9 Oct. 1648, Firebrace, p. 344.

15 cit. Firebrace, p. 153 from Thomason tracts, 669 f. 13 53.

16 cf. Robert Ashton, *The English Civil War* (1978), pp. 337–8.

17 Sir Thomas Herbert's account in *The Trial of Charles I* (ed. Roger Lockyer, 1959), p. 65.

18 Abbott, I, p. 719.

19 For the trial of Charles I I follow Dame Veronica Wedgwood's brilliant book published in 1964. I am not convinced by Professor Underdown's argument in *Pride's Purge*, pp. 165 seq., that Cromwell was involved in sending the Earl of Denbigh to Windsor to seek an agreement with the King and thus prevent his trial. In fact Denbigh did not even see Charles. Gardiner, op. cit, p. 556.

20 *The Trial of Charles I* (ed. Lockyer), p. 85, attributes this interruption to the date when the charge was made, 20 Jan. 1649; so does Gardiner, *The Great Civil War*, III (1891), p. 572; Veronica Wedgwood, *The Trial of Charles I*, pp. 154–5 attributes it to the date on which he was condemned, 27 Jan. 1649.

21 *The Trial of Charles I* (ed. Lockyer), p. 105.

22 William Allen, *A Faithful Memorial, Somers Tracts*, VI, p. 500. It has been suggested that when Allen attended this Council meeting he was present as an officer, not as an Agitator.

23 Gardiner, op. cit., pp. 554–6; cf. Abbott, I, pp. 716 seq.

24 Carlton, p. 247.

25 *Eikon Basilike*, p. 254.

26 ibid., p. 271.

27 ibid., pp. 185–91.

28 Sir Thomas Herbert's narration, *The Trial of Charles I* (ed. Lockyer), p. 146.

29 *Thurloe State Papers*, VII, p. 372.

INDEX